Love at Work

NIGEL CUTTS

Published by
Fisher King Publishing
The Studio
Arthington Lane
Pool-in-Wharfedale
LS21 1JZ
England

ISBN 978-1-906377-12-0

Editor: Mary-Ellen Wyard

Designed by **cooke**with**ane.com**

Dedication

" Someday, after we have mastered the winds, the waves, the tides and gravity, we shall harness for God the energies of love. Then for the second time in the history of the world, man will have discovered fire."

Teilhard de Chardin

To my dear friend George Freeman, whose constant yet often unconscious support for more than 45 years has made my life so much richer and so much more fulfilled.

Love at Work (a dictionary definition)

love n. **1.** an intense feeling of deep affection. a deep romantic or sexual attachment to someone. affectionate greetings. **2.** a great interest and pleasure in something. **3.** a person or thing that one loves.

at prep **1.** expressing location or arrival in a particular place or position. **2.** expressing the time when an event takes place. **3.** expressing attendance of an educational institution or workplace.

work n **1.** activity involving mental or physical effort done in order to achieve a result. **2.** such activity as a means of earning income. **3.** a task or tasks to be undertaken.

Contents

Acknowledgements

A friend is one to whom one may pour all the contents of ones heart, chaff and grain together, knowing that the gentlest of hands will take it and sift it, keeping what is worth keeping and with a breath of kindness blow away the rest.

Arabian Proverb

First, to my darling wife Gilly, who has given me so much love and support not just in the writing of this book but on our journey through life. You teach me so much. You are truly my soul mate. Thank you too for allowing and encouraging me to keep my head down and writing even when there were lots of other things we could or should have been doing together!

Next to Graham Browne and Babette Hayes, not just as my first ever personal development teachers on those amazing courses by The Bellin Partnership, called Turning Point, Point of Choice and Point of Mastery, but as my dear friends some twenty years later. Without them, it is highly likely this book would never have been written.

Then to my good friend George Metcalfe, who helped me so much in the early days of the book's preparation, spending hours sitting with me in front of a tape recorder to extract my fledgling thoughts – and also for his sage advice during our many wonderful lunches.

And to all those special friends, family members and colleagues who have contributed to the book consciously or unconsciously. All of you have taught me many things. Specifically though, those who took the trouble to read the drafts and let me have their thoughts and comments, all of which were invaluable. They are, purely in alphabetical order: Jamie Armstrong, Abbie Cooke, Gary Cooke, Liz Cornu, Gilly Cutts, Colin Hallett, Diane Hallett, Val Harris, Emily Havers, Harriet Karia, Nancy Kline, Jane Matthews, George Metcalfe, Caroline Minto and Rachel Ormrod.

Huge thanks too, to my publisher Rick Armstrong at Fisher King, for his patience and guidance through a completely unfamiliar process.

Finally, a very special thank you to Gary Cooke, the most amazing graphic designer and wonderful friend. He has added so much to the look and feel of the book. Not least when, one Sunday, soon after I had started the first Chapter, he sent me, totally unannounced and unsolicited, his draft for the cover and the page layouts with a note which simply said, "To inspire you as you write."

Foreword

At last, we can say the word "love" – at work. We can acknowledge what has been true all along: love is what works at work. Love has been just outside the office door for centuries. We have heard its knock, but we have said, "not here". Some enlightened leaders have recently moved to, "not yet". But finally, Nigel Cutts has said, "now". In this beautiful book he has opened the door.

He has done this because love is what produces results. People perform best when they are loved: when they are respected, when they can soar because of who they are – their experience, their talents, their capacity, their intelligence – is cherished. We all know this. Now we can stop believing the nonsense. We can stop putting off putting love on the top of the list of required expertise in leaders.

Love produces great thinking. That is why it produces great performance. Love, in fact, is the question: "What do you think?" And it is the generative listening that follows. Love is being with, not thinking for. Nigel knows this. And he lives it.

Don't get confused. This love is not romance or seduction or sentiment. This love answers no call from Hallmark, nor from Hollywood, or from hubris. It is the experience of starting over in this fresh never-before-lived second. It is the wanting to discover who we really are. It is the decision to be that authentic self every minute. It is the exhilaration of being still so that things can move. It is respect so deep and embodied that all good springs from it.

It is the love we find when we actually see each other, the love that stands with us as we listen, as we debate for our mutual good, as we face what is real, as we mourn, as we research, as we think for ourselves, as we find new answers together we did not think possible. This love is hard work and hard at work inside every good decision and every step human kind has made that has made a positive difference.

My first experience of seeing that love at work is what makes the difference was in 1985. "It's very refreshing," the official said, "to find the word ... er...er...'love' in a grant application." Christopher Spence needed to raise £2 million to complete what would become the world's flagship centre for people affected by HIV and AIDS. He got the money. And London got a full expression of the efficacy of love at work. The culture of listening and respect and thinking and inclusion spanned the organisation, from residents with the virus to nurses and managers and board members and cooks. Love worked. More of value was accomplished there than anyone could have dreamed possible. For thousands of people across the world, not just London, it changed the face of patient care. Love does that sort of thing.

Nigel knows this too. He knows from creating his own organisations, whose cultures under his leadership were exactly love, that it is the key thing in unleashing talent and building success. He shares with us his understanding of the teachings of many people over many eras. He brings together an important and impressive panoply of wisdom as well as his own. But what makes the book work well, besides that he writes so well, is that he is what he is writing. We can feel that as we read. We can trust him. And so we read on. And our lives and leadership and places of work can change. They can become places of love, the kind that works.

Love. This book says, 'let's say it'. And maybe even, 'let's shout it'. And 'let's whisper it'. Let's let it into our hearts and into the most laser-precise reasoning we can muster. Because if we do, perhaps work will really work. At last!

Nancy Kline
President and Founder. Time To Think Inc.

Introduction

What's in this introduction:

- The difference love makes
- The role of relationship in all our lives
- Why Love at Work matters
- A first definition of Love at Work

Love at Work

"And what is it to work with love? It is to weave the cloth with threads drawn from your heart, even as if your beloved were to wear that cloth..."

Kahlil Gibran

Why love makes the difference

Every single human being on this planet of ours wants to be loved. By love I mean to respect someone profoundly. Do we not all think better, work better, act better when we are loved? If you think back to a time when you were "in love" was not the world a rosier, gentler place? Did you not think better, work better, act with more integrity around that person and in your world? Does it cost us anything to offer love? Does it cost us anything to treat each other with respect? Does it cost us anything to respect someone profoundly? If this is truly the case then why would we not, all of us, all of the time, work to achieve this in our lives?

I have spent a lifetime working in, setting up, running, managing and leading businesses and organisations where this thing called love has been present to a greater or lesser degree. I have, often with hindsight, witnessed the enormous difference that its presence makes and the devastation that its absence causes. This is one reason why I came to write this book.

Although I had experienced much love throughout my childhood, the first time I can recall consciously experiencing it was when I was at my College of Art. I was floundering at the start of the third year of a four year course when in walked two new tutors, full of life and energy from the real world of design rather than the dust of academia. One of those two people, a wonderful man called George Freeman, set about rescuing me although I am sure he wouldn't put it that way. He talked to me for hours over my drawing board, he got me to trust myself, he gave me confidence, he asked the right questions and opened up my mind. We became friends. I even worked for him for a while and over the years we have worked together, talked together, laughed together. He has always been in my life when I needed him. I have never forgotten him and I never will. His steady non-judgmental presence through the rest of my degree meant I started to blossom. Forty five years later he is still in my life and he is still non-judgemental. We still meet. We still talk. More than anything I respect him profoundly. If that isn't love, I don't know what is. He is another reason that I came to write this book.

With the busy lives we all lead, you may be glad to hear that this is not a book you need to read sequentially. Whilst the single theme of Love at Work runs through everything, this is not an instruction manual. It is designed for you to be able to dip in and out of it as you need to or as the mood takes you – a box full of useful tools. No one has all the answers and I certainly don't! My aim is to share my experiences with you in such a way that over time you may find them useful, supportive or confirmatory. Love at Work is something I believe in deeply. It is something that, given my time again and with that wonderful thing called 20/20 hindsight, I would look for it everywhere. I would work with it constantly. I would spread the word at every opportunity. Obviously I can't go back, but I can share through the pages of this book as much as I can remember of the difference it makes. This is a third reason.

I would like to suggest to you that, in picking up this book, there is a part of you that believes my proposition that embracing Love at Work really does makes a difference. Right now it might be a very small part but, whether you choose to dip in and out at leisure or read the book cover to cover, that seed thought could grow over time. As you pick up this book as employer or employee, in a small organisation or a larger one, or just as yourself, my hope is that, as you read it and use it, that thought will grow and flourish – and so will you. My wider wish is that it supports you in some small way in your growth and your work aspirations. More than anything I hope it helps you find the courage always to be truly who you are in an organisation and in the world. I say all of this with the humility of someone who has tried, failed and picked myself up many times.

 If you knew that you were to die tomorrow, what would you be proud to have done or been?"
Nancy Kline

Open-heartedness

There will be much in the following pages about open-heartedness and it would be difficult for anyone to disagree that it makes a huge difference in this world of ours. I know it does and has in mine. Those people who have treated me in this way have had a profound effect on my life and each time it has happened I have resolved to do the same for others, be the same towards others. There have been so many of them over the years: school teachers, dance teachers, shop keepers, salesmen, bosses, employees, spiritual teachers and gurus as well as a myriad of friends and family.

"Pop" Taylor, one of my teachers at school possessed this open-heartedness. Michael Ryan, a brilliant architect I worked for in the late Sixties had it too. He often demonstrated this by quizzing you mercilessly on the thoroughness of your design and then supporting it completely once he felt it was the right solution. Above all though, I think I learnt it because it was instilled in me almost subliminally by my father, a quiet Yorkshireman of huge integrity who, in my experience, always did what he said he was going to do for people. Such was his reputation in his chosen profession as a District Valuer that he was said never to have lost a case simply because he never brought one that was unfair – a real demonstration of the principle.

Open-heartedness involves kindness, trust and understanding. Sometimes it can be as simple as letting someone out into the traffic. At others it can be total love and support at a critical physical, emotional, mental or spiritual time. It is these four levels of living that I keep in mind as I write and that I would invite you to keep in mind as you read.

Work and relationship

My core belief is that we are on this earth principally to learn about relationship. We will have many relationships in our lives – with our partner or spouse, our children, our parents, our friends, our colleagues at work and even with perfect strangers. Most of all though, we are really here to learn about our relationship with our self – our egoic self and our higher Self. If this is true and you combine it with the fact that most of us spend more time at work than we do with our significant other, then there can be no better place to learn about that relationship than at work. What better place can there be to build a world that really works for us and those around us when we are prepared to be awake and aware on every level of our human consciousness?

So, it becomes incumbent on us always to work at being the best we can by nurturing our innate desire to make a difference in the world, by being thoroughly competent, business like and highly professional and by deeply caring for all the people we work with or are touched by. What we do then is build trust and integrity through honesty and openness. In this way our work becomes a vehicle through which we can learn about life, relationship and above all ourselves.

Don't get me wrong – I know it's absolutely possible to build an organisation and make money, lots of it, without understanding and using any of the precepts I put forward. But, if somewhere inside, you yearn for a different way of doing things, a different way of being, if you want fulfilment, freedom and choice then I hope you will find what I have written useful and supportive on your journey.

The reason I feel able to help is because I have built organisations in both ways. I spent twelve years building my own business from what I can now recognise as an egotistical point of view. After it failed and, sometime later, after I had recovered from the grief of losing nearly everything, I decided that if I ever got the opportunity to build another one, I would approach it very differently. So it was that I entered a period of several years of intense soul searching and personal development. It involved reading everything relevant I could find, listening to everyone who knew anything about the subjects I was interested in and going on as many courses as I could afford. Perhaps most important was my decision to learn to meditate, something I still do every day, many, many years later.

I also recognised that swinging the pendulum too far the other way, totally away from head and towards heart, wouldn't work either. Lots of people run great organisations and lots run great people oriented ones and I wanted to learn from them too. I learned much theory by reading mountains of management books and the ones I found useful are included in either the bibliography or the reading list at the back of the book.

What I really wanted to do though was to find out what it would feel like to run an organisation from my heart in a world of money. You probably won't be surprised therefore that when, several years later, I was given the opportunity to build another business, I chose to take a very different viewpoint. I chose to do it with the express intention of making a difference in the lives of others.

Relationship matters

This second chance didn't happen by accident. It happened because of the process of self discovery I had undertaken. It happened because of the influences that the work of people like Walter and Gita Bellin, Graham Browne, Deepak Chopra, Ken Wilber, Tony Robbins, Stephen Covey, Ram Das, Jack Kornfield, Nancy Kline and many others have had and continue to have on my life, either remotely or in person. Add all this to my forty plus years of seeing and working in different organisational models and perhaps you can understand why I thought it might just be worth putting as much as possible of what I have learned down on paper.

So what is "Love at Work"? It seems timely to think about this for two reasons; the first is the world wide acceptance that we owe our children a future that is both safe and sustainable; the second is the various global crises, from economic to energy to population to war which our world continues to bump, stumble and crash its way through. We all have the innate knowledge that we cannot and must not go on this way. Unless we treat our world with love and respect, we will destroy it. If we take out of it more than we put back we will destroy it. Al Gore, as the spokesperson of many, has convinced us this principle applies to our rainforests and mountains, our seas and icecaps as much as it does to our economy. However, unless we look after ourselves – on every level; emotional, mental, physical and spiritual – we cannot look after others, let alone our planet. There is another saying that you cannot be truly in service to others unless you are in service to your self. This is simply a microcosmic perspective on the idea that we cannot take out more than we put in.

All the great philosophers and sages of our day such as Ken Wilber, Deepak Chopra and the Dalai Lama, all of the top management gurus such as Tom Peters, Stephen Covey and Jim Collins, and all of the ancient sages too are, for me, saying the same thing. It is our relationships that matter more than anything else. I would simply add that it is the one with our self that matters most.

Chapter by chapter, my goal is to let you have my thoughts and ideas on how you can create "Love at Work" through "Love in Action" to add to your own thoughts and ideas. It is the same love; it is that same profound respect that we can always demonstrate towards our fellow man, to our fellow beings and every part of our planet that creates both love at work and love in action. What it is not is romantic love or addictive love. It is the ability to see our own frailty in other people, to understand that and be compassionate towards them. Amongst other things it is compassion, caring, responsibility, understanding and humility. All of these will run as sub-themes throughout the text. If you are still uncomfortable with the word "love" in this context then you might for a while want to substitute the word "care".

Choosing exactly the right word or words to represent our place of work is difficult because such things are very diverse, not just in the type of work we do but in the size of our workplace. In an endeavour to be as inclusive as possible I have chosen principally to use two. Workplace is one but whilst that covers the physical it doesn't cover everything. The second word is organisation and I have chosen it because it covers every area of work from companies to charities to government, rather than just "business". Its shortcoming is of course that it implies a certain size, so I would ask you to stretch your imagination to think of it as covering every type of venture in any field of work from two or more people upwards.

A first definition of love at work

How do you build a business that is "Love at Work"? What is "Being at Work" as opposed to "Doing at Work"? How do you live it every day? Principally all we can do is be the example and have the courage to do what we need to do, even when it flies in the face of convention or perceived wisdom. When we:

- *Create supportive, warm, friendly environments on every level*
- *Truly listen to and fulfil each other's needs*
- *Take spontaneous right action*

we are moving in the right direction. Doing things differently, breaking the mould, looking after each other and even putting others first take courage. We need to find it though, because it is through these actions that we change our perspective on our lives and help others to change theirs. When this happens we start to see that the world is an abundant place, full of life and fun. We lose our attachment to poverty consciousness, to that debilitating thought, that idea that drags us down, that there is not enough. There is enough, there will always be enough. We just need to believe it.

Doing what we love and not getting diverted, doing what we love and not letting the glamour of fame and fortune get to us and distract us takes determination, persistence and rigour. All of which come more easily when we are working with like-minded people. So who we decide to work with or for, who we employ, who we supply and who supplies us are not just questions we should answer on a physical level, they are questions to be asked on every level.

We start a new venture or business full of hope and expectancy and with none of the worries and concerns of turnover, taxation, business getting, satisfying clients and customers. It is easy in those heady days to keep our dream clearly focussed, to talk to people, to look after people. As we grow and two of us become four, four becomes eight, eight becomes sixteen and so on it is so much more difficult to stay in touch and genuinely interested in those around us. People can so easily appear to be much less important than finishing tasks, getting work out on time or satisfying client needs. The truth of it of course is that they are not! Over time I have learned to overcome this and to understand what works for me. In passing that on, maybe it will be useful to you too or help confirm what you have always known, consciously or unconsciously.

What to take from this introduction

- **Love at Work is being in the moment, living our lives fully each day, respecting and caring for others as though they were ourselves and our family**

- **Love at Work is Love in Action**

- **Love in Action is doing what we love from our hearts**

- **Love at Work is sorely needed in our world**

Chapter 1

What's in this chapter:

- Understanding the head-heart connection
- The importance of service
- The power of connection with self
- The link between forgiveness and trust
- Making Love at Work work
- Walking the talk in our frantic world

The heart of the matter

" In a society that almost demands life at double time, speed and addictions numb us to our own experience. In such a society it is almost impossible to settle into our bodies or stay connected with our hearts, let alone connect with one another or the earth where we live."

Jack Kornfield

An Old Story

There's an apocryphal story that's been going around in one form or another for years now. It tells of a philosophy professor explaining to his students, with the aid of a large glass jar, some rocks, some pebbles and some sand, why it is important to pay attention to what really matters in our lives and, if necessary, forget about the small stuff.

For me the rocks represent all our relationships – with everyone in our lives from our families to our friends to those we pass in the street. But what are relationships? They are no more and no less than a reflection of who we are. The physical, emotional, mental and spiritual representation of everything we think and feel and do. If we look after our physical body, if we listen to our heart, if we use our mind to understand what we want to do and if we connect with whatever higher being we are comfortable describing for ourselves, then we are able to create love in our lives and more particularly Love at Work. On an energetic level we are not our physical body, we are not our brain and we are not our mind, we are pure spirit or if you find that too strong, pure energy. Pure spirit works through us for the good of all mankind. All we need to do is connect with that, listen to it through our hearts rather than our heads and the rest will take care of itself. It is only when we lose this connection that we stop doing the right thing. There is even proof nowadays that our emotions are as much seated in our physical heart as they are in our physical brain.

The head heart connection

This sense of right, of working for the good of our fellow man is, I believe, so much ingrained in all of us that it is easy to live our lives in that way. All we need is to be reminded that that is who we are. For me, the best reminders are those people who touch, move and inspire me. As Stephen Covey points out in his book, The 8th Habit, we all have choice, the choice to choose our path in life. We can choose either the lower path of mediocrity or the higher path of greatness. So we can choose to be victim, to eat Big Macs and drink full sugar Coke. We can choose to let society decide who we are and what we are. When we choose this path we will lose our connection with spirit, our ego will take over and our existence is likely to be unsatisfactory and unfulfilled. Choose the higher path and we can use our mind to truly witness our actions, to think about where we want to go and who we really want to be. Then we can also use our mind to look after our bodies by eating and drinking only things that nurture it. In doing this our body also gets to look after our brain, the physical representation of our mind within our body. Connect our mind with our heart and we get the opportunity to look at where our passion lies and do something about it!

Before we go further there is something you need to know. Within the book you will come across a series of exercises; all simple but some requiring more time than others; all connected to whatever I am talking about at the time. Your experience of the book will be considerably enhanced by doing them so please do find the space and time to try them. Here is the first:

exercise

Just stop for a moment right now, gently close your eyes and think about someone or something you are really passionate about. Allow whoever or whatever it is to come into full focus. See the scene in front of you in full colour and detail. Smell the smells, taste the tastes, experience all the sensations of wherever you have taken yourself. Then let all the emotions surface and feel them in your body wherever they are. Don't try and do anything with them – just experience them. When you are through, equally gently let the images and sensations subside and then take a deep breath or two and slowly open your eyes. ♥

That is our mind-body connection doing what it does automatically. It is a wonderful barometer for us to use to determine how we really feel about anything in our lives. My own personal experience of many years was totally to ignore this connection because subconsciously I found it too painful. Having spent a long time regaining it I now wouldn't give it up for anything. Years ago now I was working with a personal development teacher who used to encourage me frequently to get out of my head and into my heart. "I am, am!" I used to protest and no matter what I did he would continue to repeat those words. I thought I would never get it and just didn't understand what it was I was missing. Eventually I realised that "all" I needed to do was surrender. Over time I really did manage to drop from my head to my heart. It was the most amazing experience. Of course, it didn't last but over time I did manage to do it again and then again until the gap between the event that triggered the feeling and the feeling itself began to close. There is still a gap but it is much shorter nowadays and this helps me so much in being in contact with who I really am. I would encourage you to try this little exercise every day, several times a day until you can really witness what happens and then act upon it. You will then develop the ability to go to that place wherever you are and whatever you are doing. Being connected in this way will improve your decision making no end.

Mind and heart are inextricably linked. It seems to me that it is no coincidence that the universal symbol of love is a heart. It is no coincidence either that our heart is where our passions lie or that our connection with spirit is where our conscience lies. I use the word spirit deliberately. I use it to represent whatever or whoever your personal God is and however you see (or don't see) that in your mind, be it the Christian God, the Islamic one, Judaism, the multiple Gods of Hinduism or any other faith or religion across our planet. Whether your God is the Old Testament God of Retribution or none at all, the end result is that of your conscience speaking to you through your mind. It is through this shared consciousness that we develop our shared values, our vision. In case you would like to know, my personal God is a God Within but it matters not in the context of this book. What does matter is how we use our mind, our heart and our spirit in relation to ourselves, our colleagues and our team(s) to create Love at Work.

Amazingly, when we really sit down and think about who we are we find that we do actually know the answer. We can then use our mind to look forward to think about where we want to be, where we want our family to be, our friends to be, our business to be and as we do so our world expands, particularly when we do it from our hearts. I believe we can and should use our hearts to empower others. That is its greatest facility. To be there with an open heart is to be in support of others achieving what they want. What greater pleasure can there be in life?

Being in service to others

Being leadership in service is at the very heart of this book. Back in the early nineties I spent a whole year on a course teaching me how to be just that. It was hard work! It was tough going emotionally, mentally and spiritually. The sheer number of hours involved made it tough going physically as well. I remember 20 hour days over long weekends. I remember staying up half the night to complete the assignments. I remember feeling totally drained on every level. At the time I felt completely taken apart, but after I had spent the next year putting myself back together again I was absolutely clear it was totally worth the effort. Without that course (and many others) I would not have experienced the phase of my life that has brought me to writing this book. Looking back I wouldn't have changed a moment of it – though that's not how I often felt at the time! Only today as I sat down to write did I root out my final project from the course and flick through it and, my goodness, it still paints a very accurate word picture of who I am. I learned so much about myself and how I operate in every imaginable situation that I would really recommend any course with this level of rigour to anyone wanting to kick start their personal development.

So here we are setting out on a journey together, a journey to the heart. The unusual thing for so many of us, but by no means all, is that it is also a journey to our work. This thought reminds me of the time some years ago now when I was setting up a new venture in the UK for an international company and I was trying to articulate my feelings around businesses with heart. My thoughts (and what I said to everyone) went something like this:

I don't know about you but holidays and trips always give me time to think and time to assess where I am and where I'm going. For a while I've been trying to clarify my thoughts to a point where I could meaningfully tell you about them. It's something I knew you needed to know but in the hurly burly of everyday I couldn't or wouldn't make the time.

So I've spent most of the weekend looking at just that and here are those thoughts:

Many years ago I knew I wanted to be a designer. Years later I'd achieved that and also become a leader – I had my own firm. I knew how to design but what I didn't know was that I didn't know how to lead. I thought I knew but I didn't and after twelve years of various levels of power play it collapsed. I was devastated. It was like losing a child and I swore I would never go back to design.

"I'd done all I needed to do," my ego said. "That last project was my swan song," it said.

My life was a mess in every direction. I had no money, no job, my second marriage was on the rocks and my son really didn't want to speak to me.

Fortunately I had one really good friend who had the courage to help me see that my life wasn't working because of me in here not what the world was doing to me out there. Through her I ended up going on a very special personal development course called Turning Point. From then on I knew in my heart, not my head, that if I were to pull through I needed to look at every aspect of myself. I was ready to start my inner journey. For the next seven years I went on course after course after workshop. I bought and read every book on the subject I could lay my hands on. I went to every lecture I could and spent four years seeing one guru. Between 1993 and 1995 I spent a whole year on a course taking myself apart and another year putting myself back together again.

Eventually I was ready to go back into the world of work that I was good at and the universe conspired to make it happen – I got divorced and needed the money. For the next three years I put my head down and learnt new skills and started to practise my new found self in real situations. No more power plays, no more talking behind people's backs, no more manipulation – and it worked – it was so much less stressful. The world didn't need to change – the only thing that needed to change was me.

Then I became restless to try this newly built philosophy on a bigger scale and again the universe helped – I was given this job.

It's not often in life we get second chances, and that's what this feels like. Being given a second chance – an opportunity to make a real difference and I grabbed it with both hands.

So why am I telling you all this? Simply to put into context what I want to say next.

In this company, we are lucky enough to be part of an organization started by someone with a deep and abiding interest in people. My part in this is that my dream is not just a world that works for everybody but a world of work that works for everybody. I took this job not only because I wanted to do a good job professionally. I took it because I wanted to do it in a way that is a demonstration of how the world of work can really work.

Professionalism accepted, my dream was to create a supportive, nurturing, empowering place where people can't wait for the day to start. Where people are powerful rather than use power over each other. Where they talk to each other and speak up to each other not just when things are working but, equally importantly, dare to tell each other the truth when, professionally or personally, they are not – and without fear of recrimination. A place where bullying doesn't exist, a place where everyone is listened to and where everyone's opinion is valued – although that doesn't always mean acted upon. A place where true authority passes moment by moment from person to person as a project grows and changes; a place where people take responsibility for who they are and what they need to do; a place where failure is encouraged as a learning experience, another chance to improve.

We are on an exciting and fulfilling journey together - professionally, emotionally, mentally and spiritually. It won't all be plain sailing, in fact it could well get very rough at times. So my question to every one of you at this point is – do you truly have the commitment in your heart, not in your head or in your ego, to do this together? Are you fully committed to our joint vision and all that it means? Do you have the willingness to look deep inside yourself and see how you operate? If you are, we are in for a very exciting trip.

Connection with self

My questions to you at this point are exactly the same: do you truly have the commitment in your heart, not in your head or in your ego, to do this together? Are you fully committed to our joint vision and all that it means? Do you have the willingness to look deep inside yourself and see how you operate? If you are, we too are indeed in for a very exciting trip. If not, you may one day find yourself involved in a classic case of what Love at Work is most definitely not – perhaps rather like this one: Back in the Seventies I worked for a substantial firm based in Covent Garden, which at the time was the new Soho. It was family owned and still run by the man and wife, Will and Deirdre Holly (I've given them fictitious names as I will with all those in stories in the book), who had founded it. The firm had expanded considerably and they were the only two share-holding directors – the rest of us were salaried. He was Chairman and she was Finance Director. Sadly their personal relationships started to get in the way when they decided to divorce. As you might imagine, matters deteriorated so much that it was becoming impossible for them to work together. To this day I recall sitting in one particular board meeting when Will asked a question about the monthly management accounts. Deirdre's reply, looking at me, was simply, "Tell him I'm not speaking to him." Such was the tension that everyone around the table seemed to want to disappear under it. I knew in that moment it was time to leave. Any semblance of Love at Work had disappeared. Being in the right place in our world nurtures our soul. Being in the wrong place drags us down and inhibits us. It damages our soul and we don't need to allow that to happen. Whenever we feel it is, we need to take action to change it - and that's exactly what I did.

The fact is that we cannot connect with others unless we can connect with ourselves. This is exactly why understanding and working on the head/heart connection is so important. There is such a difference between self-consciousness and consciousness of self. I vividly remember listening to a speech one day, given by a very intelligent young man. Its exact content isn't important other than to say it was highly intellectual, full of clever thoughts and ideas and well delivered. The problem was that I could feel myself starting to glaze over – I'm sure you know that feeling when you suddenly start to feel sleepy for no apparent reason. Then suddenly he started to talk about cricket, I was wide awake and so was the rest of his audience! No, it wasn't the subject matter that had attracted our attention – it was his sudden connection to his change in subject. The first part of the speech was dry, full of important facts and figures but all from his head. The difference was that the second part, equally relevant to his subject, was so obviously connected to his heart, to his passion. Through this passion he was really connecting with who he was and therefore able to connect with all of us too. When we start to recognise the genuine importance of this connection and act on it we are able to go beyond human doing-ness and become human beings. It is from this place that we are able to connect with each other, communicate with each other and hear each other.

Some time back I was passed an article on project management headed "Does Your Project Have Lots Of Love?" The writer was using the word love as an acronym for his point, a very valid point, but one which is the antithesis of the journey we are travelling together. Somewhere in his wonderful writings on Unconditional Third Person Perspective, Ken Wilber talks about the meshing of heart and mind, describing thinking as the best friend of feeling and feeling as the best friend of thinking. He adds that diversity creates productivity and homogeny (his word, meaning "similarity due to common descent") kills productivity and goes on to say that operating in this way creates an accurate symbiosis of heart and mind. I couldn't agree more.

When our heart and mind mesh we do create trust, love and understanding. When we use our amazing intellects in service of our professional skills (our doing self) and of our hearts (our being self) we have the opportunity to build our relationships on a new and fascinating level. We can do this in every area of our life, not just in business. The principle applies as much to the way we treat our partner, our family, our friends or someone in the street as we go about our busy lives.

Yes, it applies in the commercial world but it works equally well in the not for profit and charity sector (which is possibly the area we see it most practiced anyway). And what about using it in our recreation time? Whether our passion is the gym, ballroom dancing or climbing mountains it matters not because whenever we are with people we get the opportunity to operate from our hearts.

Balancing the energy of our intellect, our head and our heart frees us from intrigue, that awful, deadening, sticky, mind numbing stuff of daily life that leads us to fatigue. It allows you to FLY – to Feel Like Yourself. Feeling like ourselves, being ourselves is at the heart of creating Love at Work and love anywhere else in our world for that matter. We might think that in being ourselves there is a danger that we might offend someone. The fact is that if we are truly being ourselves, being authentic, then we can't and won't offend anyone. They might take offence but that's not the same as giving offence. As Deepak Chopra says, whether we are receiving a compliment or an insult we still have the choice to feel flattered or offended – or to simply be.

Forgiveness and trust

Allowing ourselves the possibility of being wrong even when we are absolutely certain we are right is an important part of our growth. So, therefore, is learning to truly say sorry from our heart. As a child I was certainly taught to say sorry but I am sure I didn't always mean it. "Tell your sister you're sorry". "Sorry (not)". Often we say it to stop ourselves being punished and then of course it's totally meaningless. How much more powerful to see the word in a different light, in the way the Rev. Angela Tilby spoke of it on Thought For The Day. What she said was that sorry is not a response to a demand but to a gift; the gift of forgiveness. It is being forgiven that makes saying sorry possible. Forgiveness leaves you defenceless and far more open to the truth of what you have actually done. In that place there can be real sorrow which has nothing to do with self pity and self justification. Those who bully us into apologising for things they think we have done to them will never change our hearts, whereas those who love us into sorrow do change us and gain our love.

The ability to say sorry is such an important part of trust, which is an important and integral ingredient of love. Trust is the key to all successful relationships, and it can't be bought, it can't be won through technique, subterfuge or ever going behind someone's back. Trust is not something we give the first time we meet someone. Trust has to be earned before it is given. We might think we will be able to trust someone, but building trust takes time and above all integrity. Integrity is principally about always doing what we say we are going to do when we say we are going to do it. Integrity is about saying things with honesty and openness, with the minimum of ego and without thought of personal gain. Integrity is a way of life. It is above all about telling ourselves the truth and the outcome is trust. Trust in ourselves and, through doing that, others will instinctively trust us.

My experience is that, when I do my best to run both my personal and business life underpinned with integrity and trust, I can and do produce success on every level, as well as fulfilment and happiness in all I do. At the heart of every organisation are the people. On the one hand it is perfectly possible to build and run a thoroughly competent, business like, highly professional and profitable organisation from our intellect. On the other, when we also build one underpinned by a deep and caring interest in all the people who work for or are touched by what we do – clients and their staff; contractors or suppliers; our own staff and their families – we build something truly special, truly lasting. This is where organisational succession really takes place.

At the risk of repeating myself, we are not looking at love in the sense of romantic or addictive love but in the sense of caring. My understanding is that of seeing our own frailty in others, recognising that and therefore finding it easier to be compassionate towards others. Recognition includes the ability to know that we don't know and that we may very well be blind to our faults. Perhaps this is part of really understanding the need for and acting with humility. Humility is the common thread that, according to Jim Collins in Good To Great, is the trait of all great and sustainable leadership. Love in the context of this book includes many of the things we have spoken of: compassion, caring, a sense of responsibility, understanding, and humility. Humility is vital, particularly because there are always many people more knowledgeable than we are and with deeper understanding than we have.

Making 'Love at Work' work

If Love at Work is to work properly and profitably everyone in the organisation will need a high level of competence, commitment and loyalty to themselves, their role and the company. To achieve this will take time and effort combined with an unfailing commitment of the leadership to always practise what they preach, to lead by example. When such a structure is in place, issues like home-working, flexible working, childcare and work life balance no longer become issues. They become integral parts of the organisation and, because of the increased level of trust, add to efficiency and profitability. In this way both fathers and mothers get to spend time with their children, husbands and wives get to go out to dinner and couples get the opportunity to spend the time together they so badly crave.

The newspapers are frequently full of stories about the unmarried or unattached people in a company and the married or attached. They are full of stories about mothers (or fathers) that just have to leave at 5.30 to pick up the children, the implication being that the additional workload has to be taken by the unattached members of the team. Personally I don't believe it. I have never believed in stupidly long hours at the expense of the people involved. However it is handled, it creates resentment equally with those who don't want to work late and those who feel they have to. Acknowledging that there will always be exceptions, there are only two reasons for people regularly to work late or long. They are either incompetent or over-worked. In my long experience very few people are incompetent and if they are, then something can be done about that – for the good of them and of the organisation. If they are overworked then re-assessing, evaluating and redistributing their workload will solve the problem. As leaders we will be thanked and remembered for doing this and our leadership is strengthened.

Small to medium organisations have to do the best they can with the margins and resources they have. They cannot necessarily lavish huge salaries, bonuses and perks on their staff. Their major resource is their people and so in order to treat them all fairly they have to make the best of their other resources. The most valuable other resource is care and understanding and so we come back to the principle of Love at Work. Beyond a certain level (and that varies from person to person) what we all really want is not just financial reward. We want above all to be valued for what we do and appreciated for who we are. These are things we can all give to each other all of the time. In short Love at Work is nothing more, nothing less than a mutually supportive, sustainable environment.

Larger organisations, or even giants, can and do handle things differently. Google for example, in an effort to both support their staff and make the most of their valuable time when at work provide a whole array of facilities on their main campus. There are over 20 restaurants with different styles of cuisine, fitness centres, car washing, laundry, fruit and grocery delivery as well as medical and travel services. The cynical view might be that the company does this to keep people at work longer but maybe it's the start of a return to community life, of village life if you like, where you both live and work with the people you know and are interested in. So in the same way that we used to live in communities that grew crops, kept animals, talked together, developed ideas together we can now live in communities that do the same thing. Except perhaps the crops become computers and the animals become services or products. Maybe on some level we are seeing the first shoots of a return to community life. After all, many of our current commute times are unsustainable and one way through this could well be the 21st century version of the village based around technology rather than agriculture.

Believe it or not there are even leaders within banks that take the high road towards ethics and morality and therefore uphold the Love at Work principle. Stephen Green, chairman at HSBC took the view that putting its struggling US Household division into administration and leaving its creditors to carry the losses was unthinkable, so they wrote off the whole £10 billion (without cost to us as taxpayers). "Our word is our bond and the idea that you can play fast and loose with that is immoral. I genuinely believe one of the biggest issues is that we must change the culture," he says. But then Mr Green is no ordinary chairman, he is also an ordained Anglican priest. He goes on to say, "The [financial] markets, flawed as they are like every other human structure, can be used to contribute to human development. Being there also creates opportunities – to show a level of integrity that loves others as ourselves and treats them as ends rather than means."

At the end of the day the biggest contributions at work are made not by companies or organisations but by individuals and individuals coming together as a a team. If we act as human beings in our world first, then do what we need to do, we can have what we want in a much more congruent way. When we think clearly, use our thinking to influence our behaviour and then act we are capable of creating amazing results. Thinking clearly means not lying to ourselves because it is so debilitating and can occur so subtly we don't even know we are doing it. The way most of us lie to ourselves is through our beliefs but principally our limiting ones. Limiting beliefs are fiction not fact. They drag us down and hold us back.

 Our deepest fear is not that we are inadequate. Our deepest fear is that we are powerful beyond measure. It is our light, not our darkness that most frightens us. We ask ourselves, "Who am I to be brilliant, gorgeous, talented, fabulous?" Actually, who are you not to be? You are a child of God. Your playing small does not serve the world. There is nothing enlightened about shrinking so that other people won't feel insecure around you. We are all meant to shine, as children do. We were born to make manifest the glory of God that is within us. It is not just in some of us; it is in everyone. And as we let our own light shine, we unconsciously give other people permission to do the same. As we are liberated from our own fear, our presence automatically liberates others."
From A Return to Love by Marianne Williamson

These words are so powerful for me and my wife that they are framed and on the wall in our house, where we can read them every day. If they are both powerful and true why do we so often not allow ourselves to be brilliant, gorgeous, talented and fabulous?

Walking the talk

I don't know if you remember Tim Campbell, the guy who against all expectation won the first series of that dog eat dog TV show, The Apprentice. His version of what happened is very interesting in the context of Love at Work. Throughout the series he stuck to his basic philosophy that, in his words, "If I grow and help you grow, I grow twice as fast as I can on my own because together we can do far more than any other way. If I can connect with you I am twice as powerful as before." He goes on to say that he always remembers what his mother used to say – that empty vessels make the most noise. So day after day he stuck to his principle of remaining calm and taking a step back. It wasn't that he was more intelligent than his fellow competitors or that he made decisions faster, it was simply his ability to stay focused and calm in the face of pressure and make better decisions as a result of that. Through this he was able to stick with his belief that we don't have to step on anyone to get where we want to be and that we can get what we want together. "Am I as good as? Can I compete?" are the wrong questions, he says. The real ones are "What do I want? Where do I want to be?" and then not focus on anyone else. He found that when he did this with an open heart everything fell into place. It simply didn't matter to him that someone was wealthier or had a better MBA. Tim's belief in who he is is so strong that if he had felt anywhere in the series that he hadn't been able to be himself he would have left the show. Winning in any other way would never have been as rich an experience. I'm not sure I could have stayed that centred under that amount of pressure! He says of his job running one of the group companies for Sir Alan Sugar that, because other people find it difficult to understand where he is coming from, he still struggles to be himself in every given situation. His colleagues are completely engrossed in how things should be, how they should react, in telling him how to do it and how he shouldn't be there in the first place. Most of all though he says he has to do it his way because, succeed or fail, he can look back and know he did exactly as he wanted to do – from his heart as well as his head – and that is truly Love at Work!

Countering our frantic world

For a long time I have had this feeling that, to paraphrase the words of T S Elliot, we are all on a journey to return to where we started and then see it anew. In his book The 8th Habit, Steven Covey describes the ages of civilization as he sees them – The Hunter Gatherer, the Agricultural, the Industrial, the Information and finally the Age of Wisdom. My own feeling is that this Age of Wisdom is the same place that the ancient sages of the East intuited and wrote about in texts like the Upanishads. We are therefore returning to that place T S Elliot wrote about only this time we are becoming more and more in a position to prove it scientifically. The crazy thing of course is that this doesn't make those texts any more or any less true. They simply are. What is also happening beyond doubt is the speeding up of this process of what we call civilization on an exponential basis. Just look at the length of time mankind was in the hunter gatherer stage compared to the time we were in the industrial age and are now in the information age.

The more I think about this phenomenon, it is this shortening of these time periods and other related ones that strikes me more than anything. In my own working lifetime we have gone from having to use carbon paper and manual typewriters to electric typewriters to fax machines, personal computers, email, Blackberry and iPhone. Less than forty years ago we would receive a letter, think about it (often overnight) respond, put it in the post and wait for a reply. The whole process could take up almost a working week. Now we receive an email and if we don't respond within minutes we get another one asking us why we haven't. Where in all of this is the space to think?

Are we really here to react to every single piece of communication instantly? I don't think so! Perhaps we need to step back for a moment and look at our life journey as human beings thus far. When I look back over my own life I can see clearly how I have come to this point. The stepping stones of my birth into a Yorkshire family, my childhood experiences starting towards the end of the second world war, my school years, my coming south to Art College, my career, my loves, my relationships, my children, my major illness, the loss of my business and the experience and response to all these things steered me unerringly to a point where I began to look at life differently. When it finally started to dawn on me that "there has to be more to life than this" my life started to change in amazing ways. I felt like I was starting to wake up, so I did what I always do when I get really interested in something. I read, I listened to tapes, I went on courses, I watched videotapes and subsequently CDs and I went into therapy. I was like a sponge, soaking up as much information as I could. Now I don't think for one minute that this is unusual. Everywhere you look nowadays there is self-help and personal development material. Twenty odd years ago when I started on my path there might have been one shelf of such books in a good-sized bookshop. Today there are whole sections so full of material it's difficult to know what to pick up first and more importantly what's worthwhile. Back then meditation and visualisation were words used, if not behind closed doors, then only when one felt they might be well received.

Ideas like neuro linguistic programming (NLP), creative visualisation and emotional freedom techniques (EFT) were either in their infancy or not even a twinkle in someone's eye. Today they are becoming words and actions as much a part of our language and society as any other.

Meditation is a particularly powerful and ancient system of freeing the mind from unwanted thoughts. Basically it is a technique for deep relaxation and therefore renewal and revitalisation of our mind and body. It allows us to recharge our batteries and dissolve deeply-rooted stress, tension and fatigue, leaving us feeling calm, centred and vital. Every single religion in the world uses a form of it but its strongest forms emanate from the ancient Eastern ones such as Hinduism and Buddhism. It was first popularised in the west through the Beatles and the Maharishi Mahesh Yogi, until it eventually became a movement known as Transcendental Meditation or TM. There are huge rafts of other wonderful work on meditation through people like Ram Das and Deepak Chopra and the more esoteric work of amazing people like the teacher and poet Thich Nhat Hahn. I also recall Ken Wilber saying that it is the only proven method of moving from one level of being to another – and indeed there is now empirical data available to support this view. One of the great things about meditation though is that it crosses all spiritual and religious boundaries, being a fundamental part of Christianity, Judaism, Islam, Hinduism and Buddhism to name but a few. Another is probably the fact that we don't have to believe in it for it to work. Perhaps even more importantly it allows us to connect our head with our heart and to be in our lives from this perspective. My personal practice and something I have done for decades now is simple – to sit every day for at least half an hour, eyes closed, with my focus on my breath and releasing whatever thoughts come into my mind.

When you are present in this moment, you break the continuity of your story, of past and future. Then true intelligence arises, and also love. The only way love can come into your life is not through form, but through that inner spaciousness that is Presence. Love has no form."
From Stillness Amidst The World by Eckhart Tolle

Regular quiet time for myself, combined with meditation, allows me to examine and re-examine why I am here and what my life purpose might be and I have to confess that my view has changed many times over the years. As these habits set in they also allowed me to look at how I operate in the world and little by little to really witness that. By witness I mean to be in a place where, through disconnecting from life's dramas, one can really see what is happening. Through witnessing we can experience detachment and learn for ourselves in a way that best serves us, others and the world in which we live. I don't see this as an instant cure-all but simply as a mechanism that allows me to say, "There I go again!" and vow to try not to repeat whatever it was that didn't serve me.

From such a space we are much more able to have our heart and mind connected and to fully live our lives. As Goethe so beautifully puts it; "Whatever you can do or dream you can, begin it. Boldness has genius, power and magic in it!"

What to take with you from this chapter

- **The head heart connection is vital to our well being**
- **We cannot be in service to others if we are not connected to and in service to ourselves**
- **Trust is at the centre of all we do**
- **We make a difference as individuals, not as companies**
- **Always walk the talk**
- **Take time out for you**

and to remind you to...

- *Make time to do the exercise in this chapter before you move on*

Chapter 2

What's in this chapter:

- A view of who we are in the world
- Setting out our values
- Looking at morals, values, commitment and integrity
- Learning to get our ego out of the way
- Introducing a useful psychological model
- Introducing a useful spiritual model

Foundation stones

" A house must be built on solid foundations
if it is to last. The same principle applies
to man, otherwise he too will sink back
into the soft ground and become swallowed
up by the world of illusion."

Sai Baba

First principles

When I was last CEO of a substantial office and whenever anyone new
joined us I would personally give them two separate orientation sessions.
The first was based on the professional aspects of the business and its
aims and goals. The purpose of the second was to give them a brief
look into my personal philosophy, what I believe to be important in life
and the values which underpinned the working of the office on a day to
day basis. Much of what we would talk through together was around
the idea of inclusiveness rather than exclusiveness, a theme to which
we will return later in the book. It is so important that everyone in an
organisation is involved in the important issues even if at the end of the
day those with the most relevant knowledge and information make the
decisions. It is so important to take that inclusiveness all the way down
the organisation and to have as flat an organisation as possible. In that
way everyone can feel really involved and take ownership of not just
their part of the business but its whole structure.

I also talked at length with them about many things, from the principle
that we might choose our parents to choosing everyone in our lives for
the lessons we can learn from those relationships. Can you imagine what
our lives would be like if we could recognise when we first met someone
why they were in our life? However, if we were able to do this we would
most probably have learned what we needed to learn from them! Take
that thought to its logical conclusion and, when it happens regularly
enough, we disappear in a puff of smoke to await our next incarnation!

We would then take a look at the underlying principles of Maslow, Covey, Wilber and Chopra. Not bad going for a meeting of not much more than an hour. It usually affected people in one of two ways. Some people were confused and others fascinated at the thought that there was anything to work other than sheer grind. Then there were others who simply breathed a huge sigh of relief, of recognition, of feeling they had come home in some way. In one case it even turned out that we had both done some of the same courses but on different sides of the globe!

So what we are going to do now is to take a longer look at these things to set the scene even more strongly for what is to come. Before we do though, I want to emphasise something. The only thing that matters is that you take the ideas you want and need from this book – as my first ever personal growth teacher, Graham Browne, was fond of saying – you don't have to believe any of this. Pull those tools out of the box, use them, become familiar with them and make them your own. Some of the things I say will resonate, some not. Take those that do and investigate them further. Put those that don't aside for another day because you may be surprised how time and situations change our perspective. Everything I write has its background either in major teachings and philosophies or is from my own learning and understandings. Whenever possible I will identify sources but sometimes these two aspects might become confused. At that point I want to be clear that I am not claiming the work of others as my own, but simply restating their work in my own words and therefore hopefully honouring them.

Choosing one's parents

Let's start then with the very controversial thought some people have that we choose our parents. It's an ancient yet controversial idea that has its roots in places as varied as Jewish mysticism and American Indian traditions. My sense of it is that, if we are indeed nothing more than spirit which manifests through ever more solidifying bundles of energy it could well be that we decide to incarnate at a specific time and in a specific place to learn whatever lessons we need to learn for our growth and development. If this is the case then it isn't a huge step to consider that we would go as far as choosing the two people on this planet that can best give us that experience right from the moment of conception. There is of course a strong and valid counter argument based on child abuse. Setting that aside for the moment, there is an abundant supply of evidence that we are fundamentally influenced by our life in the womb and even whether we were wanted or not by one or both parents at conception. Dr Thomas Verny's painstakingly researched book on this subject "The Secret Life Of The Unborn Child" is worth a read. In it he gives strong evidence of the baby's developing response patterns to speech, music and his/her mother's emotions.

It seems true therefore that we are starting to develop our personality long before we are born. If you don't want to go along with this, then maybe the idea that we develop our personality as a result of our environment once we are born is less controversial. We are all who we are and our personality is formed because of the circumstances of our surroundings, our upbringing and particularly the influence of our mothering and fathering ones, whether they are our parents or not. Because my father was away in the Second World War when I was born, my early childhood was influenced on the male side much more by my maternal grandfather with whom I formed a particularly strong bond. It was something which ran through that early childhood, my teens and only ended when it was cut short by his death when I was eighteen. I am aware, even now, almost every day of the strength of his influence, simply because of the frequency with which a memory of him is invoked. The smell of something; the sight of someone's face; the sound of someone's voice are all triggers for our memories. Triggers which have the ability to throw us either into extreme joy on the one hand or paroxysms of fear on the other. Learning to understand this in terms of our personality, set in the hustle bustle of the everyday, is a lifetime's work in itself. To me, this compounds the idea that so much of what we are here to learn can be learned in and through our work.

As tiny babies we are physical, emotional, mental and spiritual sponges. As toddlers we are the same but as we grow over the years we become less so until by the time we are adults we are generally running our lives based on what we learned as children, whether or not that is a useful thing to do. That may not be a bad thing because it could well be that along with learning all the good things we also learn all the things we need to untangle in order to be able to learn the lessons we have come to learn.

Doing or being work

Early in Chapter One I told of how I was given the opportunity to re-run my professional life and how through that I came to the view that connecting head and heart is what makes the real difference in organisations. Growing an organisation and increasing its turnover and profitability is all for nothing if we don't do it from our hearts. I have really come to recognise how "doing" business has the weird ability to test our morality and our ethics. "Being" in business gives us huge opportunities to witness our behaviour and make the right moral and ethical choices. It gives us huge opportunities not just for us to grow but for those around us to do so as well. Many organisations are so driven to profit that cost cutting and so-called efficiency creates huge levels of stress in the people who work for them. I absolutely believe that most of us are morally sound and ethically strong, that we always want to do the right thing, to go the extra mile for our employer, to make sure that we are seen to be giving more than a fair day's work for our day's pay. The question to ask ourselves is what can we do when we reach the point where we really can't work any harder or any longer. The answer lies in being at work rather than doing work. From this perspective we are able to look inside ourselves and see how we can become exceptional. If we own the truth about whom we are and how we operate, if we maintain our integrity on every level, we create that opportunity to be exceptional in our world and achieve our dreams.

Let me give you an example of what I mean by morally sound and ethically strong. In one of the businesses I was in we dealt with a multitude of contractors and suppliers and not all of them held the values that we did. At Christmas time, when gifts in all shapes and sizes came into the office, we would auction the larger ones at the staff party and give the proceeds to our chosen charity, often raising thousands of pounds. The smaller ones were raffled in a way that whoever you were you took home the same as anyone else. One particular Christmas, one of my Contracts Managers, let's call him Nick, walked into my office in a state of shock and put a brown envelope containing £500 in notes on my desk. One of the contractors Nick had been dealing with had insisted and insisted that he took it as a gift. He was so embarrassed that, not knowing what else to do, he took the money and brought it straight to me. I simply asked him what he thought we should do with it. He said he didn't think the contractor would take it back or he wouldn't have accepted it in the first place. Nick went on to say that he thought we should write and tell the contractor that we were sure he would understand that in the circumstances we were going to give the money to charity and that we would no longer be able to work with him. When I say that that is exactly how I knew he would respond in a difficult situation, I don't just say it with the benefit of hindsight. I knew the very first time I met him that his personality was built on firm foundations and he went on to prove it many times before ending up as head of the contracts side of the business. Sound moral judgements like this make us proud to know such people.

The congruence that Nick demonstrated is such an important aspect of who we can strive to be when we connect mind and heart. It is a difficult quality to describe but when it is present it transcends beliefs, race, creed, religion and politics. John F Kennedy had it; Martin Luther King had it; Mahatma Gandhi had it. I'm sure you can think of many more people including some closer to home too. We know when it's there and we know just as clearly when it isn't. One of its interesting qualities is that agreeing or disagreeing with the holder's point of view doesn't affect our ability to recognise it. Congruence is both tangible and intangible as a quality. People develop it through understanding the concept that Victor Frankl expresses so well in his book, Man's Search For Meaning - the principle that all the circumstances of our lives are of our own creation. When we understand that, we have the full ability to direct and manage our life in every way. We are beginning to integrate our consciousness. We stop blaming others and start accepting that our lives are the way they are because of our own reactions and responses to every situation we find ourselves in. What we finally come to understand is that every time we react rather than respond we are behaving psychopathically because we are not connected to our inner self, our candle flame. Through this understanding we have the opportunity to develop more and more congruence.

Moral and professional values

Our moral values are the foundation stone of our professionalism. Of course we have to exercise our specific skills and our commercial judgement too but it is this additional quality that can set us apart in our professional lives. When it resides deep within us, all our other actions are carried out with integrity, humility and kindness. In my last company we discussed this idea at length over a series of meetings and came up with the following rather long set of values for us to work with:

Our values as individuals

We value our business success so we:

- *Ensure our personal goals are aligned with those of the company*
- *Always look to enhance our competitive advantage*
- *Focus on outcomes rather than inputs*
- *Focus on solutions rather than problems*
- *Focus on effectiveness, not efficiency*

We value change and learning so we:

- *Learn through our mistakes and those of others*
- *Seek feedback on our performance*
- *Are proactive in our own development*
- *Encourage differences of view*
- *Embrace new ideas*
- *Question the way we do things*
- *Do our very best all the time*

We value integrity and are committed to:

- *Creating trust in all our relationships*
- *Being true to our word*
- *Listening carefully and without interruption*
- *Treating people with respect*
- *Appreciating others*
- *Telling people the truth*
- *Creating a thinking environment*

We value all our work colleagues internal and external so we:

- *Know they are central to our success*
- *Act with integrity in all our relationships*
- *Clearly identify others' needs and act on them*

- *Take all feedback seriously*
- *Value ourselves as well*

We value commitment and motivation so we:

- *Respect our need for work/life balance*
- *Respect and value individual and group achievement*
- *Are positive and committed*
- *Are passionate, energetic and engaged*
- *Take responsibility for our career development*

We value cooperation highly and so:

- *Take responsibility for our work*
- *Solve problems through ad hoc meetings, strategising and brainstorming*
- *Engage constructively with colleagues*
- *Value everyone's contribution as highly as our own*

We always value initiative and so:

- *Take responsibility to show it*
- *Always resolve problems*
- *Actively seek help when we need it*
- *Find ways to enhance everyone's performance*

Commitment and integrity

What perhaps matters most though is our commitment. Our commitment to be the best we can, do the best we can in every given circumstance and to support others in being and doing the same. One definition of the word commitment which I really like is, "Having the integrity around the intent to do something". Integrity is something every human being is capable of. We sometimes forget that in the rush to earn a living. Not forgetting to live with integrity means we have to wake up and stay awake, something which for most of us is easier said than done simply because we are fallible. Once we do decide to wake up we notice this fallibility more and more. We could therefore go down a path of beating ourselves up but it really doesn't help! All we actually need to do is to notice what happened and say to ourselves, "There I go again". The more we do this the more we will notice how we operate and we are on the path to Witness Consciousness, the path many consider to be the first stage towards transformation and eventually enlightenment. For me, there is no doubt that our future is determined by our present actions, so being able to see in the moment what one is doing, how one is behaving is absolutely key. This is where our karma, as it is called in the Eastern traditions, is formed.

Wouldn't our world be a wonderful, stronger, more powerful place if every business were run as much for the physical, emotional, mental and spiritual well being of every one who worked there as for the financial bottom line? Wouldn't our lives be so much more exciting if every company had a declared set of values, created by its employees, which upheld our worth as human beings? There are the first green shoots of this new corporate consciousness happening in companies like Microsoft, Boeing, Intel, even The World Bank and in leading consultancies such as McKinsey and Co. People like Gita Bellin, who did so much for the Eighties personal transformation movement, are now moving into the corporate arena to great effect.

Such ideas make absolute corporate sense. Nowadays we are seldom if ever employed for our manual ability alone, as we used to be in the industrial era. Very often we are employed for our intellectual ability but it is absolutely clear that this cannot be separated from our emotional and spiritual needs. Whether we work in business, the not for profit sector or the caring professions, the truth is that, when these needs are met too we are happier, more content and therefore more reliable as employees. Everybody wins. An upward spiral is created in which all our properly met needs feed off each other resulting in us thinking better, becoming more creative and producing outstanding work. Love at Work really does make sense.

One of the biggest issues in moving forward in this way is that it does demand a willingness from everyone in the organisation to take full responsibility for their personal growth. Even more importantly, change of this magnitude has to be led from the top. If the leadership isn't up for it then it is doomed to failure. Jack Welch and others talk about the importance of employees holding the leadership's values. I actually think this is very much a two way street. If we are to be truly fulfilled as individuals then it is just as important that the company we work for upholds our values as it is the other way round. Organisations are no more than collections of people there for a specific purpose, to paraphrase Anita Roddick. When we are looking for help or a product, people principally buy people. Companies don't buy companies even if the company name or brand becomes synonymous with the qualities and values of the people and we should never forget that.

In this respect the relationship between the employer and the employed has changed beyond recognition since the height of the Agrarian Age when the Lord of the Manor held sway over his tenants and serfs. This relationship didn't change hugely even in the Industrial Age either but, following the First World War, people's individual autonomy gathered pace rapidly until by the turn of the 21st century very few jobs for life were available or indeed sought. That's not to say that there weren't good landlords and great benefactors. Of course there were; people with names such as Cadbury, Rowntree, Terry, Lever, Ford, Rockefeller, Kellogg, and then lately Packard, Gates, Soros and Buffet. By now though, most of us have become used to the idea of having a number of jobs of our choice over our lifetime. Choice is the key word here and something we will return to again and again as we go on.

Getting our ego out of the way

 Remember that fear always lurks behind perfectionism. Confronting your fears and allowing yourself the right to be human can, paradoxically, make you a far happier and more productive person."
David M. Burns

There is no doubt that the biggest stumbling block to developing an organisation that demonstrates love in action is our individual egos. That's because it's also the biggest stumbling block to our own development. In this case I am using the first part of the Oxford English Dictionary definition of "a person's sense of self-esteem or self-importance". When we are ego free (if that's at all possible) we are able to:

* *Recognise all others as equals*
* *Act with compassion as though others were our self*

- *Work with humility because there are always others more knowledgeable and more aware than we are*
- *Trust ourselves and others which encourages others to trust us*
- *Act responsibly in every situation*
- *Care deeply about other people and the effect we have on them*
- *Understand others' feelings and actions*

Since Jim Collins wrote Built To Last and then Good To Great many of us in business have come to recognise the importance of putting one's ego on one side and thinking first of the people who are the very reason for an organisation's existence – whether they be employees, contractors, suppliers, clients, customers or members of their families. He proved beyond any doubt that lack of ego, particularly in the top leadership, was and remains the biggest single factor in the long term success of any company. That's not to say you can't have a strong ego and enormous success. However this sort of success is likely to disappear with the CEO when he moves on to climb his next mountain. Others, such as Marcum and Smith in their book Egonomics, have since looked in much more detail at the effect of the ego right through an organisation, drawing astounding conclusions on its debilitating effects on efficiency, productivity and profitability.

Getting our ego out of the way is, therefore, absolutely key to creating Love at Work and building a successful business, but what is this thing we call ego? Let's ask the Oxford Dictionary for its full definition:

ego /eego, ego/ • noun (pl. egos) 1 a person's sense of self-esteem or self-importance. 2 Psychoanalysis the part of the mind that mediates between the conscious and the unconscious and is responsible for the interpretation of reality and the development of a sense of self.

It seems a good answer because it really covers everything. The fact is there is nothing wrong with our ego when it really does what the definition says. After all it has got each and every one of us to where we are today. The problem for most of us lies not in that it mediates between our conscious and unconscious but that it is responsible for our interpretation of reality. If it doesn't get that right it will falsely develop our sense of self. I suggest that it is virtually impossible for it to interpret our reality accurately because everything we think, feel, say and do is affected by our desire to get our needs met. The most fundamental need is that of love. When that isn't met we settle for attention and this is when it begins to get sticky because, whereas true love only comes in an unconditional form, attention comes in as many forms as we can create situations to get it. Whether we get attention by doing things to please others (conforming) or by doing this against the will of others (rebelling) they are both different ends of the same stick. Think about when you were a child. Which version did you use most? One of them produces praise, the other at least disapproval and sometimes so violently it becomes physical abuse. Although neither of them is love in any form I have to ask why on earth we would do such a thing to ourselves. The answer lies in deficit need. When we lack anything enough we will do anything to get it, but more of this later.

 A loving person lives in a loving world. A hostile person lives in a hostile world. Everyone you meet is your mirror."
Ken Keyes Jnr

The importance of attention

Fundamental to understanding the affect of our egos is our listening and thinking skills. These are completely and inextricably linked with each other in ways which, when we begin to understand them, can make mind blowing differences to our performance as human beings. Really listening to someone is one of the greatest gifts we can give them. I learned this many years ago from a dear friend to whom I used to teach competitive dog training. Her name is Muriel Dwyer and she is synonymous with Montessori teaching worldwide. She actually worked very closely with the Montessoris from the very beginning of their work and with Maria Montessori in particular. At one of my training classes she said to me, "You know, this is no different from the most fundamental Montessori principal of teaching children. If you don't have their attention you can't teach them anything." That thought became my absolute mantra when teaching handlers to teach their dogs. I needed the handler's attention but they needed the dog's attention. So they were taught to understand the importance of not progressing with proper obedience exercises until such time as they could demonstrate 100% attention from their dog. It still resonates with me just how much attention is at the heart of everything we learn. What is more, the more fully someone places their attention on us the more fully we are able to place our attention on our thoughts. The experience is exponential! We will go into a really effective way of how we can do this in a later chapter but what might be of interest to you right now is to understand a little about how our brain decides what to listen to and what not.

In simple terms there are what might be called the old brain and the new brain. The old brain responds to every stimulus totally unconsciously, instinctively and intuitively. The new brain is conscious and alert, logical and reasoning. It is the old brain that initially filters our response to everything we experience in our world but is only able to analyse what it sees, hears, senses in very basic ways, part of which is our fight or flight mechanism. So it will decide for us whether we need to attack, submit, run away, procreate, nurture or be nurtured. All of which sounds pretty limiting. It builds and adjusts its responses based on our experiences, particularly those of our childhood. This is why we tend to choose our friends and our relationships to conform to those nurturing experiences of our early lives. It explains why we can so often fail to get our needs met. It also explains why we can switch off in an instant in learning situations. It is usually nothing to do with feeling tired after lunch or dehydrated (although that does of course have an effect) but directly to do with how our old brain perceives the person we are listening to. The challenge to trainers, teachers and even sales people (and we are all that on some level) is the same: to present what we have to say in a way that the recipient finds nurturing. Otherwise that reptilian brain, as it is sometimes called, will decide metaphorically to attack, submit or run away. The more we understand these issues the more chance we have of getting the non-serving part of our egos out of the way and being present for ourselves and others.

Taking the high road

So, in that hour's orientation, what else do I say and what do we discuss? There are principally two things, one of which we have touched on and the other not. The one we have is Stephen Covey's principle of taking the road to greatness rather than the road to mediocrity. The other is the psychological principle of levels of consciousness as expounded particularly in Maslow's Hierarchy of Needs and in Ken Wilber's work on what he calls Levels, Lines and Quadrants. During the 1960s Abraham

Maslow published his important contribution to modern psychology, explaining how human needs were hierarchical in nature and introducing the concepts of order, truth, goodness, beauty, unity, aliveness, uniqueness and justice. Originally believing that each of us has five categories of needs he finally settled on six: physiological, safety, social, ego, self actualisation and transcendence. Today however, many people group the first two together, seeing safety as a part of our physiological needs. His theory is that, only when the lower level of needs was at least partially met, would a person move on to fulfilling their needs in the next level. Whilst it is possible to work on more than one level of needs at a time our primary concern is to fulfill those at the lower level first but with the focus being on our dominant concern, which may well be at a higher level. Maslow also believed that the biggest obstacle to self actualisation was the society in which we live. Ken Wilber's work is very well articulated in his CD set, Kosmic Consciousness. You could say that in it he takes Maslow to a whole new level, seeing a much more complex reality but one which answers a whole load more questions than Maslow's theory can.

Wilber is, in my mind, a master at taking the vast amounts of research and theory on every aspect of human development, together with the wealth of ancient religious and philosophical texts, and making sense of them. The heart of his theory on human development seems to me to revolve around his concept of levels, lines and quadrants or what he calls AQUAL – all levels, all lines, all quadrants. In brief, he says that levels represent the stages of our development as individuals, lines represent the elements of that development and quadrants our relationship to our self, to others and to the world. I wouldn't for one moment want to begin to interpret what he says any more than this and it isn't the purpose of this book. What I would say is that the CD set, Kosmic Consciousness, is absolutely fascinating. If you want to broaden your understanding of how we operate as human beings it is more than worth a listen.

As we transform our energy from the spiritual plane to this plane of consciousness, this level of energy, we come in to it knowing that we are all powerful (and I mean that in the sense of using our power well and wisely, not in the sense of power over). From the time we manifest in our human body, that sense of our innate power slowly disappears one way or another - through our upbringing, through our environment and so on. We come in knowing who we are and knowing that we can

do anything we want to do. But, over the first few years of our life that sense is, if not forgotten or lost, eroded and we begin to believe that we aren't powerful. We begin to believe that we are in fact inadequate. Part of our journey in this life is to regain that sense of power, that sense of wisdom, that sense of being able to do anything, achieve anything and have anything that we want. The whole purpose of the orientation session I was talking of earlier was to help people understand that the office was built on the premise that we can be all those things.

Maslow's hierarchy

The question I was constantly asking myself was how do we build an organisation in which people are able to fully express themselves, are able to feel their genuine power and at the same time able to integrate and live in the world in which we do live, without having spent however many years meditating on a mountain top to regain that power. This is where Maslow's hierarchy theory comes in. The idea that our personal development on a physical, emotional, mental and spiritual level is linked to everything we can achieve. The same needs are also mirrored in the corporate world. For example:

- *On a survival level if a company isn't able to pay the bills the business does not exist*

- *On an emotional level if an organisation doesn't have relationships with others it has no identity*

- *Without a sense of self esteem the organisation cannot grow*

Just by taking those first two levels we can see huge parallels between our individual needs and our organisational needs. As we move through those states of consciousness as individuals, physically, emotionally and mentally so we come at the higher mental level to want to connect with our higher self or our spiritual state.

The same applies in an organisation. We begin to be able to move from a win/lose mentality, one of domination and submission, of right and wrong, of blame and shame to one of win/win. Once we move from that place of self interest, lack of choice, people doing it to us, all those various things, to a place in our emotional body, our heart, we shift into a different level of understanding. We create different levels of relationship, different ways of doing things and a different way of being in the world. We start to think about our achievements in the world, about our desire to grow and about finding meaning. When we do that we are coming to a point of personal transformation. If you apply those things on an organisational level you start to look at a different way of running a company for example, a different way of achieving results and a different way of being in the corporate world. We start to look at the win/win reality and eventually the win/win/win reality. Recognising that we can both have what we want, we start to look at doing things together rather than separately, to transcend the concept of right and wrong by accepting things just are. We know that things are perfect just the way they are. That we don't have to take offence when somebody does something to us and that taking offence is just as debilitating as giving offence. As we start to flex our emotional and mental muscles and are able to think about maximising our potential, we have the opportunity to move from our earlier state, where we were in agreement and a win/lose reality, to one of alignment and one of a win/win reality.

If all this sounds a little simplistic, let me assure you it's not! At no time do we move sequentially from the physical level to the emotional to the mental to the spiritual and stay there. We live our lives all over the place, dipping in and out of them as our circumstances and emotions catch us. It may be, for example, that on a physical level we are surviving, but on a spiritual level experiencing enlightenment. Imagine the whole thing as the most complex wiring diagram of ideas and thoughts and consciousness there could possibly be. Now it becomes easier to see that whilst we can spend much of our time in the lower levels we can still experience the spiritual. That may simply be sitting on a cliff top watching a sunset - and then we lose it. So we are not embedded in that world. We are still embedded in the physical, but occasionally we get touches of the higher levels and begin to know that we can have it wherever we are we, whatever we are doing. As we grow in our stability and alignment we move, if we are ready and willing and able, towards the spiritual level of Maslow's Hierarchy diagram (which you will find at the beginning of chapter 3). We start to think about making a difference in the world, we start to think about being of service in our business, in our community, in our family and exactly the same thing happens on a corporate level. When we have an organisation which is more than surviving, has good relationships, internally and externally, has a level of self esteem and is looking to become a meaningful organisation then it starts to think about the community outside. It asks what it can do for its community and eventually to what it can do in the wider world. This is one of the reasons why we are moving very rapidly from people talking about corporate social responsibility to people talking about sustainability. There is a fundamental difference between the two. Corporate social responsibility is more about our individual communities. Sustainability is about the whole planet and all our futures.

Win/win/win

At this point we stop thinking about win/win and start thinking about win/win/win – I win, you win, and the world or the community wins. This is power as a shared phenomenon rather than something that we fight over. We are talking about clear vision; about authority in its truest sense; about really having choice; about fulfillment; about attunement. If you change that word slightly it becomes atonement. Atonement in the biblical sense means the reconciliation of man and God. Break it back to its original meaning – at-one-ment – and it's easy to see what a very powerful place it can be. The last thing that I want to say here about our individual and corporate development is not an original thought and I'm not entirely sure where it came from, but it strikes me as a really good analogy. If you think about our human potential and what is possible as we move from agreement to alignment to attunement you might like to look at it like this. If you imagine it in terms of light, "agreement" is the equivalent of a 40 watt lamp, something you have on your bedside table, "alignment" is like a searchlight and finally, "attunement" on the spiritual level is as powerful as a laser beam. Now isn't that something worth aiming for?

 There are two ways you can die. You can stop breathing or you can stop dreaming."
Rocco Casciato

Moving towards spirit

In my mind all of this meshes nicely with one more major thought line or set of principles that I have found really useful for over twenty years and is embodied in the work of Deepak Chopra. Even now I remember starting to read his book, Quantum Healing, on the mind body connection in medicine and being blown away by it. Things have moved on since but it is still a pioneering work. From then on I was hooked and scoured the shelves of bookshops to see whether he had brought anything else out that I could devour. Finally he brought all of it together in a wonderful little book called The Seven Spiritual Laws Of Success. It was given to me by a dear friend within weeks of it being printed and I couldn't wait to get home to sit down and read it. It didn't take long because if you have also read it you will know it is small, concise and yet full of all the wisdom we need for a lifetime's work. That first reading brought together for me and articulated perfectly all the personal development and spiritual work I had done up to that point. I read it again and again and again and even bought the audio version. I still read it to this day (it's always on my bedside table) and can't even begin to remember how many copies I have given away to friends and acquaintances – it must be dozens. You may have guessed by now how significant I feel Deepak's work is! Although he has gone on to write many more books, both fact and fiction, it is The Seven Spiritual Laws Of Success that I recommend you read even if you read nothing else of his. In fact it is so important that I hope he won't mind my paraphrasing it and précising it here, particularly as in and of itself it does this of the great Indian traditions:

Being a very visual person I often see ideas in my head in the form of pictures or diagrams. Whenever I think about the Seven Spiritual Laws I picture them as a circle of circles, each one interconnected with the next and dependent on every other one. Perhaps they are a bit like people in that we need relationships or maybe it's more to do with what the ancient and great sages have always known and western scientists are beginning to confirm:

The essential communication mechanism of the universe is a quantum frequency connected to a giant matrix or "quantum energy soup" (sometimes called the Zero Point Field). If this is so, and it appears to be, this means that we are all connected at an energy level and that our thoughts and intentions, particularly when collective, can influence our world."
Lynne McTaggart

1 The first law is that of **Pure Potentiality,** or the idea/concept that our essential nature is nothing more or less than pure consciousness. This gives us the opportunity to watch in stillness, with non-judgement of our world, of others and of ourselves. To do this we need to be in touch with ourselves and with nature. We can achieve it through meditation or simply sitting in silence and enjoying the beauty of the world that surrounds us. When I was a boy my unconscious way of doing this was to sit on the end of the pier or lie on the cliff top watching the sea roll in and out, instinctively knowing how to make that connection to the field of pure potentiality.

2 The second law is that of **Giving and Receiving.** What we observe when we sit in stillness and simply watch is that nothing is ever static and that our world works through constant exchange. We are all connected at an energetic level and our thoughts and intentions, particularly when collective, can influence that world. Accepting this leads us to understand the concept of giving and receiving - the more we give the more we receive because we keep the abundance of our world circulating. Rich or poor, we always have something to give, even when it's as simple as a compliment or a flower or a prayer. Although many of us find it more difficult to receive than to give, it really is just as important. Without receiving there is no giving and without giving there is no receiving. In this way we keep wealth in all its forms – love, joy, friendship, money – circulating. Perhaps you can begin to see where my image of a circle of circles comes from.

3 The third law is **Cause and Effect.** One of the principal reasons I see the laws as a circle of circles is because of the law of cause and effect – or Karma. Newton's 3rd Law of Motion translates from the Latin as "For every action, there is an equal and opposite reaction", or as my mother was fond of saying, "We sow, yet we know not where we reap" which is probably not the exact biblical text! When we live our lives in full consciousness of these ideas we can ask ourselves, of every thought and action, "Is what I am about to do going to bring happiness to myself and others?" Ask our hearts for guidance and we can safely go ahead if the answer is yes and have the opportunity to stop and think if the answer is no. When we work at creating happiness, love and success for others in this way, we create it for ourselves. Whatever we give out we get back many-fold – and that applies to both positive and negative issues so choose wisely. But know too, that when we look at our world in this way we can begin to accept that life isn't meant to be a struggle.

4 Fourth is the law of **Least Effort.** When we stop struggling and accept our world the way it is rather than wanting it the way it is not, then something happens. We realise we don't need to let the past affect the present and we don't need to worry about the future. However we do need to take responsibility for events and problems by not blaming anyone (including ourselves) for the way our life is. All we need to do is remember everything is the way it is and not the way it isn't! When we understand this principle we also get to understand the principle of Defencelessness and come to recognise that when we let go of our ego we don't need to justify ourselves, don't need to be right, don't need to have the last word. My goodness, there are times when I for one still need to learn that!

5 Next is the fifth law, that of **Intention and Desire.** Intentionality is about setting out your hopes and dreams, whatever they are – new car, new house, new relationship, commitment to your growth or to meditate, in a way that you can make them real. One of my ways of doing this is to create a list around the specific thing or action but beware; you will get precisely what you ask for! We need too, to create it in the present tense. Create it in the future tense and that is exactly where it will stay. (I'll cover all of this in much more detail in Chapter 4 when we deal with creative visualisation.) Carry the list around with you, pin it to the wall, put it where you can see it, but the ultimate secret is to release our attachment to it, which brings us to the next and sixth law, the law of Detachment.

6 **Detachment** means letting go of expectations and not wanting things to be different, not forcing solutions on problems or intentions, not insisting things be the way we want them to be. By stepping into uncertainty again and again, we of course become more uncertain but the strange thing is that the more we do it the more secure we eventually become. The answer is to simply let go and trust that all is well.

7 The last law, the seventh law, **Life Purpose,** brings us to the final link in this mobius band or never ending chain of laws; the eternal question, "Why are we here?" I would suggest we are here because we need to learn on a soul level how to truly serve others and our self. One way of doing that is by knowing what it is that is special about each of us, because there is no doubt in my eyes that each one of us is special.

The Seven Spiritual Laws

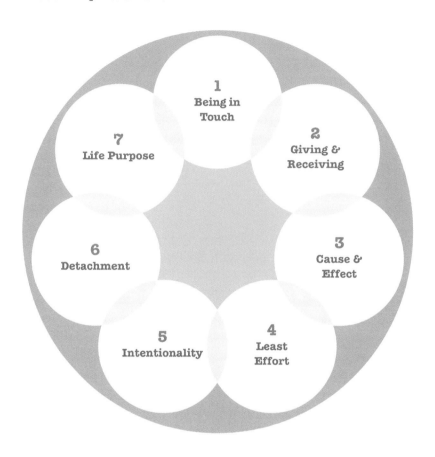

exercise

Stop reading for a few minutes and make a list of your unique talents, the things you really love to do. You may well surprise yourself because we all have unique gifts, qualities and passions. The secret is to recognise them and use them, whatever they are, in the service of others. Whether we are lawyers, doctors, bankers, nurses, social workers, carpenters, bricklayers, architects or the local shopkeeper, doing what we do best to the best of our ability and with an open heart will always bring joy and light to us and to the world. ♥

Once we decide we want to transform our lives we can do it the easy way or the hard way. It's not the cards we are dealt that are important but the way we play them. We can all live in abundance. The road to enlightenment does not have to be travelled on our knees clad in sack cloth and ashes. Living your truth through the Seven Spiritual Laws is not a religious philosophy. It's just one way of living your life.

That is why the Circle of Circles is so important. When we are in touch with the world, giving what we seek, creating our good fortune effortlessly and easily, fulfilled in our intentions and desires, content everything is as it should be, we can create what we want for ourselves and others. We constantly complete the circle and the circles within the circle – unceasingly – never endingly.

 There are many paths to enlightenment. Be sure to take one with a heart."
Lao Tse

Moving towards understanding

Everything I have spoken of in this chapter is aimed at helping us as our business lives become more and more demanding, as we have come to the point where we have worked smarter, harder and longer and it still isn't enough. We really have to ask ourselves what else we can do if we are not to end up in exhaustion. There is something else that thinkers in this field are beginning to realise we can do, and that is for us to tap into our innate power, the power that we came to earth with when we were born and which, as we closed down in order to handle the vicissitudes of life on this planet, we either forgot or lost. For all I know there may be as many ways of doing this as there are people on earth, but as with all the great spiritual traditions, they distil to the same thing. That distillation is as clearly and concisely expressed in The Seven Spiritual Laws Of Success as you are ever likely to find. It also debunks the idea of poverty consciousness; that spirituality and poverty walk hand in hand; that one cannot be truly spiritual unless one denounces material possessions. What's more, it is a perfect definition of Love at Work.

At the end of the day no matter what the outer manifestation, everything we say, do, feel, touch, taste, experience in any way on a mental, physical, emotional or spiritual level is there for us to understand ourselves as "human beings", not "human doings". It comes back to relationship; with our friends, our family, our work colleagues and our clients. In fact everyone we come into contact with. And they are there, as is everything, to reflect ourselves back to ourselves so that we can understand more about ourselves. I touched on it before, when it comes right down to it relationship is about nothing but our individual self, which has manifest itself on this physical plane in order to understand itself and its relationship to all things.

Somewhere in the Upanishads it says, "All this is that, all that is that, and that's all there is." Simple, isn't it? Oh, that it were! If we were really able to understand the true meaning of this one sentence, our struggle on the material plane would be over! Our working life, with all its ups and downs, profit and loss, bigger and better, stock market positioning, sales and manufacturing, service provision or whatever, is there ultimately only for us to learn more about ourselves. We could of course take the opposite view; that we don't need any of it and that we can learn just as much by sitting on a mountain top. Maybe it's just as valid, but the evidence is that we have chosen on some level to live in a complex society with all its accompanying pressures, or we would be somewhere else doing something else. This thing called work is therefore an ideal place to not only do a good job, contribute to the company and be well and justly rewarded; it is the place above all others where day by day, minute by minute, we have the opportunity to learn about ourselves, to constantly challenge ourselves and push ourselves beyond our comfort zones.

What to take with you from this chapter

- **Our personality starts to develop from the point of conception**
- **Clear, strong, moral values are the cornerstone of who we are**
- **Live with integrity**
- **Get your ego out of the way**
- **Rigorous attention is fundamental to our success**
- **A well developed world view supports us in our endeavours**
- **Everything is the way it is, not the way it is not**

and to remind you to...

- *Do the exercise in this chapter before moving on*
- *Read and reread Deepak Chopra's Seven Spiritual Laws Of Success*

Notes

....

....

....

....

....

....

....

Chapter 3

What's in this chapter:

- The grace of Agreement, Alignment, Attunement
- The power of witness consciousness
- Our need for love, or its substitute, attention
- Understanding how we operate

Building on up

" Because our minds seek each other through limbic resonance, because our psychological rhythms answer to the call of limbic regulation, because we change one another's brains through limbic revision – what we do inside relationships matters more than any other aspect of human life."

Lewis, Amini and Lannon – A General Theory Of Love

Maslow's influence

In the last chapter I spoke at some length about the principles underlying Deepak Chopra's Seven Spiritual Laws Of Success. Now I want to back track and delve more deeply into some of the principles that I have come to understand around what makes each of us who we are. Such understandings can help us be more fulfilled as human beings and therefore, better employers, better employees, better wives, husbands, fathers, mothers, friends and lovers. They are principles I learned many years ago from several sources and I hope, when you have read and absorbed them, they will resonate with you and start to make as much difference in your life as they have in mine.

To return to Maslow for a while, he believed that we could only move to what he called self-actualisation if we could set aside the hindrances placed on us by society; issues such as biased education, parental upbringing and unnecessary interference by the state. He foresaw that over the time of several generations it would be possible to replace the ego's need for self esteem with self worth or inner confidence. His vision was vast and included, through the concept of respectful teaching; the building of an individual's authenticity, transcendence of their cultural conditioning, vocation in life, the joy of life, acceptance of one's inner nature and recognition of needs, appreciation of beauty, respect for others and the importance of choice.

Whilst his is only one perspective it is, I believe, a very useful starting point and opens us to the possibility of achieving our full potential from a different perspective to that of Deepak Chopra. Maslow's Hierarchy of needs is a terrific tool through which to build a picture of how we each develop different perspectives, different motivations and different priorities. Without that picture we can't begin to take the first steps on our personal journey of development and self-actualisation.

In the previous chapter we looked at the basic principles Maslow was expounding. Now I'd like us to take a deeper look at some of the other principles associated with it. It feels like there are nearly as many diagrammatic interpretations of his theory as there are people who have written about it, so I guess another one won't hurt. My version is a bit different though because what I have done is add a view that includes not only the Seven Levels of Personal Consciousness but also what I am calling the Seven Levels of Corporate Consciousness. It is also different because it attempts to demonstrate the closing of the human psyche through the first three levels and towards the fourth and then the reopening or reawakening as we move upwards from there. Take a look at it on the opposite page and you will see just how strong the parallels are between our individual needs and those of an organisation. Although I've called it corporate consciousness it obviously applies equally as well to any group of people coming together in common interest or for the common good. Unfortunately there doesn't seem to be a word that covers every type and size of group, even the word organisation implies a size that is not always relevant

Agreement

Take a close look too at some of the words and phrases particularly in the three levels defined as Agreement, Alignment and Attunement and see how different they are. Agreement sounds like an OK word, after all it's something we all do with each other every day but in this context we can see just how debilitating agreement can be. That's probably because we can agree to something without believing in it or its truth.

	Common-interest	Group-interest	Self-interest

Common-interest
- I am you, you are me
- Win/win/win reality
- Power as shared potential
- Wholeness
- Clear vision and expression
- Authority
- For the good of the whole
- Being choice
- Being liberation and fulfilment
- Total involvement in whole

Group-interest
- If it benefits you, it benefits me
- Win/win/reality
- Together
- Transcends right or wrong
- Accurate self image
- Congruence
- Maximising potential of you and me
- Having choice
- Doing freely
- Freedom and satisfaction
- 100% Participation

Self-interest
- Me v's you, us v's them
- Win/lose/reality
- Domination/submission
- Right/wrong/blame
- Self-promotion delusion
- 'Driven' by conflicting
- Desires
- My self-interest
- No choice
- Doing compulsively
- Compulsion and Dissatisfaction

Human needs	7 levels of individual consciousness	7 levels of corporate consciousness	Level
SPIRITUAL	Service	Society	7
SPIRITUAL	Make a difference	Community	6
MENTAL	Meaning	Organisation	5
MENTAL	Personal growth / Achievement	Transformation	4
EMOTIONAL	Self-esteem	Self-esteem	3
EMOTIONAL	Relationships	Relationships	2
PHYSICAL	Security	Survival	1

Attunement
- Synergy
- Win/win/win
- Power as who we are

Alignment
- Autonomy
- Win/win
- Power as a shared phenomenon

Agreement
- Compliance
- Win/Lose
- Power as something to fight for

At this level of win/lose or right/wrong we are actually in adversary, not agreement. It's me versus you; us versus them, a world of dog eat dog, of conflict and gangs, whether they are of the playground, the street or on a more global basis. In this space of not enough, of poverty consciousness we are deluded, we strive to dominate others driven by our conflicting desires. Our world is full of compulsion and dissatisfaction and whilst we may think we have choice, we absolutely do not. Our lives are full of self interest and the over-riding idea that power is something to fight for. It's a place where satiating our physical and emotional needs comes first.

Alignment

At the point where we start to search for meaning in our lives and genuinely work not just for the benefit of ourselves but of our family, friends and work colleagues, things start to change. This new win/win reality transcends right and wrong and contains the opportunity to maximize not just our own potential but that of others. As we do things for ourselves and others more freely, we develop a much more accurate self image. It is this image which creates both congruence and genuine choice for us. In doing things freely, we create freedom and satisfaction as opposed to compulsion and dissatisfaction. We can live, if we so choose, able to participate fully in our world. In this new world of Alignment we have autonomy and can appreciate the idea that power is something we can share and in sharing it we become stronger.

Attunement

Our growth continues and as our needs are met more and more on each of the lower levels so we start to seek to make a difference not just in our immediate world but in our communities. Eventually that desire transmutes to a desire to work for the good of mankind as a whole and for our planet. This happens as the veils of separation between us dissolve and we recognise that each of us is no different from the other; that I am you and you are me. Where before we felt that win/win was a great way to live our lives, we suddenly see that the potential of win/win/win is amazing. We live in authority rather than with authority for the good of the whole; we feel whole. In Attunement we create synergy, we create exponential power, power as who we are, who we really are. Our human potential becomes exponential, we feel liberated and fulfilled, totally a part of and involved in everything around us. Power is not something we use over people; it is something we use for the good of us all. Can you sense what an amazing place that would be to live our lives in - and who on earth wouldn't want that? From here there is no doubt that we can truly create Love at Work.

Having read the previous few paragraphs, do take another look at the hierarchy diagram. Can you now see in it the benefits of striving to work in attunement, even when we don't or aren't able to achieve it? Whenever we shift from doing things out of self interest or wanting to prove ourselves right, the level of power available to resolve whatever challenges are set us is increased dramatically. Whenever we recognise the benefit of telling ourselves and others the truth, of doing things congruently and for mutual benefit, our clarity of vision and expression of authority changes gear. Choice, fulfillment and involvement become the norm.

Within this paradigm our needs vary according to the stage of consciousness we are operating in at any given moment. In my experience those needs that always drive us most and hardest are around our need for love. As I explained briefly in an earlier chapter, when our need for love isn't met, what we seek is attention. It's easy to imagine how fraught with danger a need as powerful as attention can be. Physically abusive relationships of all types revolve around this single issue and until, with help, the victim can step back far enough to be able to see this they will go on repeating the pattern either within that relationship or in a subsequent one.

Witness Consciousness

How then do we get to see what our patterns are and what our unfulfilled needs are? The short answer is through a lot of very hard work until we are established in something called "Witness Consciousness". The fuller answer will follow! Whilst we have long intuited the way our needs build up in us even pre-birth, we have only recently developed the scientific and medical tools to allow us to look inside the brain and begin to understand what happens. We don't need to go into that area in depth now but if you do want to know more then I suggest you read

"A General Theory Of Love" by Lewis, Amini and Lannon. What I do want to look at though, is what those mechanisms in us are and what we can do about them, if we so choose. If our need, neediness or lack of need significantly affects the way we behave and operate in our world then they will also affect everything we are involved in or with. Until such time as we can understand and release these needs, their affect will be detrimental rather than positive. Therefore, it would seem very useful if we could first of all learn to watch our thoughts and then decide whether they are supportive of our actions and progress or not.

 Not causing harm requires staying awake. Part of being awake is slowing down enough to notice what we do. The more we witness our emotional chain reactions and understand how they work, the easier it is to refrain. It becomes a way of life to stay awake, slow down and notice."
Pema Chodron

This is by no means a new thought! Indeed, Witness Consciousness is one of the three great principles at the heart of all the Indian spiritual and philosophical traditions and of yoga and meditation. In this sense the Witness is the non-attached, non-judgmental observer that is not bound by ego. On a day to day level we could think of it as our own personal observer, so all we need to do is awaken it. We will delve more into this and the specific process of meditation in a later chapter. For now however let's focus on uncovering how our needs affect everything we do.

On some level everything we do every day is based on what happens to us in early childhood and how we react to that in terms of getting our need for love met and in its absence our need for attention. Until we recognise that and start to work on those issues then nothing will change. We will remain stuck wherever we are. Furthermore, simply having the knowledge of how we operate as human beings and having the knowledge of what to do about it is not enough. In fact it's more than possible to use this knowledge to stay even more stuck than we already are.

So how does this need within us operate and what can we do about it? Principally it affects us in three ways: first in terms of how we react, second in terms of how we feel (what might be called our Feeling Cycle) and third in terms of how we act (what might be called our Action Cycle). Whilst the explanations I am giving you are my interpretation of what happens, I give them because having heard them and worked with them, I know both intuitively and intellectually that they are as close to the truth as anything I have come across. Whether they resonate for you, only you will know.

Although all of us are a complex mass of reactions, feelings and actions which change femtosecond* by femtosecond we all develop over time, particularly pre-birth to the age of around seven, what might be called default settings of behaviour. The scary thing is that until we are willing to witness our behaviour and choose to do something about our reaction we have but two alternatives which we use to get love or attention.

Conform or rebel

One of these layers of behaviour is to conform or rebel and every human interaction at this level is based on them. Imagine a simple interaction with your mother when you were very small. She gives you her attention and then asks you to do something and you willingly do it – her response is praise and love which reinforces the behaviour. Over time this conforming to get love or attention develops into a very strong pattern. Now imagine the same situation but this time she doesn't give you her attention and tells you to do something. Because you don't get the attention you were wanting you don't do it and maybe even stamp your little foot. You most likely will get her attention now but in an unwanted way, possibly through a scolding or worse. But you did get her attention and most times any attention is better than no attention. Over time this rebelling to get attention (or love substitute) develops into a very strong pattern too. Although both patterns become imprinted, one of them becomes the dominant one. On one level it really doesn't matter which because they are both simply different ends of the same attention stick. It is on such patterns that our personalities are formed. It's easy to test this out, see the exercise on the following page.

*A femtosecond is defined as one billionth of one millionth, or one quadrillionth of a second.
A femtosecond is to one second what the diameter of a human hair is to the distance between the earth and moon, or a grain of sand to all the sand on all the beaches of the earth.

exercise

As you did earlier, simply close your eyes. Take a moment to relax and then reflect on a recent situation when you were asked to do something – it's easy enough because it was probably no more than minutes ago. How does it feel? Can you sense whether you rebelled or conformed? Now think back over another time when you were told to do something. How did that feel? Did you rebel? Did you feel angry? Or did you just do it? It doesn't matter who we are or what we do – it happens to us – all the time, and we react – all the time. Now, staying with your eyes closed, go over a few more times when you were either asked or told to do something and work out which is your dominant pattern – to rebel or to conform – we all have one. Now think about your partner or someone else you know really well and see which one they use most. Then try thinking of a few friends and see which of the two they use most. It can be both interesting and revealing but the purpose behind this little exercise is to get you to look at it in relation to your self. Once you have tried this a few times you will most likely never look at yourself or your friends in the same way again! ♥

The feeling cycle

The second and equally deeply ingrained layer is around what I referred to earlier as our Feeling Cycle. It is developed around the amount of love we are given or is taken from us when we are very small; some would say so small that it starts pre-birth. The result of all of which is, at our core, a feeling of either abandonment or neglect at one end of the spectrum and smothering or invasion at the other. I'll do my best to explain this through some examples.

Imagine you are lying in your cot as a tiny baby and on some level feeling lonely or hungry or in need of changing. Your reaction is to make a sound, to cry, to attract your mother's attention. She comes, she picks you up, she cuddles you, she feeds you and perhaps changes you, then puts you down again. Your needs are met and you settle down to sleep. All is well in your world.

Now imagine this. You cry and your mother doesn't come so you cry even louder. Still no one comes, so you cry even louder. Still no one comes and this goes on until eventually your mother arrives and does all the things I wrote of above. The result is that whilst you are left with a feeling that all is well in your world you are also left with a niggling feeling that it isn't quite. This is the start of us feeling neglected. Should you cry and cry louder and louder as you did in the last example and still no one comes and you carry on crying that feeling of neglect will get stronger and stronger until it is replaced by one of abandonment. The result is that we feel that there is never anyone there for us. We feel isolated.

What we are also likely eventually to learn in this extreme situation where there is nobody there for us is a lack of purpose, a sense of "What's the point?" We will carry this through our life until we recognise it and choose to do something about it. It is through layer upon layer of this experience of neglect or abandonment that the needy personality develops and in extreme cases develops a belief that there is never anyone there for them. For those of us who take this pattern with us into later childhood and adulthood we will always feel that there is never enough – enough attention, enough love, enough money, enough material things, or even enough sunshine! Returning to the point about pre-birth experience, the development of this aspect of our personality could well also be affected by the sense we might have of whether we were or were not wanted when we were conceived and indeed, throughout the whole gestation process.

I am sure it will come as no surprise that should your early experience lie at or towards the other end of the spectrum you will develop entirely different patterns. This time imagine you are lying in your cot as a tiny baby and on some level feeling lonely or hungry or in need of changing. Your reaction is to make a sound, to cry, to attract your mother's attention. She comes, she picks you up, she cuddles you and continues to cuddle you. Doesn't that feel good? Now imagine you are lying there content and quiet and enjoying just being when, whoosh, you are picked up and held tight and cuddled and cuddled. On another occasion you may even be asleep when it happens but you get woken up because mummy or daddy in their need, has to have you awake. When this goes on time after time, when we experience too much attention on a grand scale we develop a sense of being smothered. Where the neglected or abandoned child can't get enough attention, the smothered child just wants some space. The emotion can be so strong that it can affect our physical being and our breathing to the extent that we may, through the psychosomatic connection, develop asthma. This is very much my experience. As a 2nd World War baby, with my father away in the RAF and our town being bombed, it must have been a huge sense of comfort to my mother to be able to pick me up and cuddle me at those and many other times. The point is not my personal circumstance or whether what my mother did was right or wrong, but that any child in this situation is being taken from when they are in need of being given to.

At the far end of this side of the spectrum is a place where we feel so totally invaded by our parent that to alleviate it we develop a part of our personality that says we don't need or want anyone. This is just as much a place of isolation as the person who experienced abandonment as a child. Thankfully most of us didn't experience such extreme forms of early life experience and therefore don't have to live in those extreme worlds.

What is affected through all of this is our ability to get our needs met, which we do through the use of our will. This is why for example once I start to witness my behaviours I am able to choose to change them. In this I have but two choices of action: for me to satisfy my will or to satisfy your will. In the circles where I heard and learnt about this stuff, those actions are called I-centred and U-centred. I-centred means my ability to get you to react to me; the way I want things to be; the way I want the world to be; the way I want other people to be. U-centred means my ability to react to you; to your values, attitudes, ideas and expectations. On a societal level it also means values, attitudes, ideas and expectations. This is why we will now take a look at our Action Cycle.

The action cycle

Which type of personality we develop, either I-centred or U-centred, is linked in part to our early experiences around the spectrum I have described earlier. Whilst we might know we want to get our needs met or meet the needs of others, we also need to develop strategies to enable that to happen. In the event, whether our basic personality is I-centred or U-centred there are two ways we can do this. They are "overtly" and "covertly" and which one we principally end up using is tied directly back into our experience of the Feeling Cycle in relationship. Both personality types will use both. The nearer to the centre of the spectrum we are, the more likely we are to operate overtly. The nearer we are to the extremes of the spectrum the more likely we are to operate covertly.

You may well be saying to yourself that this is all very well, but how does it connect to what you thought you might find in this book. It's simply that unless we have some basic understandings of how our personality works, we cannot witness our behaviours. If we can't witness our behaviours then we certainly can't change them when we need to. Nor can we witness those of others and the affect and effect it will have on our growing business.

exercise

Why don't you put the book down for a moment and try this? Gently close your eyes and bring to mind some people in your life you know really well and think about them in the light of these ideas. Can you see whether they rebel or conform? Can you see whether they are needy, extremely needy, not needy or totally isolated? Can you see whether they are covert or overt in their behaviour? ❤

I know I have friends who are absolute masters at getting all their needs met and sometimes I still wonder how they do it. Equally I have friends who are always there for everyone else, very often at their own expense. Working with these understandings will give us much more flexibility in the way we interact with people, particularly those who can affect the growth and development of our business whether they are colleagues, suppliers, customers or clients.

Understanding how we operate

I have long believed that it is not the cards we are dealt that matter in our lives but how we play them. Whether those cards are high, low or court cards is not important. It is how we react or respond to every given situation, what we learn from it and subsequently apply.

Once we can even start to glimpse the variety of ways in which we all operate we can also begin to imagine the endless possibilities of need and reaction in all of us. Through this understanding, I hope you will, over time, develop an insight into how we cannot move ourselves or our work forward unless we get our needs met; of how those needs arise within us and how that is profoundly affected by our upbringing; of how through our feeling and action cycles we strive to get them met; and how we do that through rebelling or conforming which are as I said but opposite ends of the same stick.

Understanding that each of us individually and as families, businesses or organisations has inbuilt needs and that we have learned a multitude of strategies (some devious, some not) to get them met is very powerful. We do it all the time on our physical, emotional, mental and spiritual levels around survival, relationships, stimulation and recognition. When we can start to see all of this, particularly in our selves, and at the same time not judge ourselves or make ourselves wrong we are opening up our head-heart connection and the possibility, once more, of Love at Work. Doing no more than this, means there is hope for our individual futures, the future of all of us and our planet.

What to take with you from this chapter

- **We all develop patterns pre and post-birth that may or may not serve us**
- **We run our lives by conforming or rebelling in order to get our needs met**
- **As we learn to witness these patterns we have the opportunity to change them**
- **As we exercise our opportunity to change, so do those around us**
- **As we move from agreement to alignment to attunement our perspective changes**
- **There is no one and no thing to change but ourselves**

Notes

Chapter 4

What's in this chapter:

- Meditation – powerful beyond belief
- Creating what you want through visualisation
- Getting what we want in our lives
- The power of the mind

Useful tools

" You are what your deep, driving desire is.
As is your desire, so is your will.
As your will is, so is your deed.
As your deed is, so is your destiny."
The Upanishads

The power of meditation

By far the most important and effective tool on our personal journey is meditation. Indeed it is the only proven method of pushing forward with our development on every level – physical, emotional, mental and spiritual. Organisations such as the Integral Institute, founded by Ken Wilber, have been carrying out research in this area for years and have emphatically stated that meditation is the fastest and only proven way to ground ourselves in the higher levels of self development. It is also proven, through research carried out by the Maharishi Foundation International into the efficacy of their Transcendental Meditation system, to reduce symptoms of stress, anxiety, and high blood pressure as well as decrease visits to the doctor and hospital admissions. Their claims are backed up by more than 600 scientific studies conducted at 400 medical schools in 33 countries in the past 40 years. Many of the principles of TM, as it is known, appear in many other systems of meditation so it is fair to assume that the benefits will accrue just as much from those as it does from using the Maharishi Mahesh Yogi's system. In addition there is an absolute plethora of other studies confirming the truth of the power of meditation.

This is not surprising, because the ancients were using meditation at least five thousand years ago and probably even pre-history to understand many things which only now are we even beginning to prove scientifically. Most, if not all religious traditions, including Christianity, Islam and Judaism contain some form of meditation practice. However, those currently used in the west owe much to Buddhism on the one hand and to the Hindu

Vedic traditions on the other, where the oldest written records exist. Behind each one is the intention to create a deeper connection to a higher power and to a deeper state of consciousness by freeing our mind from our life conditioning. That higher power is defined and described in different ways in the many and varied disciplines available to us today.

Had I been writing this book twenty or thirty years ago there would have been a whole raft of people who had never heard of meditation, other than perhaps to think that it was something weird that only the Beatles and hippies did. The need to convince you of the benefits would have been far greater. Not so now. I can't think of anyone who wouldn't have heard of it and I guess that a lot of people reading this book will already have tried it or are practising it. If you are one of those people and are happy with your current practice, and that may well be in one of the other religious forms, I wouldn't dream of doing anything but encouraging you to continue. If you do want to try something new then you could try the method further on in this chapter – you can always return to your previous practice later.

Meditation works

What really matters though is that meditation works. Twenty minutes a day, twice a day can become a life changing experience as I know personally. Back in the early Seventies, as a young man, I developed Crohn's disease along with all its debilitating side effects. For years and years I tried everything I could find in both western and eastern medicine, short of major surgery, to alleviate it but to no avail. It was so bad that at one stage I was taking 19 different pills and potions a day! Eventually in the mid Eighties I came across acupuncture and through my practitioner, an amazing healer, I also learnt about meditation. By the end of the eighties it had become a part of my daily routine. There is no doubt in my mind that it was the combination of acupuncture and meditation that allowed me to come off all my drugs and eventually heal my body. For over fifteen years now I have had none of the signs and symptoms of Crohn's. Western medicine says that it is incurable. I am living proof that it is not. Anyone who meditates regularly will tell you how important it is in their life and the various influences it has had. They will also tell you how it is even more important to meditate before a particularly busy day. Once settled into the routine you will be amazed by how calming and refreshing it can be.

Learning to meditate

I consider it such an important element in creating Love at Work that I think it worthwhile to describe in detail the way in which I was taught to meditate. If we are truly serious about being at work in this way we need all the tools we can find. This is the single most powerful one! So I suggest you read this section through a number of times before you try the meditation so that you are pretty clear as to what you are going to do. That way you will be able to focus much more on the meditation. I've also added a prompt sheet at the end of the procedure.

The first thing you need to know is that there is nothing you can do that is either right or wrong when you meditate. Everyone's experience is different and every experience is different, every time. All you need is the time and the space and you.

The second thing is to understand that you cannot achieve a meditative state using this method through concentration or trying to meditate, any more than you can by using control. Equally resistance will negatively affect your meditation. So let go of resistance, let go of control and don't try to concentrate.

The third is that the space you use is important. It needs to be quiet, gently lit and say to you that you matter. It needs to be free from any form of interruption whether that's your partner, your children or your pets. Pets and particularly cats and dogs love the energy created by meditation and will lap it up given the opportunity – don't let them. It's your energy and you are meditating because you want to increase it, so don't give it away easily! That's not to say that if you and your partner are both learning to meditate you can't do that together – my wife and I do so much of the time.

When one learns letting go and letting be
When one learns sinking
When one learns emptying and being emptied
One necessarily comes face to face with
NO- THING –NESS"

Matthew Fox

Meditation – the first stage

1 One last thing before we proceed, working through this series of exercises over a period of weeks doesn't need to stop you from reading the rest of the book.

exercise

Telephone, mobile, laptop and Blackberry all need to be off. Heavy meals, tobacco and alcohol before your chosen time should be avoided too. For your morning meditation be sure to have showered or bathed but not eaten before you start. Next you need to be dressed in loose clothes, sitting comfortably with your back straight and your feet (shoe-less if you prefer) firmly on the ground. An upright chair without arms is ideal - arms on a chair always seem to be in a position where they distract us. There is no need to assume the lotus position if you aren't used to it because it will only add another distraction. You are likely to have plenty of those from your mind without the help of your physical body! Other people use meditation stools and others still lie down. I don't recommend lying down because the very fact that you are going to be attempting to let go of your mind could easily send you to sleep.

Now gently place your hands together on your lap, close your eyes and focus on your breathing. Simply watch in your mind the rise and fall of your chest and the quiet in and out of your breath. With your eyes closed and your mouth closed, breathe out through your nose and as you do so let go of all the stress and worries of the day. As you breathe in take in clean, fresh renewing energy. Do this four or five times and then relax even more, simply focusing on your breath. Continue to focus on your breath as you inhale and exhale through your nose and, as you do so, just watch any thoughts or feelings that arise, any sensations in your body and let them be, let them go. Each time a thought arises just notice it and return to your breathing.

Sit like this for twenty minutes or so, trusting that you will know when the time is up. If you really don't think you will know then you need to find something that gives you a very gentle reminder - your normal alarm or phone is not OK. The last thing you need is to be shocked out of that quiet state! After those twenty minutes, take two or three deep breaths before slowly opening your eyes. You have just successfully completed your first meditation. Easy, isn't it? That's all you need to do every day for the first week other than repeat it morning and evening.

If you are finding it difficult to settle into your routine try this simple technique. Start as above by closing your eyes but for just 30 seconds, then half open them for 20 seconds, close them for 20 seconds, half open them for 15 seconds, close them for ten seconds, open them slightly for 10 seconds then close them again and allow yourself to be fully in your meditation. ♥

You have spent a week now doing your best to still your mind by letting your thoughts go. Some days it may have been easy and others hard. You may have felt frustrated by the sheer number of your thoughts – as though they were a never ending shopping or to-do list. Let me reassure you that although it may not have felt like that, it is as much meditation as the times when all seems calm and still. Whenever you notice a thought, return to your breath again and again and again.

Let's review those first sessions and try and uncover what has been happening. For the moment imagine your mind as an iceberg, floating one-eighth above the water and with seven-eighths below it. The eighth above is your conscious mind, the seven eighths below is your unconscious waiting for you to delve into it. As you breathe and relax you start to let go of your conscious thoughts and descend into the unconscious, which is full of millions and trillions of stored memories, reactions and feelings. As you descend your mind comes across one of these thoughts, bumps into it and releases it and it make its way upwards from the depths of your iceberg or ocean like a bubble. This happens time after time as we meditate – descending, bumping, releasing – until we slip further into meditation, our mind stills and we move unconsciously, unknowingly into the gap, something we will come back to later. It is in the subconscious releasing of those memories, reactions and feelings over time that we begin to feel less stressed, less worried, less anxious. Can you see now why meditation is such a powerful tool; why when we are calm and clear we will make so much better decisions in and for our lives?

The tip of the iceberg, our conscious self is how we see our self, how we think others see us and how others do see us. The subconscious self is the part of us that is hidden not just from others but from ourselves. The process of meditation allows us to release those childhood beliefs and assumptions and let go of the related stress, leaving us free to probe the unlimited energy of who we really are.

Meditation – the second stage

The first stage is very simple and straightforward and quite honestly you can stick with that as long as you like. If you do want to move on then this is the next step used in many systems. It involves what is known as a mantra. Mantras are no more and no less than a sound, syllable or group of syllables used to create a vibration which has the power to transform. They originated in the Vedic traditions of India and are an integral part of the spiritual practice in Hinduism, Jainism, Buddhism and Sikhism. There are literally hundreds and hundreds of them in many forms from single words to salutations to sentences to complete prayers. Because essentially they represent pure sound, many of them are to be found in Sanskrit, the oldest and purest language still in existence. In the context we are going to use them, the sounds or syllables are chosen specifically because they do not represent words and therefore cannot be interpreted through previous knowledge. The fact is that we will give meaning to any word that exists in our own language. Just try not creating an association for ice-cream or dry-white-wine! If you want to hear some traditional ones simply type www.sanatansociety.org into your web browser and follow the links.

exercise

In some westernised meditation systems gurus and course leaders charge very large sums of money to give you your personal mantra. My own view cuts across this in that I believe that given the right circumstances, no one knows better than ourselves what is best for us. I believe that all that matters is that you have a mantra available to you which resonates and that given reasonable choice you are the one best placed to decide what that is. This is why you will find, a little further on, a whole series of mantra sounds for you to choose from. What I am going to say next may sound tedious and unnecessary but I promise you it is not and that it will repay your effort a thousand fold and more. Ideally what you need to do is write them all out in capitals on separate pieces of paper and look at each of them in turn. Do this by settling yourself in your meditation position and then looking at them one at a time through half closed eyes and say each one quietly to yourself several times. Set aside only those that resonate with you. Yes, you will know when they do. When you are left with only the few you felt drawn to, repeat the process until you are left with just one. This is your chosen mantra, something to be respected and used with reverence. Do not be tempted to change it because you think it isn't working or because it becomes uncomfortable. Such things are absolutely part of the process of using a mantra in meditation and are absolute proof that it is working. Here is the list chosen at random from some of those used by Self Transformation Seminars:

SAAN-YUMM	SHAA-LOM	AA-REE-HUM
SAA-MEEMM	SAA-LAAM	SHAA-RAA-NUM
DAY-VUMM	SAA-VOOM	SOO-VEE-SHAAM
JAA-NUMM		SHAA-TOO-REEM
SHAA-RING		SOW-NAA-SHAAM
HAAS-YUMM		SOW-MAA-HUM
SOW-MAAH		HAA-NEE-MUM
DOE-NUM		SHEE-RAA-YUM
KREES-TUM		BRAA-CHE-UM

Now that you have chosen your mantra we can move to the next stage of meditation. Have the piece of paper with it written on handy on your knee. First of all settle into your usual meditation procedure and begin your practice. Once you are fully settled and are watching your breath, then watching your thoughts arise and returning to your breath (probably but not necessarily after about ten minutes). At this point you are going to introduce your mantra into your meditation. If you can't remember it half open your eyes and look at it on your lap then close your eyes again. So far your routine has been to focus on your breath; recognise that a thought has arisen and that you aren't focusing on your breath; then return to your breath. From now on you are going to use your breath as a cushion onto which you introduce your mantra. The sequence therefore now goes as follows. You are settled in what is called the breathing cycle; watching your breath, watching your thoughts, letting them go and returning to your breath gently and rhythmically. At this point, with your breathing in the background, introduce your mantra into your mind, saying it gently to yourself on each out-breath. When a thought arises recognise that you have stopped using your mantra and return to it, reintroducing it gently. That's all there is to it! Every time you witness a thought, return to your mantra. At the end of your meditation take a few deep breaths in and out, open your eyes slowly and bring yourself back into your world. ♥

Meditation – Stage Three

3 You have been meditating for several weeks now and are settled in your routine. You start each time by taking a few deep breaths, letting go of all the problems, stress and worries of your life as you exhale, and inhale calm clear energy as you settle into your routine. Then you move your focus to your breath and settle even further, returning to your breath every time you notice a thought.

As you go deeper into your meditation and you introduce your mantra, saying it to yourself as you breathe out, you may find something close to the following happens. You return to your mantra every time you notice a thought; a constant repetition of breathing - mantra - thoughts. As you slip from your conscious mind to your sub-conscious your breathing becomes shallower still and your mantra a gentle pulse with just the occasional thought. Then you may notice a sensation. It may be peaceful, it may be troubled, you may want to laugh or you may even want to scream or run. Just notice that you aren't using your mantra and return to it. Your breathing becomes even shallower until there is almost no breath, no mantra and no thoughts. This is the place referred to as The Gap. It is that place of stillness where we have the opportunity to be in touch with our true self, our higher Self. Then in an instant there is a sudden intake of breath and it is gone. Sometimes it lasts for what seems like eternity but it always fades. Don't expect to experience it every time though. Simply be open to it happening. We will talk more about this place when we look at visualisation as a tool later on but all you need to know is that, as with all meditation, the place of The Gap is no different from or more important than any other place. For now though there is nothing more to do than maintain your practice, twice a day, day in day out, week in week out until it becomes a totally ingrained habit – as much a habit as breathing, eating and sleeping.

Meditation – a short checklist

- *Find a quiet space free from distraction*
- *Gently close your eyes*
- *Take a few deep breaths*
- *Let go of your body*
- *Let go of your mind*
- *Focus on your breathing*
- *Let your thoughts go as they arise*
- *When you are settled introduce your mantra*
- *Let your thoughts go as they arise*
- *Allow yourself to drop into the gap as it occurs*
- *Allow yourself to simply know when time is up*
- *Focus on your breath*
- *Focus on your body*
- *Bring yourself fully back into the space*
- *Gently open your eyes*

Don't give up

Before we leave this subject I want to say again; take what you want from this book, what is useful for you but do not give up on meditation! Not everyone will find the meditation method I use right for them. If this one doesn't suit, please, please go out and find a method that does – it may be in a book, on a CD, a DVD or in a class of like-minded people. Indeed if you haven't meditated before, attending some classes will help establish your practice much more quickly and answer your questions as they arise. Meditating has a cumulative effect, so the important thing is to keep on doing it. This really is the only thing that matters, as illustrated by the following parable.

A student once said to his Zen Master, "Please write for me something of great wisdom." The Master picked up his brush and wrote one word: "Attention." The student said, "Is that all?" The master picked up his brush again and wrote, "Attention, Attention."

This is the real purpose of meditation – to bring our attention or awareness to the present moment, for this is all there is – no past, no future, just the perfect moment of now. In our busy lives we forget this and in doing so we damage our thinking, our relationships and our world. This state of pure attention is a million miles from the world of continuous partial attention that most of us live in today. If we could only live in this fully attentive state we would not worry, we would not be upset, because we would truly know that each moment is exactly as it is meant to be.

Stopping the world is the whole art of meditation and to live in the moment is to live in eternity. To taste the moment with no idea, no mind is to taste immortality.
Osho

The power of visualisation

One of the great benefits of regular meditation is that we can use its benefits to support another great tool – creative visualisation. It's something I use all the time to help me achieve my goals. It's something that has become common place in sports training and much has been written about it in relation to achieving our life's dream and building the business we want to support that. Films like The Secret and the follow up book, The Answer, go into much more detail than I intend to here. Let me start though, by telling you a couple of stories – a personal one first and then a business one.

A personal story

Some fifteen years ago there were two people who had recently come out of long marriages that no longer worked for them or their spouses. These two people had also met, in passing, on a number of occasions over the time of a number of courses. Unbeknown to each other, these two people, who both believed in lasting relationships, decided to write a list of everything they would like in their ideal partner. The lists included height, weight, looks, style, children, interests, attitudes, music, hobbies and much, much more. One of them was actually at the point of placing an advert in an appropriate newspaper (this is in the days before the internet or speed dating!). The day before the ad was to be placed the woman in the story took a phone call from the man who asked her if she would like to meet. For various reasons like holidays and moving house it was actually a few weeks before they did get together. She actually came to help him settle into his new house and after the usual dates and dinners they became a couple. Two years later they started to live together and three years after that they got married with all their seven children present. Seven years later they are more deeply in love than they were then and still learning about each other and life. Now in one respect this story may not be remarkable but in another it is. Every single thing on both their lists written all those years ago was there in the person they married and occasionally they still pull them out to marvel at their accuracy. That couple is my wife Gilly, and me.

A business story

You may recall me saying in an earlier chapter that, after I lost my business in the last recession and after I had spent a lot of time dealing with my personal issues, I realised that if I were ever to get the opportunity to build a business again I would do it very differently. It's over ten years now since that opportunity came but what's important is not that it did happen but how it happened. I had eventually got myself back into the world of business that I knew and was working in a small architectural practice, doing fairly ordinary work – not that I wasn't grateful, it just wasn't very satisfying. So one winter's day I sat down and wrote a list of what I wanted in my next job, which I fully intended to be my swan song in the world of corporate interior architecture. The list contained absolutely everything I could think of – from the type of firm I wanted to work for (because I had long ago decided I didn't want to start up on my own again), how long my commute would be and the position of the office in relation to a park (to take those walks I need to clear my head) and a church (as a quiet place to meditate). I put the list in a place in our house where I could always see it and a copy with me in my briefcase so that I could read it as often as possible. Then I carried on with my life knowing that something would happen when the time was right.

One day, out of the blue, in the October of that same year I was on my way home when I took a call on my mobile from a recruitment agency. "Would I be interested in meeting some people from a global architecture firm who were looking to set up in London?" they asked. It didn't take me long to say yes (I think it was milliseconds) and after a long telephone interview at some unsociable time in the morning and several further interviews in person I got the job. This wasn't any job – it was to set up and run as Head of Office their UK operation. It was a job that lasted more than nine years, until my retirement from the profession – it was indeed my swan song. Not only was I to be virtually my own boss again but I got to pick the location too. Office space was in short supply at the time because we were in the middle of the dot-com bubble but eventually I did find exactly the right first office with the right rent, the right location and a level of fit out appropriate to the business. But best of all it was within a fifteen minute walk over the River Thames from my train station, right on the edge of Trafalgar Square and had a church and a park nearby. Not just any park or any church though! St James's was the park and St Martin in the Fields the church – two of London's great landmarks!

 Whatever you can do, or dream you can do, begin it. Boldness has genius, power, and magic in it. Begin it now."
Goethe

When visualisation works as well as that, why wouldn't we want to use it? Perhaps I'd better tell you what I know about how it works and how to use it. I came to the conclusion long ago that we all visualize all of the time but just don't know it. In some way and on some level it's how we got to be here in the first place. I'm convinced that it happens as much in your life as it does in mine and many of you could already be using it. The difference between us may simply be that I have made it a conscious part of my life. The good news is that you can easily do the same and you can learn over time to increase its power and intensity. Most importantly though it is your personal vision that will help you achieve what you want in your work and in your life.

 Your vision will become clear only when you look into your heart. Who looks outside, dreams. Who looks inside, awakens."
Carl Jung

Creating what we want

If we are going to create what we want in our lives we first of all have to know what it is we want. We can discover that in several ways; through meditation; through guided meditation or simply through thinking. Every one of these relies on one thing more than any other: focusing our attention, which as I've already said is not something that very many of us are very good at much of the time. It takes rigour and effort and in this modern western world there are far, far too many distractions. I wonder just how many of us set New Year Resolutions that don't even see the month of January out. I used to wonder why that was until I stopped wondering and did something about it. Now at the beginning of each year my wife and I, together with a close friend sit down together for several hours to look at our aims and goals for the coming year. In addition we have all, most likely, spent several hours collecting our thoughts and ideas prior to meeting. The outcome of us all listening to each other and asking for clarification is a very clear set of goals and objectives for each of us which we review through a similar process once a quarter. As we've honed our skills it has amazed all of us just how many of them get met and the increasing speed with which it happens. When we did our first quarter review for this year no less than 16 of the 27 goals I had set had already happened. I'm not talking small stuff here either – I'm talking about major issues around my work, health, finances and relationships. Doing this does take focus and concentration so here is one way of doing it:

exercise

The first thing I suggest you do is to keep a small notebook handy at all times, or if you are of that generation, your PDA. Find some time when you won't be interrupted and relax your mind by using the opening part of your meditation. Equally you could do it immediately following your meditation. This time let your mind go wherever it wants to go but focusing gently on what you want by asking that very question "What do I want for my life?" You can follow this session up later with other sessions about what you want for your family or friends or work colleagues or even your community or the planet – but start with what you know best – you. As you let your mind flow, record in whatever way suits you best what you uncover. When you come to a stop and you think there is nothing more, ask yourself the question again. You will be surprised just how much more there is so go on asking yourself the question every time you feel there is nothing more until you know absolutely that there isn't. Don't try to make sense of it at this stage – just allow it to settle in your mind over the next couple of days and continue to add to your list as new thoughts arise. ♥

Then when you next have some uninterrupted time sit down quietly and sift through all that you wrote, grouping it, crossing things out, adding other things until you have a clear picture of how you want your life to be. I suggest you do this in pencil on a large piece of paper or use Post-It notes so you can move things about, rub them out and rewrite them until eventually you can link them together however you feel appropriate.

Making it visible

exercise

One of the most powerful things you can do now is to find images in magazines, newspapers, catalogues, brochures or even on the internet that represent all those hopes and dreams you have uncovered then cut them out. Next, stick them all on a piece of board that you can put somewhere you will see it as many times a day as possible. Ideally you should always look at it when you first wake up and just before you fall asleep. ♥

Do make sure you put it in a place where you can see the whole board. My wife, Gilly, once got three quarters of the way through the year and couldn't understand why some of her goals weren't even beginning to happen. It was then that I noticed that the bottom third of the board was hidden by other things like books and the answering machine. As soon as she moved the board to a place where she could see all of it, those other things started to move too.

The fact is that we always attract to us the things we focus on. I'm sure there have been many times in your life when this has happened to you. There you were looking for a new car in a particular model or colour, say a VW Golf GTI in silver or a pair of new red shoes. Suddenly over the next few days all you see is not just VW Golfs but GTIs in silver or loads of women wearing red shoes. This is the Law of Attraction at work, a key element of creative visualisation.

We absolutely do need to focus on what we want and not on what we don't want. This is because our subconscious mind does not recognise the difference between positives and negatives, it only recognises words. So if you include in your description of something you want in say, your next partner, that they must not drink or smoke, you will attract smokers and probably heavy drinkers, rather than someone who cares about their health and enjoys an occasional glass of wine in just the same way you can attract silver, VW Golf GTIs. For me this is simple confirmation that whatever words we focus on are taken literally by our mind.

The more we practise

Like everything we do in our life, the more we practise visualisation the better we get at it and the more rapidly we get results. Take my annual goal setting I spoke of earlier as an example; one year, one of the things I wrote down in January was, "Cut down my work to four days a week" and another was "Resolve my retirement plan". All of this I held in the context of The Seven Spiritual Laws and what I call the circle of circles (see chapter 2). By March that year I had agreed with the group directors that I would hand the office over to my successors by the 1st of May. The following January I wrote, "Continue to be paid by…until I can replace this income". By the end of that month I had come to an agreement with my chairman to retire a few months early! And my income was replaced.

Occasionally in the grander scheme of things, no matter how hard we try we won't succeed. It may feel that the universe is saying to us "No, that's not in your plan this time around" but more likely what is happening is that what we are aiming for is not aligned with either our karma (the effect of our deeds) or our dharma (our life purpose). When this happens no amount of pushing and shoving and hard work will help us achieve our goals and the sooner we wake up to that the better. This is another reason we need to be wide eyed in our awareness to what is happening around us and in our lives – and on all levels; physical, emotional, mental and spiritual – all of the time. The more rigour we apply to this and to our thinking the faster we will move forward.

Recognising when we have achieved a particular goal and then moving on, even though it isn't in the way we first envisioned it and may even have become attached to, is vitally important. In this way we eliminate the possibility of wasting huge amounts of energy or even becoming depressed or lifeless. Knowing what we want in life is a gift we can all give ourselves and is the key to unlocking the potential and power within us.

Equally importantly we need to share our goals and ambitions, our hopes and dreams, only with those people we can trust with them. They are fragile things at this stage and attracting negative energy towards them and to you through ridicule and disbelief will only damage your success, if not destroy it.

What do you want in your life?

Another really useful and successful way in which you can uncover what you want in your life is through guided meditation. It's a relatively simple technique and there is a multitude of such CDs out there in the marketplace. Just so you get the idea, here is one you might like to try around your job, as it is Love at Work which we are focusing on.

exercise

The following guided meditation will work best if you ask someone you trust to take you slowly through it or failing that, dictate it yourself (again very slowly) into a tape-recorder or onto a CD and then play it back, after you have settled into the first part of your pre-meditation relaxation. Here it is:

Feeling calm and relaxed with your eyes closed, allow yourself to relax even further. Then starting at the top of your head, relax your scalp, relax your brow then your eyes, your cheeks, chin, neck and back of the neck. Now relax both your shoulders, your upper arms, your forearms, wrists, hands and fingers. Focus now on your upper back and let it relax, followed by your chest, lower back, stomach and each of your hips. Then move down and let your pelvis go, your thighs, knees, forelegs, calves, ankles, feet and toes. Just totally relax…

Allow all your senses to be there – your senses of taste, touch, feeling, smell, sight and sound.

Going even deeper now imagine yourself standing on the edge of a vast plain with the grass in front of you gently blowing and whispering in the breeze. Step onto the plain and begin walking in the sunshine cooled by that breeze.

As you walk on you can see in the distance a city or town – a wonderful, inspirational place, its towers and spires glinting in the sunlight. As you draw nearer there is a sense of familiarity which grows as you step off the plain and into the shade of the buildings.

It feels even more familiar now as you smell the food cooking in the restaurants. You touch the coolness of the masonry of the buildings, see the people moving about their business and listen to the clamour of them talking. You sit down at a café and order a cup of coffee. It tastes exquisite. It's the best cup of coffee you have ever had.

Finishing your coffee you pay the waiter and walk on through the streets, in and out of the sunlight, feeling the buzz and excitement. Eventually you come to a building which seems somehow familiar yet isn't. Can you see what it looks like? Look carefully and remember every detail.

This is a very special place where you work in your perfect job. Where is the entrance? When you find it walk inside. Say hello to the concierge and stop and speak to those you meet as you walk through the space and towards your workspace – it may or may not be a desk. What is it like about it? What are your surroundings like? Sit down and take a good look around. What is it you do in this special place? What do you feel about your work?

Who are your colleagues and what are you working on? Using all your senses remember all that you see. What do you feel about these colleagues who are more than just workmates? Notice how well people interact, how supportive and understanding they are of each other, how much they appreciate one another.

Time moves on – it's time for a break – you've been working hard but don't realise it because you so enjoy what you do. In fact you enjoy it so much that the whole day has passed. What is it that you do that is so fulfilling, so engrossing?

Stand up and walk around knowing that you will be just as excited when you return tomorrow. Say goodbye to those people you need to, safe in the knowledge that you can come back here anytime you want.

Walk out through the space, past perhaps the coffee machine or photocopier, past perhaps the meeting rooms and reception and eventually out into the street.

Feel the air again, so different from the air in the office. Smell, hear, see the town or city all around you and feel them fade away as you come to the edge of the city. Feel them change to country smells, sights and sounds as you start to walk back across the plain.

Feel yourself floating. Floating up and up and up until you are securely back in the room you left a little while ago. Feel your toes and legs, your pelvis and stomach, your back, your shoulders and arms. Start to loosen your neck and head and when you are absolutely ready gently open your eyes.

Before it all starts to fade and with your eyes half closed, if it helps, write down everything you can remember of that place and what you did because these are real clues as to what you want to do with your life. ♥

If you are lucky enough to find that these things match with what you do now, then that's wonderful and it's obvious you already understand much of what you need to do to create the life and work of your dreams. If not then you have gained some real clues, some real insights into what it is you really want to do and what your life purpose might be. Add all of this to what you have already uncovered through the previous exercise and you are stepping nearer to having your life the way you want it, including Love at Work.

Without such visions we wither and die. Vision is the one thing that takes our human race step by wobbly step. Lack of it is the greatest single factor that stops all of us achieving what we want. When we go along with the herd, when we listen to all those naysayers who lack vision and are inhibited and hide bound we end up where they are – not getting the results we want and blaming everyone else but ourselves for it. When we have vision, focus on it and take action we become exceptional human beings with an opportunity to make a real difference in the world.

Placing our attention on the intention, as advocated in the book, The Secret, is absolutely essential to successful visualisation. It takes on a new level though when we set this in the context of our overall growth. I have learnt through working with The Seven Spiritual Laws Of Success that, when my visualisation (Law 5 – Intention and Desire followed by Law 6 - Detachment) is set in the context of the other five laws and I work with the circle of circles I described in Chapter 2, the speed at which things happen is amplified quite startlingly. In fact it can be quite un-nerving.

Of course, it also feels sensational when we notice the speeding up of our desires being met but it brings with it something that we need to be very conscious of and that is to be absolutely sure we are focusing on what we really want.

Having what you want

We really can have what we want! I know it to be true because I now have a long list of my visualisations that have manifested successfully. My wife (the love of my life), two different houses at two different times, a flat in London, the car I always wanted, a hugely successful public speaking club, my perfect job and even my retirement from major business are but some of the examples I can think of. Seeing these written down could appear to be egoic bragging but I promise you it's not. I am always in awe of how we can all make this happen for ourselves. Think negative thoughts and you will get negative outcomes. Think positive thoughts and you will get positive outcomes. This is not happy-clappy nonsense – it is fact.

Moreover, you will also find that the clearer you are in your intentions the more help you will get in ways we can't even begin to understand. I remember a stage in one company where the office had grown to a size where we felt we wanted to push out into Europe. Without us even advertising, out of the blue came an email from someone who had all the right qualifications and attributes in that area. We took him on and, here's the interesting bit, before he had even started we had unsolicited enquiries for three jobs in Russia, one in Greece, one in Spain and one in France. On another occasion I recall one day simply thinking about a particular specialist we needed and within hours a member of staff had come to me and asked if I would like to meet someone they knew who was looking to change jobs. I did meet them and they were absolutely perfect for the role I had been contemplating. For me this is synchronicity at work.

I really can't stress enough how important it is that we understand we can use all of this knowledge not just for what we want but for what we want for others. When we use our power well, wisely and with loving responsibility the world around us responds with positivity and expands and grows. Knowing that we can create what we want in our lives brings with it grave responsibilities. Such abilities should not be used frivolously or worst of all, negatively. They should and must be used for the good of our communities, our societies and our world.

As our ability to create what we want in our lives increases so does the level of synchronicity. Although the dictionary definitions are very similar, synchronicity is not the same as coincidence, at least not in my mind. Most people use the word coincidence to mean simultaneously occurring events and for which there is no logical or scientific reason. Synchronicity on the other hand is used to define those events that arise naturally but unexpectedly when one has taken action around one's intention and yet that is the only influence. Carl Jung determined that such events reveal an underlying conceptual framework greater than that which the person had any conscious thoughts on. As William Hutchinson Murray of the Scottish Himalayan Expedition said:

Until one is committed, there is hesitancy, the chance to draw back, always ineffectiveness. Concerning all acts of initiative (and creation), there is one elementary truth the ignorance of which kills countless ideas and splendid plans.

The moment one definitely commits oneself, then providence moves too. All sorts of things occur to help one that would never otherwise have occurred. A whole stream of events issues from the decision, raising in one's favor all manner of unforeseen incidents and meetings and material assistance, which no man could have dreamed would have come his way. Whatever you can do, or dream you can,

begin it. Boldness has genius, power and magic in it. Begin it now."

There have been many examples of synchronicity in my life as I am sure there have in yours. Let me give you just three that will probably spark in your mind some of your own. The first one that comes to mind is when, one year I was looking for another person at senior level and hadn't had much success because although there were plenty of people available who were professionally talented I didn't feel they held the values we stood for as a company. Almost as soon as I focused on this, a young woman came for interview who not only held those values but had done the same personal development courses in Australia that I had done in the UK. The second one is around writing this book. I had absolutely no idea how I would get it published but once I started to tell people about the project several totally disconnected people I met either were publishers, had clients who were or knew someone who was. The outcome is self-evident.

My favourite story though concerns a friend of mine who is fortunate enough to be particularly well off. His father had always had Lagonda cars – the sort that used to race at Brooklands in the thirties, shiny dark green with leather straps over the bonnet and huge headlights. When George decided he wanted one of his own he, on some level, started to put it out to the universe. As he told the story to me years later, what he said came as no surprise: One day as he was driving down the road he found himself following exactly the sort of car he was looking for. Being the man he is, he overtook it and flagged the owner down. Looking admiringly at the car he asked if it was for sale. Unfortunately the poor chap had only picked it up that morning and certainly had no intention of getting rid of it. George gave him his business card and asked him, if he ever did decide to sell, to call him. Fast forward a couple of years and George had a phone call – it was the man with the Lagonda and he was ready to sell, so they arranged for an inspection. As George was looking over the car he opened the bonnet to look at the manufacturer's plate all old Lagondas have there and stared in disbelief – the name of the person the car was made for was unbelievable. It was his father's car of many years ago. Now that really is synchronicity through intentionality! Before we leave this subject I want to add two things. We've spoken about the way the mind doesn't differentiate between negatives and positives. What it does take equally literally is past, present and future tenses. So, if you create your visualisation or affirmation in the future tense it will literally never happen because it is just that – in the future. Make sure that whatever it is you are focusing on is couched in similar terms; for example, "I am full of vitality and health right now" or "My perfect job is within my radar now". There was never a truer saying than the old one that "Tomorrow never comes." Remember – present tense only or you will wait literally an eternity! Then work with visualisation or affirmation with a sense of gratitude for what you know will manifest.

The power of the mind

There are many other tips and techniques within the esoteric field available to us to help us develop our ability to create Love at Work. What you will find is that as you develop your interest you will also naturally develop an instinct as to which, if any, interest you and which you would like to add to your expanding set of tools. My suggestion would be that you certainly choose meditation and visualisation and become really familiar with them. The other one I would add is Neuro Linguistic Programming (NLP) and we will move onto that next. As for any others, in my experience it is easy to get side-tracked into investigating everything out there, in the same way we can become religious or spiritual seekers rather than practitioners. A few well honed tools we are really familiar with are worth a whole box full of little used and therefore unfamiliar ones.

When I was learning to water ski in the late Fifties it was a relatively new sport and we learned by a combination of trial and error. The British Water Ski Federation was in its infancy (I went to its first ever meeting); skis were primitive by today's standards and instruction scant or non-existent. So much so that I fell off 67 times before I got to stand on a slalom ski – and yes, I did keep count. I guess much of the modelling I was doing was wrong! That experience taught me that the best and most sustainable results are achieved through a regular process of immersing, modelling and repeating the desired behaviour or action, whether that has been in sport, business or my personal life. What that means is first finding the best and then spending as much time as you can watching them, learning from them and getting them to teach you everything they know (immersing). Next you need to make sure you really understand what you are seeing and then break it down into a form that you can precisely repeat every time you do it (modelling) and then repeat it – and repeat it and repeat it until it becomes second nature. I took the same approach to dog training many years later and the results were equally powerful. Nowadays we can achieve much faster and more efficient results through adapting the techniques of NLP.

So what exactly is NLP? It's a very good question because it is certainly not the exact science its title would perhaps have us believe. That, however, doesn't lessen its usefulness in certain areas of our personal growth and development. It originates in the early 1970s through the collaboration of Richard Bandler, a philosopher and psychologist with John Grinder, a psychologist with a special interest in linguistics. Both were heavily influenced by the work of Fritz Perls (founder of Gestalt), Virginia Satir (a highly revered family psychotherapist) and Milton Erickson. The latter was a psychiatrist who did much to advance the power and usefulness of hypnotherapy, believing that the unconscious mind was susceptible to suggestions so long as the suggestion could be phrased to resonate at the appropriate level in someone's psyche. Their ground breaking book, Frogs Into Princes: Neuro Linguistic Programming (1979), is still in print today.

This is not the place for a detailed discourse on NLP so, suffice to say, that many of the techniques and models now taught within the variety of NLP organisations were first brought to light by Bandler and Grinder through their work with Erickson. Some really useful tools using names like anchoring, swish patterns and reframing as well as meta-models, nesting loops, chaining states and sub-modalities owe their existence to these two men. All of this work has been taken up and developed by, amongst others, people like Anthony Robbins and Paul McKenna. The latter is currently working with Richard Bandler. TonyRobbins' books, tapes, CDs, videos and courses are all particularly good value.

On a day-to-day basis, anchoring, swish patterns and reframing are in my mind by far the easiest to learn and the most practically useful for us. They rely heavily on an in-depth understanding of our auditory, visual and kinesthetic senses. At home we use all three techniques on a regular basis. We have had endless successes with them, both personally and in our work on everything from public speaking to memory to health and even sexual issues.

Taking public speaking as an example, being in your power from the moment you step onto the stage is vital. It's then that your audience instantly senses whether you are fully present or not. So when I was first mentoring at competition level the young man who has now won the UK and All Ireland Speaking Competition twice and represented us in America, I used a very simple anchoring technique to put him in the best possible state to walk onto the stage. It's explained in more detail in the following paragraph. The outcome was and still is that he can put himself into his most powerful state with one simple move. From the moment he uses the "trigger" for this, he can walk up to the front and onto the stage, fully confident that he will give his absolutely best performance. Through a great deal of his own hard work he has become a fabulous speaker so I'm not claiming this is the only reason he wins. It absolutely does support him though in his goals and ambitions.

On another occasion a few years ago, I was talking with a senior member of my office, let's call him Pete, who was a keen Skeet shooter and on the verge of making the England team. Skeet is a specialist segment of clay pigeon shooting. The problem was that over the previous few weeks his scores had dropped from 98 or 99/100 to at best 90 or 91/100. Now for me as a complete amateur in this world anything over 60/100 makes me feel terrific but of course, he was pretty distraught as he watched his dream fading week by week. So that Friday evening, after our working day was finished, we went in the conference room and shut the door. Pete described to me in detail what he saw as the problem and I instantly recognised that we could cure it quickly and easily. So we set about a simple anchoring process. If you don't know what this is, basically it is a way of being able to recreate your optimum performance at will. It is achieved by bringing into the sharpest of sharp focus your best ever performance and then anchoring it as an accessible "trigger" in a convenient part of your body or through a discrete action. I say discrete because there are many occasions when for example shouting Geronimo as you leap in the air is not appropriate! The use of the word "trigger" is simply coincidental to this story and applies in all such processes. You then repeat the process with as many of your best performances as you can, metaphorically nesting them on top of each other in the chosen place on your body.

In this particular case, Pete had a hidden but enormous advantage. When you shoot clays you pull the gun up to precisely the same place in your shoulder every time you take a shot. Combine this with the need for an accessible trigger; put that trigger in the right place in the shoulder and bingo! The following Monday morning he came back into the office with a huge grin on his face – the day before he had shot a 98 and a 99 for the first time in months. He continued to shoot like that until I lost touch with him after he left the company. As far as I know he still shoots that well and probably always will. He may be shooting even better, particularly if he has continued to add his more recent best performances to those we used that Friday.

Because I believe it is important to be fully trained in something to be able to teach it and this is not one of my specialties, it would be disingenuous of me to give you detailed procedures for the three different NLP tools I have described, in the same way I have for meditation and visualisation. I have always believed that if you are going to learn something then the best way is to learn it from the best available source. If you do want to know more then there are literally dozens of books, CDs and training courses out there. In fact so popular has it become that there is probably one every weekend somewhere in the country – so do your research and choose wisely. Simply type NLP into Google or your favourite search engine and you will soon find what you are looking for.

What to take with you from this chapter

- **Meditation is the only proven transformative tool**
- **Take the time and make the effort to meditate regularly**
- **Visualisation used in context is extremely powerful**
- **We can always have what we want**
- **Learn to use the power of your mind**

and to remind you to…

- *Make sure you meditate daily for at least twenty minutes, preferably at the beginning and end of your day*
- *Make sure you do all the exercises in this chapter before you move on*

Notes

Chapter 5

What's in this chapter:

- Embedding the concepts of Love at Work
- Values, people and diversity
- Understanding people through really listening
- Instincts, integrity, acceptance and choice
- A sustainable life

People are paramount

"Embed in your DNA a desire for others to succeed and you will succeed too."

Anon

Aiming for love at work

Whether you are starting an organisation from scratch, wanting to move towards the values espoused in this book or wanting to work somewhere that does, you should have gathered by now that the biggest task is in understanding who we are. There is a lot of hard and never ending work to do on ourselves and, repeating what I said earlier, there is no better place to do that than at work. Whatever our role in the workplace, we are embarking on a journey travelled by relatively few people and talked about even less. We are going to need all the help and support we can get.

It doesn't matter whether you are an entrepreneur owner, organisation leader or an employee – the values you choose for yourself and the organisation at the outset will wither and die on the vine unless you constantly nurture them. Express those values from the very first day, make them public and take measures to be able to ask the question, "How do we keep these values as we grow?" It's a great question and one you should never tire of.

When you start a new venture, every time someone joins there is the potential to increase or decrease the power of the organisation through the power of that individual. Obviously we want to increase it for the benefit of everyone. It is vital therefore that, from the very first time you meet a prospective employee or employer, you talk with them about your values and go on doing so until they understand that it is a part of your ethos. On a larger scale, so many company take-overs and mergers fail not because the numbers didn't stack up but because the values of the two organisations didn't match. If their values are not your values you probably shouldn't have to think very hard about the worth of joining forces. If you do decide to go ahead you will however need to think hard about how to ensure that your values match, that everyone understands what they are and buys into them. The hardest part of all will be engendering trust – and that of course is a two way street.

So we come to leadership, which we will deal with in detail in the next chapter. At least 75% of leadership is by example, by intensely careful listening, by loving feedback and through your consistency as an individual. How you behave in every circumstance will affect others perception of you, how they behave towards you and towards others. If you demonstrate love in action, Love at Work, the likelihood is that they will too. At the very least, they will begin to notice and step out of their comfort zone towards the fiery furnace of self-awareness. None of this will happen overnight. You will not establish or change the culture of any organisation with anything but constancy and repetition. This is because the culture of any organisation is an amalgam of its combined wisdom which has to be accepted by everyone. Different people gain knowledge and understanding at different rates, so progress will happen at the mean speed at which people understand.

To digress from culture building to cultural change for a moment, my sense is that there is little difference in what it takes in the long run – but it will be a much longer run. Bringing Love at Work to a new workplace is so different from introducing it to an established one. Just think for a moment how long your personal growth and change can take. Occasionally we make lightening break throughs, but in the main we get there the same way you eat an elephant – a bite at a time! Love at Work is cultural change so don't underestimate the enormity of the task of achieving it. Naturally the leader will need the power to change. The best way to achieve this is surely going to be through consensus – on every level. I would go so far as to say that without it your aims are doomed to failure – and hopefully that is the only negative in this book!

Overcoming the system

What is even worse is that employment law in this country is not set up to support small companies and even less so for those that want to take on the philosophy of Love at Work. This is because it is all written to resolve the traditional level of confrontation between major companies and unions; the idea of the overlord and the underdog. All of which makes it incredibly difficult for any organisation that wants to treat people fairly and equally as decent human beings. Let me give you an example. We had been having a particularly difficult time on a project and it eventually became very apparent that Jerry, the manager concerned, had not been performing. He was completely out of his depth but instead of asking for help he simply lied about it. No wonder the job was in trouble! When someone has been taken on in all good faith and yet they aren't doing well, you give them the appropriate training and support and this is what we did. If they still aren't doing well for various reasons, you need to explain that to them too. My way, and hopefully yours, would be to sit them down and talk to them about what I saw and discuss with them how they could improve performance or attitude or whatever. In this case it still didn't work and so we had that final conversation where we mutually agreed that he would most likely be better off working in another company or doing something else entirely.

When you are working to develop an organisation based on Love at Work you don't need people who don't hold your values. You don't need them in any other business either! Talking behind people's backs is taboo. That doesn't mean we don't talk about each other. It means we talk about each other in a supportive way, trying to discover and understand more about what makes us tick, in the way we often do in our families. It does mean though that we don't talk about each other to people outside the team whatever the circumstances. For example, when I went to see the client concerned I did not talk about Jerry and his failings. I simply said that he was leaving us and that I would be introducing them to his replacement. The client may very well have known why but if you do this about one person they may well think you would do it about them and it breaks trust. Deal with issues in this way and you end up with happy staff and happy clients.

Under current legislation you are taking a serious risk if you do what I did. You have to follow a set of procedures that were laid down for large scale company disputes and that means the very first time you need to speak to someone seriously about their performance you have to give them a formal warning. I find that very sad because it immediately sets up a level of antagonism that cuts completely against the grain of the organisation you are trying to build. Their morale goes through the floor and the likelihood of turning them round disappears in an instant. On the other hand, fail to follow the prescribed route and you risk legal action.

Whilst my view on employment legislation may appear negative in what is intended to be a very positive book, my intention in including it is to focus us on the importance of retaining our best people. You can now see just how important it is to truly build an organisation with values that everyone subscribes to, even to the extent that someone can recognise when they don't fit through either ability or style. In fact when we communicate clearly and openly and people can see they don't fit, they will move on with much more ease. It is difficult, but it is not impossible and it has to be something we aim for if we are to create Love at Work.

Hold your values

I recall one situation where a professionally talented senior manager, who came under my aegis, just didn't hold the values that I wanted for the team. He was incredibly competent and could also be incredibly caring. In fact I remember him once going to collect and take home a young woman who had had an accident on her bicycle. He simply stopped what he was doing, jumped in a cab, took in the whole situation and dealt with it – and became the office hero. On the other hand he was so sure he was always right that he became a bully of the first order and staff would end up terrified of both his outbursts and insinuations. His personality could be quite dysfunctional and yet I knew he had a heart of gold. So we worked and worked together to try and resolve these issues. We talked for hours and hours over a period of time and when the more subtle approaches failed to work I stopped pulling punches and gave it to him straight. Things would improve for a while and then it would happen again. There really was no alternative but to move him on and so we did. Maybe it was a couple of years later when I next saw him at an industry dinner. When he made a point of coming up to me I didn't know what to expect. What he said was that whilst he had been very hurt at being fired, on reflection he understood quite clearly why I had done it. He went on to thank me for everything I had done for him, how much he had learned from me and how much of a difference it had made to his career ever since. As my mother was so fond of saying, "We sow, yet we know not where we reap."

I can accept failure, everyone fails at something. But I can't accept not trying."
Michael Jordan

Keep your best people

The single most fundamental way in which we can create Love at Work is through retaining our best people. Surprisingly perhaps, in many sectors of employment, most people are not totally money motivated. They are far more motivated by having their potential recognised, being given responsibility and by being acknowledged for their efforts. We can only do this by spending time with them and that can feel like we are moving too slowly towards our target – but the reverse is true. When we get to know people and what makes them tick, when we get to understand how they work rather than how we work and what gives them pleasure in their work, they become capable of things we never imagined. With people there is no doubt that taking your time, taking things slowly is actually the fastest way forward. Be prepared too to let them see who you are –nothing builds trust faster than allowing your own vulnerability to show. No matter what size your organisation is, there is no reason why you should not meet them one to one over coffee, over lunch, over a beer or glass of wine to get to know their career goals, their personal goals. Be genuinely interested in them, let them talk and make sure you listen. Most importantly recognise a job well done verbally and by practical acts of appreciation. There are a hundred ways you can do this – praising them in front of others, flowers, theatre or cinema tickets, a meal for them and their partner, sending them on a course they particularly want to do – the list is endless.

One of the biggest potential dangers for the people in any organisation is the politics which will raise their heads whether we like it or not. People are people and, until the day we are all transformed or enlightened, some of us will always set others against each other, wittingly or unwittingly. They will want to put others down so they themselves look good, to enhance their prospects of promotion or even out of pure maliciousness – though such cases are rare. It is absolutely vital therefore that we develop not just an innate ability to spot and reward behaviours that support our cause of Love at Work but that we develop the same level of vigilance towards those who don't. Then we need to be prepared to take action and fast.

We all need to be politically competent, to understand what we can and can't control and to understand the political and psychological maps of the company we work for. Without this we would lose our persuasive powers and on some level become autistic as an organisation. In the same way that our egos have positive and negative sides, so do office politics. It's about working with those who support us and removing those who don't. Unless we understand this we will be far less successful in making things happen. The fact is whenever we make a decision we are laying ourselves open to criticism. We reduce the risk by openly and with integrity building support from like-minded people.

This is as true in client relationships as it is with our colleagues. Relationships are complex enough on a one to one basis. They get more so the more people we communicate with inside our business – probably by the power of the number of people involved. Add those of the clients or customers we work for and suddenly the issues are multiplied exponentially. I'm not for one second suggesting any of this should be seen as unmanageable. It's more that I am emphasising the need for rigour in all aspects of our business, not just the financials. Whether it is in professional or personal relationships, the way through is most definitely by knowledge sharing and collaboration. I suggest it is one thing never to forget.

Personality diversity

Every day we meet and work with people as diverse and as different from whom we are as we can possibly imagine. Doing our best at all times to understand them will go a long way to improving their lives and ours. If you want to delve deeply into the world of personality types and how to use this information to build your business then the almost classical work of Myers Briggs is a great place to start. It is a psychological profiling technique intended to help you determine your personal preferences so that you (or your prospective employer) can decide your suitability for a particular role. This superficial description is not meant to belittle its usefulness and power both as a recruitment tool for companies and a career defining tool for individuals. Most people (including me) undergoing the interview process at major companies will have taken the test at least once and probably several times in their lives. Developed in the 1940s and based in Jungian philosophy, it was originally intended to help women in particular, discover in what sort of job they would be "most comfortable and effective". Like all such tools it is predominantly useful in conjunction with a variety of others. Neither as an individual or an organisation should you use it as the deciding factor.

My personal concern with it is that it appears to say that our personality is a given and therefore extremely difficult, if not impossible, to change. All change takes hard work and of course some more than others. It may simply be that the Myers Briggs Type Indicator (MBTI) was created at a time when it was popular to think that our Intellectual Quotient (IQ) was the only real measure of who we are. As our understanding of the human mind has increased, so the widening of theories associated with it has developed. Today we talk not just about IQ but also about PQ (Physical Quotient), EQ (Emotional Quotient) and SQ (Spiritual Quotient), each one having its place in understanding who we are as human beings. In terms of Love at Work, you won't be surprised to learn that I believe that it is our EQ which supports the concept.

Until very recently no one had attempted to measure emotions and behaviours alongside intelligence, concentrating instead on IQ or personality assessments. The more recent models attempt to understand how our behaviour can affect our success. From previous chapters you will know just how much I believe our emotions and self-awareness affect our success. This move towards understanding our EQ fits nicely with this view in that it propounds the very valid thought that, depending on the issue or circumstance, rigour around our IQ may not always be as important as rigour around our EQ. Indeed, a recent article in Harvard Business Review said: "EI (Emotional Intelligence) plays a far greater role than IQ in determining leaders' and organisations' success. One can't do much to improve IQ but you can boost EI by understanding which skills define it."

One development in this area that deserves more than a mention is EBW – Emotional Behaviours at Work, the brainchild of Brentfield Consultancy. Not all ideas suit everyone and if on some level you struggle with some of the concepts I put forward then you may want to take a look at something more measurable. If so, this is probably the direction for you. Although it doesn't use the exact words, it is grounded in the same ideas of witness consciousness that we looked at in Chapter Three. For me, any work that helps us understand more clearly how our emotions affect our decision making and therefore the effectiveness of our business gets my vote – particularly when it also supports the idea that we can change those behaviours through increased self awareness. All of which will aid us in assessing our own and others' self awareness and talent as well as our leadership and management potential.

Personality types

Having looked in Chapters Two and Three at a model of how we might build our personality and in Chapter Four at some suggestions as to how we might change it if we so wish, let's look for a while now at the broad types which might manifest as a result of all that. It is important to have this understanding because it affects everything from leadership to personal relationships; to teamwork and on to customer relationships and sales performance. In other words virtually everything that matters including the balance sheet. Most of the models and diagrams I have either seen or worked with in this area (and there are many) divide us as people into four major groupings. Here, in as simple language as possible, is my personal interpretation of those.

You will remember from the earlier chapters that our personalities as young beings develop according to how well we manage to get our needs met. This then tends to knock on into the personality type we develop – and that will vary enormously according to our very own personal experience. The differences can be very marked even within the same family. I remember once administering some personal development courses and on each of three consecutive courses were two brothers and their mother. The elder brother was on the first course. He was a very successful salesman with all the trappings of his own flat and a beautiful sports car. At some point on the weekend he stood up and told the story of his childhood and how he felt that as a result of it he could not have grown up to be any different from the way he was. His mother was on the second course and her story corroborated his. The younger brother was on the third course and, as his elder sibling had done, he stood up and told the story of his childhood and how he felt that he could not be any different from the way he was. Now here's the interesting bit – this brother was a drug addict who had been let out of open prison for the weekend to take the course. I can't think of a more startling example of how differently we all see our world.

The need for an accurate self image rears its head again. It's a tall order, but before we manage to do anything well, and consistently well, and before we can contribute to a team or lead a team, we need to understand both ourselves and others. Even if we know very well both our strengths and our weaknesses we may not have given a thought to the fact that it is our character, and how we show our character in the world through our behaviour, that counts! It pays therefore for us to make sure that what we think those characteristics are, are in fact true.

The most comprehensive and at the same time simplest method I have come across for doing this is the Peoplemap System™ Personality Type Questionnaire. It is made up of just seven questions, taking less than five minutes to complete and self score. Developed and validated by Andrew Mathis, Ph.D. and Michael Lillibridge, Ph.D., the Peoplemap™ Questionnaire has a 95% accuracy rate in identifying the personality types of Leader, People, Free Spirit and Task. Let us take a moment to look at some of the strengths – and the potential 'Achilles' Heels', of these types:

The Leader Type will recognise themselves as someone who is accomplishment-oriented, focused, motivated, and who likes to take charge; hopefully others will too, but they may see someone who is impatient, demanding and quick to find fault with them!

The People Type will be quick to sign up to a long list of sterling qualities- he is considerate, friendly, helpful, honest, kind, a good listener and someone who just can't say "No"; others will most likely agree, but may add that he is too sensitive and easily hurt, or just too damned interested and talkative!

The Free Spirit Type doesn't hide his qualities; adventurous, creative, an out-of-the-box thinker, easily bored, independent and a risk taker; he can ignite a team or leave them reeling at what they see as outrageous and impossible ideas and demands!

The Task Type loves the small print and the set timetable, and may even see himself as mundane and 'wanting' for his very qualities. He is organised and dependable, precise, self disciplined, responsible and constantly busy and thrives in an ordered environment; often others depend on him to create order from their chaos – and give him small thanks for it!

Personality Types

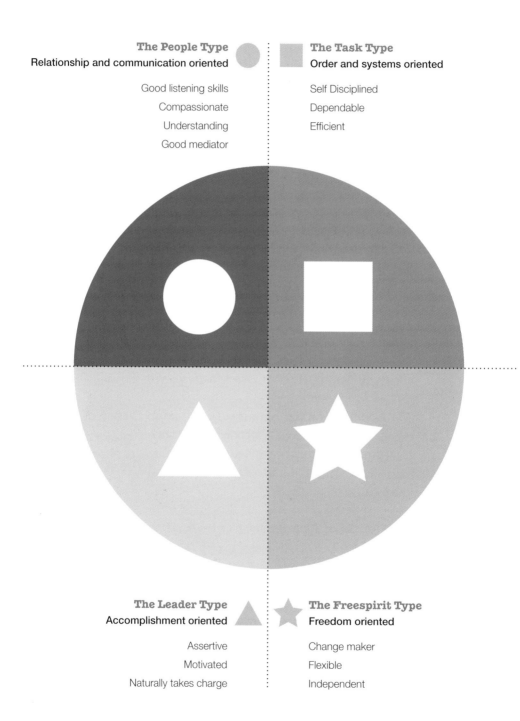

The People Type
Relationship and communication oriented

Good listening skills
Compassionate
Understanding
Good mediator

The Task Type
Order and systems oriented

Self Disciplined
Dependable
Efficient

The Leader Type
Accomplishment oriented

Assertive
Motivated
Naturally takes charge

The Freespirit Type
Freedom oriented

Change maker
Flexible
Independent

Just as the human body has mostly two of everything, so our innate personality is, thankfully a matter of two of these types. We come in any conjugation; for example we may be People – Free Spirit or Task People. To add to this sublime mix, we tend also to have an element least evident in our behaviour, to be aware of and to acquire as a learned trait. For many Free Spirit types it tends to be the Task element, and interestingly, when the rather unusual combination of Free Spirit – Task is the main personality, we find a person who is doing battle with themselves; one part of them wanting adventure and risk, while the other part of them has heaped opprobrium and caution upon them. It is a truly exciting and gratifying moment during Peoplemap training to witness a participant harnessing these polar strengths, determined in the future to get the best out of themselves.

We cannot afford to just pay lip service or give a passing nod to work of this quality and the information it provides - it is a vital tool in being in command of ourselves. From the outset of Peoplemap training, not only do these traits begin to make sense for us, but we can also identify them in our relatives, friends and colleagues. The result is our interactions with them and our understanding of them changes and becomes fun-filled as our previous prejudices and preconceptions - not to say antipathy and animosity - fall away. One Peoplemap™ Trainer was told, "Three months ago, if we had given them guns, they would have shot each other". If you want to take a closer look, the Peoplemap System™ Questionnaire is available on line at www.Peoplemapsystem. com, together with information on their training programmes. I need to make you aware that there is a charge for the questionnaire.

Having a working understanding of all of this will be enormously helpful to your understanding of yourself and of others in every aspect of your business life. Take for example something which we will discuss in more depth later – networking. It isn't, as many people seem to think, about getting round as many people as you can as fast as possible and pushing a business card into their hand. It works best when people know, like and respect us enough to become our personal ambassadors and that they feel there is something in it for them too. It takes time to get to know, like and trust someone and we can do this more efficiently when we understand our own personality type and have a pretty good idea of that of the person we want to recommend us or introduce us to someone. Matching what we say and how we say it to the way in which someone can receive it makes a huge difference.

Really listen

Everyone likes us to show an interest in them, even if their personality type is not effusive. Knowing how to ask questions they feel comfortable with and really wanting to hear the answers, goes a long way to establishing liking and respect – and eventually trust. When we ask questions we need to really want to know the answers. The only way we can do that is to listen with our full attention. Ask the question in a way you think the person will best hear it and just listen – never interrupt! There is that wonderful story in the classic Dale Carnegie book, "How to Win Friends And Influence People": A man goes to a cocktail party and is introduced by his host to an elderly woman. He sits down beside her and asks her a question. Every time she stops talking (which isn't often) he asks her another one and hours later he feels able to excuse himself and moves on to someone else. The following day his host rang him to say that the woman had called her to say how enchanting and interesting he was. We both know he had hardly said a word but what he had done was show genuine interest and above all attention. Listening and attention are at the heart of Love at Work so we will return to them much more fully in Chapter Six.

This question of us being able to hear each other – or not – is at the epicentre of every misunderstanding, disagreement, argument and eventually war that there is or ever has been and much of the time it comes down to personality types not being able to hear each other. I recall one such situation between a Director and an Associate, both highly creative people. He, the more senior and her boss, was a Free Spirit Type with some Leader in there. She was very ambitious People-Leader type, and therefore strongly staff and client orientated. Although on the surface they rubbed along well for some time, with hindsight a clash was always going to happen. His personal freedom came before everything; he started late and you never really knew where he was at the end of the day but it was usually in the pub having fun with other Free-Spirits, he would work from home at any excuse; she was motivated, strong, accomplished and wanting to see the big picture and liked to be in charge. She had every opportunity to be so because to him responsibility came second to his freedom. In the end of course one of them had to go and I confess to making the mistake of choosing the wrong one. I kept him instead of her!

Stick to your guns

Differences in attitudes as blatant as this spell disaster and who in their right mind wants that? It was something Jack Welch of GE talked a lot about. One of his favourite diagrams demonstrating how he saw the importance of people holding your values looks something like this:

People who...

1	Share your values	and	make you money
2	Share your values	and	don't make you money
3	Don't share your values	and	don't make you money
4	Don't share your values	and	make you money

The question he asked was simply, "What do you do with each of these categories of people?" His answers were: do everything you can to keep the first ones, train the second and fire the third. I guess we can all see that, but the real question is what do you do with the fourth ones -those who don't share your values yet make you plenty of money? Whilst your first reaction might be to keep them your considered response to this has to be fire them too. It's not too difficult to see why. In not sharing your values they will, over time, undermine everything you believe in and stand for – a situation potentially far more dangerous than a lack of profit in one area of your business, though this is far from desirable. Why would we ever allow anyone to do that to us? It's a view endorsed by Richard Barrett in his book "Liberating The Corporate Soul" and which absolutely underlines a point I made in a previous chapter - whether employer or employee, always thoroughly question your own and the other person's values.

Expectations move so fast nowadays that what was good yesterday needs to be excellent today and what is excellent today needs to be outstanding tomorrow. This applies as much to people as it does to things. For this reason alone we need to have confidence in people's qualities rather than their competencies. Competence has to be a given in our fast moving world. As we saw in the personality models earlier, people who are well balanced emotionally can manage their impulses well, communicate with others effectively and manage and solve problems with ease. They often use humour to build rapport and reduce tension. This "clarity" in thinking and "composure" in stressful and chaotic situations is what defines top performers – not their professional competence.

Being in the workplace with integrity is never easy. I repeat, it takes rigour, conscientiousness and, above all, a level of independent thinking. Choosing the right people for your organisation can be a daunting and sometimes demoralising task. How often have you despaired of finding the person you really wanted? Let me take a step sideways for a moment and give you a parable. For many years I was a Championship judge in Dog Obedience, judging up to 60 dogs a day at the highest competitive level. There would be days when I stood in the ring for hours not seeing anything that really met what I was looking for, beginning to doubt my own standards and then, out of the blue, a handler and dog would walk in and put in a stunning performance. It always took patience and sometimes courage to stick to my guns but I never once regretted it. The same thing applies to finding the great business people you really want to work with.

Great business people are like great athletes. They are rare, but you always know them when you meet them because of their confidence, self belief and focus, none of which should be mistaken for arrogance. Another of their qualities is the ability to maintain their level of performance over long periods of time. It comes out of them knowing who they are and therefore always knowing what to do to stay at their peak. That's not to say they don't have off days - of course they do, but it's guaranteed that they will have fewer than most people and they will always know what to do to get back on top. Keeping such people isn't easy unless you too are on top of your own game and your leadership skills are up there with the best. Team building is all about leadership and that means getting the best out of people. When you do, you can be proud of them and proud of yourself.

People like this don't want to be controlled, don't want to be told what to do but they really do want to be involved – and on every level. They want to have their say, they want to express their ideas and you need them to do this because it leads to them taking responsibility too. With high quality people, the more responsibility that they are given and that they take, the more willing they are to share ideas and help grow a culture of openness and confidence. What starts to happen then is that, even in times of crisis, confident people will express certainty. That is vital in high speed modern business because there simply isn't time to vacillate and of course confidence, by its very nature, breeds success.

Trust your instincts

So that I am sure you really do get this message, here are a couple of salutary tales. The first concerns a senior manager with whom I was really struggling. I rely a lot of the time on my gut and my instinct, my sixth sense, to tell me what's really going on in an organisation. In this particular case, here was a man whose cup was always half empty and that is so disruptive. I remember him saying about one prospective client he was courting that we wouldn't get the job and he got to be right. None of the rest of us thought we wouldn't get it but he certainly proved his point by screwing up on a done deal and then blaming everyone else. People were scared of him and didn't tell him the truth for fear of bringing his anger down on themselves. To be honest there were times when I felt scared of him too. Time after time he fell out with clients and it became like a cancer spreading through the business with people whispering in corners and not even telling themselves the truth about what was going on. My guiding principle, of always getting people who are struggling with someone to speak directly to that person, started to fall apart. Part of the problem was that he could also be charming, friendly and thoughtful but of course that was always covertly on his terms (do you remember getting our needs met covertly?). All my high ideals around building a business with heart were disintegrating around me until one Monday morning. I had spent the whole weekend thinking about what best to do and not surprisingly concluded that if I really was the business head then I needed to deal with it and deal with it fast. I had spent more than a year trying to turn this man round and to no avail – everyone was suffering and none of it was his fault or so he kept on saying. So I stopped thinking and took action to cut out the cancer. Within 24 hours the office was a different place. All the whispering had stopped and people were laughing and joking, having fun as they worked.

The second and even more salutary story involves another manager. It has a different slant but involves the same underlying principle of personal dishonesty around acknowledging who he was and how he behaved. In this case there was a complete lack of openness around what he was doing and an awful lot of him saying what he thought people wanted to hear rather than discussing and sharing his business problems. One of his favourite phrases was, "Leave it to me". So it took all of us quite a long time to realise that this was really just his way of not doing things. By a mixture of bonhomie and putting the blame elsewhere, he survived for a long time. He was what my wife would call a "charming deceiver". Far too often nothing happened simply because he didn't possess the appropriate skills. For example tasks were left unfinished, budget reports were late or just not prepared, schedules were missed and staff were not reviewed or coached. Whenever I did uncover inadequacies in his performance, other senior staff would defend him and even protect him by saying he was far too important to a particular project to let go. My anger started to spurt out inappropriately towards him. I spotted it and stopped doing it to make sure he felt part of the team but still nothing changed. After more than two years he eventually messed up two really large and important projects and that's the point at which he got himself fired. The moral to the tale is that, as leaders, we must always trust our instinct and not let our judgement be swayed by others no matter how much we value theirs. Never has Jack Welch's principle of the importance of people holding your values been more clearly underlined.

In neither of these cases were the people displaying the characteristics we ourselves need to display or look for in others if we are to build strong organisations demonstrating the principles of Love at Work. When we do uphold our values, the characteristics we display in business become self evident. We lead from the front, put our clients and customers first, focus on solutions that are at least win/win and by being both participative and decisive we get the best out of everyone and they get the best out of us. By keeping communication open and our goals in mind we will also be able to adapt to changing situations when we need to. After all, change is the one thing that is certain in life.

Look for the right qualities

Establishing rapport with people becomes so much easier when we openly and honestly communicate with others on this basis. Knowing that we can get on with colleagues, clients and suppliers and that we have common interests leads to the creation of trust – the most highly valued component of any relationship. Nor will you go far wrong if you look for the following qualities in the people you choose, no matter what your expectations of their professional skills:

Score each attribute: 1 = low and 10 = the best you can be.

exercise

	1	2	3	4	5	6	7	8	9	10
Passion for what they do										
Strong work ethic										
Strong personal ethics										
Deep interest in people										
Clear communicators										
Clear thinkers										
Experience of life and business										
Excellent leadership attributes (whatever the role)										
Enjoy teamwork										
TOTAL										

You might find photocopying this page several times and scoring yourself and other people you know to be a useful reality check.

Building a strong culture of genuine teamwork and personal responsibility creates a clear but rugged path for people. Nothing can be second best whether it's in our private life or our company life. Having the courage to be who we truly are, to speak up to each other in good times and in bad and to say when we are struggling or excited will always make a real difference in our lives. Whatever our chosen career path, the more we work as team, the more successful we will be individually and corporately.

Dropping our defences

One of the biggest killers of cultures of this type is defensiveness. It's something we all fall into at least from time to time and I've seen it become the downfall of some really good people. For whatever reason, perhaps things aren't going as well as both they and their bosses wanted for them – they've lost that "purple patch" or their "golden touch" and they start to blame clients, other staff and even the weather for their diminishing success. The result is that things go from bad to worse. So the question is: what can we do to help them out of it? Any solution isn't going to be easy because their defence mechanism has kicked in and whilst they may not actually be behaving physically like a wounded tiger, they are probably doing a pretty good impression emotionally!

Somehow we have to get them to lower their defences and help them look at where this behaviour is coming from. My guess is that it isn't from the adult but from the five or six year old deep inside them. It takes tact and diplomacy plus the ability to put our own stuff on one side to help them see what is going on. I remember once having to deal with a team leader who was constantly over optimistic about his level of potential business, which time after time failed to materialise. When we started the session he was, not surprisingly perhaps, very defensive and feeling under attack not just from myself but from some of the shareholders too. All I could do was go into my heart and listen quietly to what he had to say. Very slowly I got him to move back through his life and identify when and where he had first become falsely optimistic. What he said was revealing. He had learned to be this way as a small boy in order to stop himself getting hit by his Father. I was shocked and sympathetic but he needed to understand that the adult world doesn't work like that. After several sessions he recognised that he had to be prepared to face life squarely and take responsibility for his actions. You can imagine we covered a lot of ground and spoke of many things in those sessions and he worked hard to make the necessary changes. It takes more effort and courage than we ever realise and the universe will always present opportunities to test our learning.

We will find those tests easier though if we: understand what needs to be done in the context of what's right for the business; develop an action plan with clear deadlines and communicate it succinctly; and ensure everyone understands the plan and who is responsible for which actions. So much of the time we spend communicating is in meetings. That makes it absolutely vital that we make sure they are 100% productive for everyone involved. In a later chapter I shall talk much more about how to make this happen.

 There are no mistakes. The events we bring upon ourselves, no matter how unpleasant, are necessary in order to learn what we need to learn; whatever steps we take, they're necessary to reach the places we've chosen to go."
Richard Bach

Acceptance

The most important thing of all though is that we understand more and more about ourselves through the actions we take, the consequences of those actions and our interactions with everyone else in our world. We can do this by being truthful with ourselves about our feelings and then recognising the patterns in our life that don't work for us. Finding a safe and trusting place where we can reach a level of vulnerability that allows us to release the underlying hurt that drives our behaviours isn't easy but it is possible. Once we do find that place we need to do what we do whenever we are learning anything new – practise and practise until the changes we are making replace the old debilitating patterns. Only then can we start to develop our true potential and become Love at Work, not just for others but for ourselves.

So much of developing this ability is about acceptance – of ourselves and of others. When we accept that we are all doing the very best we can, given all the circumstances of our lives and that if we weren't, things would be different, we have come a long way. Blame, resentment and guilt are amongst the biggest killers of personal happiness – ours and other people's. Why would we want to spend time in such debilitating states? Much better that we acknowledge our fear, our anger or our resentment and take appropriate action. This takes commitment and a willingness to do what it takes regardless of the fear – and that is what courage really is! We can do this by being self critical rather than self condemning, by seeing ourselves and others from the same side of the table – and we make it so much easier on ourselves when we do.

When we understand this, we can live our lives more and more in a state of grace known as interdependence. As babies we come into the world totally dependent on others and that's the way we stay for some years. As we grow we learn that we can survive more and more without reliance on our mother or father and start to stretch our muscles of independence. Later on we realise that the world is much less frightening if we have people to fall back on and we develop key relationships, friendships and loves. So often though, those loves are founded on codependency which, although it may seem to work at first, is in fact a very toxic place to live. Understanding and acceptance of our self is the way through to living with real respect for one's self and others – that place of interdependence.

Interdependence can only be reached once we understand the principle of victim consciousness (of which I spoke in chapter 3) and begin to witness our behaviours. One of the ways which will help us move from victim to witness consciousness is to engage with other people and show genuine interest in them. Through this interest we start to expand our world and change our perspective. This will naturally lead to an understanding of how we operate emotionally – whether we are principally I-centred or U-centred or come from a position of need or no-need. We can also benefit from an understanding of what Jung called our mask and shadow. The mask we present to the world is based on a combination of what we would like to be and the opposite of what we would most dislike being and being seen as. It is in the acceptance and integration of all those things that lie in the shadow behind the mask that we react less and less to all the emotional buttons that get pushed. When we start to accept all those parts of us we can, day by day, move closer to a level of congruity and integrity which allows us to stand firmly on our feet and speak up for ourselves in an ever-changing world.

Pyramids and whirlpools

This is particularly important within a growing organisation. Maybe it's my original design background but I often visualise an organisation living by the principles of Love at Work as a pyramid sitting in a sea of speaking up. I use the words speaking up because it is through this that we allow people to see who we are, what we believe in and what matters to us, in fact to tell our truths. This Pyramid of Responsibility starts small and rises from the sea as the workplace you are creating grows, with the newer people pushing it up from underneath. Each layer of the pyramid floats on an air gap which allows everyone to breathe and expand so that they do and think about the things that only they can do.

The Pyramid of Responsibility

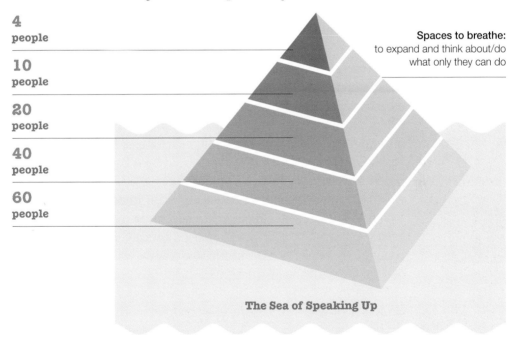

4 people

10 people

20 people

40 people

60 people

Spaces to breathe: to expand and think about/do what only they can do

The Sea of Speaking Up

Whilst this pyramid is pushing up through its sea of speaking up it totally relies on people taking personal responsibility. Stephen Covey talks about this as a Circle of Influence but, when I imagine it, my 3D mind comes into play again and I see it as a Whirlpool of Influence. It has the same elements that he describes except in my mind the person at the centre grows by drawing more and more responsibility to themselves and into the funnel in the middle of the whirlpool.

The Whirlpool of Influence
Pull more and more responsibility into the funnel of Autonomy

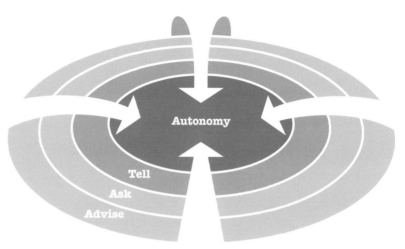

All of this is to remind us that life is about choices. We can choose to be in a good mood or a bad mood; we can choose to be angry or joyful; thoughtless or thoughtful, kind or mean, positive or negative. We can even choose to live or die. In my experience those people that get things done and achieve the most, with the least effort, choose the positive route – the one full of joy, thoughtfulness, kindness and love. Perhaps you've noticed that people like this think big yet don't seem to need much; are always helping others, yet are surrounded by people who willingly help them; are constantly open to seeking the truth in themselves and others. They don't need to be the exceptions if we believe in a world of abundance. There is enough; there will always be enough and we can all have our lives the way we want them. We simply need to believe it and take action.

So much of what we believe is embedded in our language. When we help ourselves and others to change that language we can move mountains. Get rid of words like "should", "shouldn't", "can't", "ought", "have to", "must" and all those other debilitating injunctions and negatives. Changing "but" to "and" helps enormously. Remember our internal critic was established at the same time and at the same speed we learned to speak and it will take real determination to do this. Most of all, respond to others from your heart, trust your intuition. Genuine honesty is still a rare quality and people will recognise it and respect you hugely for it.

A sustainable life

It ain't easy being green."
Kermit the Frog

No matter how much effort we put into our personal growth it can be really useful to take a reality check every now and again. We all grew up with phrases like "Charity begins at home" and so, I would suggest, does sustainability. If our own lives are not sustainable, then what chance is there for our planet? Now is not the time or place to get into the wider debate on climate change, global warming or GM foods. It is a good point though to stop and reflect. A good friend of mine, Jamie Armstrong, has developed the following model and I include it here for you to use.

exercise

Sustainability is the interaction of four strands of a working life, a working team or a working community. Those four strands are:

- Natural Resources – the things we use such as energy, materials and even our health
- Environment – how we affect the physical environment and how it affects us. This includes our living, working, local and natural environments
- Finances – the money we make, create, spend, invest, save and share with others
- Society – how we relate to ourselves and others – those close to us, in our community and in the wider world. Our values, support, encouragement and engagement

When answering the questions Jamie suggests:

"Some of the questions appear simple, think deeply about them. Some of the questions appear deeper, think simply about them and let your heart answer. Remember we think with our hearts as well as our heads."

Now simply score each of your answers on a scale of 1:5, where 1 is the best case and 5 the worst.

How sustainable are you?

IN YOUR SOCIETY

Social responsibility

How socially responsible are you? e.g. by being a 'good neighbour', contributing time or money to good causes	1	2	3	4	5
How easy does your lifestyle make it for you to help the people/ causes you want to?	1	2	3	4	5
How much do you keep up to date with news and current affairs at a global/national/ local level?	1	2	3	4	5

Relationships

How well do you keep in touch with people you want to?	1	2	3	4	5
How easy does your lifestyle make things for you and the lives of those around you?	1	2	3	4	5
How well do you understand the needs and desires of those around you, and change your behaviour to help meet these, when appropriate?	1	2	3	4	5

Stress

How comfortable are you with the level of stress and anxiety in your life, and how this affects others around you?	1	2	3	4	5
How well do your working hours match your ideal work/ play rhythm and your family and social needs?	1	2	3	4	5
How well do you feel your travel/commuting fits your life?	1	2	3	4	5

Communication

How well heard and understood by others do you feel?	1	2	3	4	5
How well do you listen to what other people have to say?	1	2	3	4	5
How well connected do you feel to the rest of the world?	1	2	3	4	5

IN YOUR ENVIRONMENT

Living environment

How closely does the place you live match your needs and desires?	1	2	3	4	5
How safe, relaxed and comfortable do you feel with your living surroundings?	1	2	3	4	5

Environmental practises

How environmentally aware do you consider yourself to be?	1	2	3	4	5
How effective are you at putting good practices in place in your home to reduce your impact on the environment?	1	2	3	4	5

Natural Environment

How good is the access you have to high quality green/natural space?	1	2	3	4	5
How much use do you make of your nearby green/natural space?	1	2	3	4	5
How much do you do to help improve your local natural environment?	1	2	3	4	5
How far do you go beyond your own backyard in helping to improve th natural environment?	1	2	3	4	5

Working environment

How much is your working environment fit for purpose?	1	2	3	4	5
How comfortable are you with your working environment?	1	2	3	4	5
How well do the facilities in your working environment suit your needs ?	1	2	3	4	5

AROUND NATURAL RESOURCES

Physical and Mental Health

How good are you at maintaining a good level of health and fitness?	1	2	3	4	5
Do you spend enough quality time on yourself when you want to e.g. quiet time, time for prayer or meditation?	1	2	3	4	5
Do you get enough exercise and recreation?	1	2	3	4	5
Do you drink and eat healthily, nurturing your body?	1	2	3	4	5

Wellbeing

How close are you to having everything you need right here, right now?	1	2	3	4	5
How much do you feel in control of your life?	1	2	3	4	5
How well is your life in balance? e.g. are you having enough fun/love in your life?	1	2	3	4	5

Purchasing

How much do you support your local shops/ businesses and buy fair trade/ organic/low environmental impact products?	1	2	3	4	5

How much do you try to reduce the
amount of packaging waste you buy
when you shop?   1   2   3   4   5

Resources (usage)

How well do you minimise the amount
of energy and water that you use
in your activities?   1   2   3   4   5

How much do you avoid/reduce/re-use/
recycle the waste that you produce?   1   2   3   4   5

How much attention do you pay to
using sustainable forms of transport
whenever possible?   1   2   3   4   5

IN YOUR FINANCES

Income v's debt

How good do you think your approach
to money is?   1   2   3   4   5

How well are your finances organised
so that you don't have to worry about
them on a day-to-day basis?   1   2   3   4   5

How manageable do you consider your
level of debt to be?   1   2   3   4   5

Planning for future

How well do you think your regular
savings provide for you and your
dependents upon your retirement?   1   2   3   4   5

How well do you think that you could
cope financially in the event of an
unexpected happening or emergency?   1   2   3   4   5

Job satisfaction

How satisfied are you in your job/
career/role   1   2   3   4   5

How personally rewarding do you find your job/career/role?	1	2	3	4	5
How much do you feel valued or recognised by others for your ontribution?	1	2	3	4	5
How much do you value or recognise yourself for your contribution?	1	2	3	4	5

Self advancement

How clear is your vision of the future/aspirations/a sense of purpose in your life?	1	2	3	4	5
How likely to be fulfilled are your hopes for the future?	1	2	3	4	5
How well do you utilise all your skills and talents?	1	2	3	4	5

All you need to do now is apply these numbers to the chart (right) to get a snapshot of the impact you make in your life on this planet. We all make an impact; the question is how lightly we can tread or as Jamie would put it, how big the splodge is that we make. It's a great word and somehow describes our attempts at sustainability perfectly. How big is your Splodge Print and what can you do to create a controlled explosion? ♥

When you've completed the exercise and evaluated it you will probably see how important it is to do the things you want to do and stop doing the things you don't. The fact is they will also be the things you do well. For me, this understanding was life changing. Even now though, there are times when I forget this principle and life starts to drag but the great thing is the more I do it the easier it is to spot the repeating pattern. I simply stop doing what I don't enjoy and go back to doing what I do enjoy. Take it from me there are enough people in the world who like doing the things you don't for you not to worry about it. Make sure though that those people around you also know what you are and aren't doing and why!

Splodge Chart

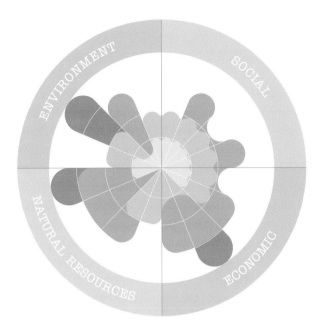

Now you can live with real power. The question is what is power? Basically I see three types, all of which you can look at again in relation to Maslow's hierarchy described in Chapter 2:

Power as something to fight for: Its roots are in the physical and emotional parts of our being, in that part of us which fights for survival. The part that believes we can only have what we want at the expense of others, resulting in everything from playground bullying to megalomania and the Third Reich. The win/lose mentality.

Power as a shared phenomenon: This develops in us once our physical and emotional needs are met and we begin to understand and feel there is meaning to our lives. It is an understanding that begins to transcend right and wrong and comes once we start to form an accurate self image through witnessing our behaviour. We do this through our mind as opposed to our physical being and emotions. It manifests in a sense of self transformation and is often expressed as win/win.

Power as who we are: Once we have achieved a level of personal growth and start to connect with Spirit we begin to see the connection between ourselves and the wider world and want to make a difference out there. We develop clear vision and are able to express our authority in the true sense of the word. At this level we reach a state of attunement, atonement or at-one-ment. The place of win/win/win.

It is this last one, "power as who we are", that I want to encourage you to strive for and work with constantly. It is the place of autonomy from where we can see clearly what we want in our lives and careers – and what we don't. I believe that we all want to be responsible for our own growth and development, our individual destiny. This is why the most fundamental commitment every single leader needs to make is to the development of the people he/she works with. Those people are hugely diverse in nature, background and ethnicity. In fact they are all different and we should celebrate that every single day. It is what makes our cultures rich and our businesses succeed.

Living with diversity encourages people to get out of their comfort zone. Constantly seeing and being with diverse people gives us constant opportunities to see things differently until it becomes the norm and no big deal to try something new. All successful people, whatever they do, live much of their lives outside their comfort zone – athletes, cricketers, rugby players, architects, accountants or lawyers. As Simon Barnes, sports correspondent for The Times once wrote, "The comfort zone is always the most desirable place to be. But in settling for comfort, there is a price to pay and it comes in the death of ambition, of hope, of youth and the death of self."

What to take with you from this chapter

- **Always aim for Love at Work - you know it's the only thing that works**
- **Hold your values and stick to your guns**
- **Do whatever it takes to be the best and to keep the best people**
- **Trust your instincts above all else**
- **Look for balance in all you do**
- **Look for sustainability in all you do and say**

and to remind you to...

- *Make sure you do both the exercises in this chapter before you move on*

Notes

....

....

....

....

....

....

....

....

....

Chapter 6

What's in this chapter:

- The qualities and characteristics of leadership
- How leadership affects a team
- Learning to keep a steady heartbeat
- Identifying and dealing with strengths and weaknesses
- Diversity, commitment and equality
- Knowing what not to do

Leadership – the lifebloood

" Leadership is lifting a person's vision to higher sights, the raising of a person's performance to a higher standard, the building of a personality beyond its normal limitations."

Peter F Drucker

The qualities of leadership

The growth of any organisation is both exciting and challenging, particularly that first step of becoming a team leader, however it manifests. In a small business it could simply be the move from sole trader to employing someone else. In an established organisation it might be a promotion that puts you in that position. Whichever way it happens, it demands as much character and courage of the individual as any other step they will take in their life. Having taken it, future ones may be easier emotionally but they will remain as demanding mentally.

How we view our business in these early stages will affect its every aspect. What I always found really useful was having an idea, a schema, a diagram, a design in my head of how my growing company might look. Because a business is three dimensional, the model I chose was our planet with its tectonic plates. It works because even with four or five people you can visualise how they can move and interlock. In the same way the earth's tectonic plates (admittedly over millennia) move, shift and overlap, so do the people in a business. Every time you add someone else, all the other people on the team need to adjust their position, skills and responsibilities to accommodate the change. Whether you are talking about a whole company or a team within a company, I found looking at it three dimensionally a really easy way to visualise the developing structure and explain it to other people. It even works of course as a model for a much larger company where the plates could represent the various departments or divisions. If your natural style isn't visual like mine then I am sure you could, if you wanted, develop a model that is based on one of the other key senses such as the auditory or kinaesthetic.

Let's get this out of the way early in this chapter - the difference between managing and leading. The following, anonymously written poem provides a good starting point:

The boss drives his men; the leader inspires them.
The boss depends on authority; the leader on good will.
The boss evokes fear; the leader radiates love.

The boss says "I"; the leader says "We".
The boss shows who is wrong; the leader shows what is wrong.
The boss knows how it is done; the leader shows how it is done.

The boss assigns the tasks; the leader sets the pace.
The boss says, "Get here on time"; the leader begins on time.
The boss makes work drudgery, the leader makes it interesting.
The boss says "GO"; the leader says "LET'S GO".

I would simplify it even further by saying that, in today's business world we should manage situations or processes and lead people. By its nature, leadership takes real creativity and a very high level of understanding of people and their personalities. We will need all of the elements of the previous chapters – and much more – if we are to become true leaders. Part of our responsibility will be to help imbue these understandings and traits in others. As our organisation grows, and whether we like it or not, we will be unable to maintain the level of relationship we have with a small number of people, when the numbers are much larger. It's no different really from the number of friends or family we are able to have such relationships with. Sadly, there will come a point where we will no longer be able to speak meaningfully to, and have long conversations with, everyone in our extended team.

Of course we should always aim to keep close contact with everyone for as long as possible and there are people with the most incredible memories for people and all they hear. For us mere mortals though, what is fundamentally important is that when we are with people, we really listen to them. Feeling really listened to is something we probably appreciate above everything else. We feel validated, understood and loved. Listening is an essential part of creating Love at Work. Interestingly, when we do truly listen we always remember far more than we would otherwise do if our mind is in several different places at once.

Leading by example

There is no greater way of leading than through example – in everything. In fact, it's the only way. We demonstrate it particularly through our integrity, our truth telling and promise keeping. Remember, business is but a metaphor for life; life is about relationships; the ultimate relationship is with one's self. When we maintain integrity with our self we maintain it with the world. It is something that flows back and forth, back and forth like the tides, the energy of the sun and the moon and the seasons that go with them. By leading in this way everyone gets to understand what needs to be the unshakable ethos of the organisation, or the company, or the team. The specific work they are doing may principally involve their IQ. Underpinning that mental ability with theirs and the organisation's EQ makes it that much more powerful.

We need to accept though that everyone is at a different level of personal growth and that this will affect the speed at which our growing organisation can progress. Having a personal accurate self-image allows us to more ably lead by example and demonstrate Love at Work. This becomes more important as the business gets bigger, because it is those essential qualities of leadership that need to rub off on those we are going to rely on to hold our values. This ideal was encapsulated by one of my team saying during a presentation debrief, "The thing I take from all of this is that it doesn't matter whether we are talking about facts, figures, programmes or anything else, we need to do it with integrity and passion." Never a truer word was spoken.

Those around us are the mirrors of who we are, warts and all. They encapsulate all our traits – good and bad – our mask and our shadow. They reflect back to us the qualities we need to encourage and the qualities we need to work to improve. You will find people who are naturally great ambassadors for the business, people who are commercially savvy, others who really understand clients and others who are financially hard-nosed. You need them all – to learn from and to recognise yourself in. If you are building a service organisation (and what business isn't nowadays) the ability to understand those people within the business will rub off on your ability to understand your clients, customers and suppliers. And the closer you are to the client, the more they will want to talk to you and the more likely you are to win the work.

Relationships

People always want to deal with people. People want to create relationships, they want to create friendships, want to feel loved, want to feel cared for. All of these things are such a part of the human condition that we all want to work with people we get on with, people we understand and who understand us. I absolutely believe that, if we stick with this belief through the times when cost is king and loyalty frequently meaningless in the face of it, we will win out. We will return to the real values, the ones that give our lives meaning as human beings. People will begin to trust again, deals will be done on hand shakes and repeat business gained on things other than price. Head or head/heart – which will you choose?

Honesty, consistency and integrity are the core values vital to long term success – and profit. They are what demonstrate authenticity. Inspiring others by seeing things through their eyes as well as your own builds a shared vision. Encouraging their questioning and decisiveness helps resolve even the biggest challenges together. In this way people become more fully engaged with the organisation. Such engagement lifts it several fold. People's commitment directly affects the bottom line. As Jim Collins said, "Resolve and humility are the key, not charisma."

A word of caution

However, it is the ultimate leadership in any organisation that affects the overall outcome and the return on investment. No matter how good individual heads may be, if they are constrained by unenlightened views, even energetically, they will fail in the long term. Over time the leader becomes worn down, their beliefs become weakened and they become a mouthpiece, an administrator or eventually leave. I've seen it happen time and again. Often the result is an organisation kept small by the controlling energy of its leader and it even dying as a result. Certainly, such an organisation has no real chance of surviving beyond its original ownership.

Learnng about leadership

Being a leader means supporting others not just in their professional but also in their personal development and in creating organisational excellence. Building political understanding and sensibility within the organisation is a part of that too. With these three things leaders at all levels can, with good mentoring support, encourage the principles of Love at Work. A strong mentoring programme will create the right environment faster than anything else. It will help us align our personal vision with that of the company and thus exercise real leadership. Part of the mentor's job is to know when to supervise, coach or consult on whatever the issue might be. It is also to bring a level of experience that isn't available elsewhere and to know how to disseminate it in the most useful way – one which empowers the recipient.

There is much for us all to learn about leadership – always. Without a doubt though, it is the catalyst for great teamwork. However big or small your team or company, whatever its focus and whatever your business, the underlying principles are always the same. Great leadership comes when people feel responsible for success, so identifying those people with the right character traits is essential. Good leadership results in:

- *Problems being raised and tackled early and creatively*
- *Free flowing information in all directions*
- *Leaders changing as circumstances change*
- *Proactive risk assessment*
- *People working for the good of the whole team*
- *Personal motivation towards excellence*
- *Group learning*
- *Higher achievement levels all round*

Leadership and learning are indispensible to each other."
John F Kennedy

Leading the team

Leading colleagues in this way means a much higher likelihood of team success because everyone shares the same goals and values. Accusation, blame, criticism, interrogation, offering solutions and jumping to conclusions are all put-downs and amongst the biggest killers of teamwork. On the other hand, listening carefully though asking open questions and not interrupting will allow you to separate the issues from the person and hear past the emotions to the underlying cause of whatever is really happening. Your team will fly when you combine really listening with genuine recognition and appreciation with welcoming conflicting views and wild ideas.

Your team will fly because you believe in yourself and in them. They will know this because you are prepared to live by your personal values and communicate your higher purpose. They will know it because you treat them as equals, no matter what role they play or level they are at in your organisation. They will know it because you are always prepared to listen, because you don't allow hidden agendas and because you always point people at each other to resolve their differences of opinion, never taking sides. When you do these things you will find that people fall into their natural authority and willingly take things off (not out of) your hands. There is no faster way for a team, including its leader, to learn and grow.

Leadership and influence has to be earned. People need to feel confident in you, to trust you. It involves risks and if you want others to lead too then they need to feel secure and totally supported. It is so much about first taking people with you and then, as they grow, them taking you with them. This will happen naturally because as you consistently demonstrate your leadership qualities your team will start to demonstrate theirs too. Helping people to get to a place where they act on their own is always satisfying – it is also much more effective and productive.

Once you are confident your team is starting to take responsibility – and risks – it's time to step back and allow the space for them to step into.It's a law of nature that vacuums always get filled. The key lies in creating the vacuum, not in filling it. You may not feel comfortable but it is essential for your growth as well as theirs.

A steady heartbeat

 Start with the premise that the function of leadership is to produce more leaders, not more followers."
Ralph Nader

The ultimate leader of an organisation, its founder, principal or CEO, determines its heartbeat. He or she needs many qualities; entrepreneurship, vision, personal energy, sales and marketing ability, financial understanding, good judgement, tenacity and perhaps most of all, outstanding communication skills. Don't forget integrity, self-confidence, commitment and PASSION. People like this quite naturally develop a learning culture, a collegiate atmosphere and as flat a structure as possible. They simply wouldn't have it any other way. They encourage Love at Work.

Picking those natural leaders at all levels, from CEO to receptionist, is what makes a huge difference. The receptionist who welcomes you with a smile in their voice when they answer your call, or on their face when you arrive, is just as valuable as the CEO. They are so often the public voice and face of the organisation. Recognising the importance of their contribution and working hard to help them make it, will pay huge dividends. Keeping this level of enthusiasm and rigour can sometimes be difficult though. I remember entrusting the setting up of a new mobile phone contract for senior staff to an office manager and being very specific about the make and model of phone we wanted. When the deal was done and my new phone was handed to me I knew something wasn't right but was much more focussed on other issues. It took me two days to realise it was the wrong one – whatever that says about me! It went back of course, but that's not the point. The point is that we need those around us to be as rigorous and as passionate about everything they do as we are ourselves as leaders.

The need for rigour

The idea of Love at Work can sound soft and a bit warm and fuzzy round the edges. If that's what you are thinking then you are missing the point! Love at Work involves a serious level of rigour not just around the organisation and its processes but around oneself; how one behaves, reacts, performs and responds all of the time. This makes a 360 degree vision of the world in which we work essential. In most businesses (and any other type of organisation for that matter) this means that the owner has to be a consummate professional in whatever it is that they are providing – unless of course they are prepared to genuinely be a sleeping partner. For example, a managing director who doesn't totally understand what it is you are providing, has never written a proposal, been face to face with clients or provided the service you are offering spells disaster, if not immediately, then in the long term. Yes, you can have specialist businessmen within the organisation and they can play a hugely important role in questioning the accepted norm. However I firmly believe they should not have control of it. Whether your specialisation is in IT, law, accountancy, architecture or anything else the only way someone can truly understand it is by knowing how to do it. The firm's whole professional ethic is built around a total understanding of whatever its particular skill, service or product is. Its whole philosophy, its raison d'être can only be truly understood by people who have been there, seen it and done it. This is why, for example, someone like Sir Stuart Rose has been so successful at turning round the fortunes of Marks & Spencer. The value of his knowledge of their particular market through on the ground experience should not be underestimated.

Getting to know your people, what their interests are, what they want out of life is highly rewarding for both sides. Treat them with kindness and respect and you get kindness and respect back. It is something we all need to do. Not because we will get more out of people but because we and they will benefit as human beings. There is absolutely no substitute for this.

Leadership is not a process."
Nigel Cutts

Maintaining the dream

I have heard Chief Executives ask, "How do I reignite the spark? How do I get people to think and work as they used to?" Sadly, by the time they are asking these questions it is nearly always too late. Their own energy has gone and with it the collective energy of the organisation. They have forgotten the most important thing, the people, and in doing so they have forgotten that Love at Work works. Thinking about and caring about people is a first principle of leadership. It may in fact be the only principle that matters. It works because it is from this place that we best communicate our vision and give them the opportunity to see how this aligns with their own. Being such a leader means constantly sharpening the arrowhead and keeping the arrow true so that it flies exactly where we need it to. Michael Tilson Thomas, music director of the San Francisco Symphony Orchestra put it like this:

"A conductor's authority rests on two things: the orchestra's confidence in the conductor's insightful knowledge of the whole score; and the orchestra's faith in the conductor's good heart, which seeks to inspire everyone to make music that is excellent, generous and sincere.

Old-school conductors liked to hold the lead in their hands at all times. I do not. Sometimes I lead. Other times, I'll say, "Violas, I'm giving you the lead. Listen to one another, and find your way in this phrase." I'm not trying to drill people military style, to play music exactly together. I'm trying to encourage them to play as one, which is a different thing. I'm guiding the performance, but I'm aware that they are executing it. It's their sinews, their heartstrings. I'm there to help them do it in a way that is convincing and natural for them but also as part of a larger design.

My approach is to be in tune with the people with whom I am working. If I'm conducting an ensemble for the first time, I will relate what it is I want them to do to the great things they've already done. If I'm conducting my own orchestra, I can see in the musicians' bodies and faces how they're feeling that day and it becomes very clear who may need encouragement and who may need cautioning. The objectivity and perspective I have as the only person who is just listening is a powerful thing. I try to use this perspective to help the ensemble reach its goals."

This bears a direct correlation to the idea that companies don't succeed, people do. You can imagine therefore how important it is to develop leadership across the whole of an organisation. Mentoring, coaching and independent thinking have a major part to play in this development as you will see in later chapters.

Feeling the fear

One issue that all leaders face and is seldom talked about is fear - their own and that of their team. The team can show theirs but the leader absolutely cannot show his or hers. They can share joy, laughter, fun and even concern but never fear. It is as dangerous as any contagious disease and can be life threatening to an organisation. Our only response to fear comes from our reptilian brain – to fight or run. Neither of which is often useful in our modern world. So when you are in a corner, stick to the facts, tell the hard truths, make the difficult decisions and take the sometimes even more difficult actions. The ability to do those things is the real reason you got to be leader in the first place and why people on your team will continue to respect and trust you.

Integrity and consistency are everything, never more so than when you are dealing with people's perceived conduct. Acknowledge, appreciate and praise people publically but never ever criticise them in front of others. Not only will you lose their trust but also that of everyone else. Their single thought will be, "If he/she can do that to them, then they can do it to me too!" Take it from me, it can and does happen. I have on more than one occasion seen people, very good people, wither and die overnight in such situations. The worst I saw was a public dressing down in front of the whole company by email. What was most terrible about it was that the person giving the dressing down had got their facts completely wrong but by the time they realised it irreparable damage had been done. No measure of apology could ever restore the broken trust. The result is that the person leaves and the company is the poorer not just by the loss of a brilliant, loyal and sometimes long serving employee, but also by the collateral damage caused by a totally avoidable error of judgement.

Keeping focus

The more we work at our leadership and the more we work at being a team, the more successful we will be. The more we speak up to each other personally and professionally the more we can raise our game. Asking ourselves this question will help us keep on track: "Is what I am doing right now getting me closer to my goal?" Teams can of course vary in size enormously and it may seem obvious but they need to be kept as small as they can to achieve their goal – be it for a specific project, for a department or that of the whole organisation. Keeping a team tight increases the likelihood of everyone knowing what is going on. I have found it useful to imagine a department or even a whole organisation as a team of teams, all pulling together, shifting organically and overlapping in the way I earlier described tectonic plates. The outcome is a series of smaller platelets forming a larger one and the larger one being one of a group. This reduces the possibility of building a linear organisation based on silos or one in which you suddenly realise walls have appeared overnight and you have no idea why. Once they are there they can by very difficult to demolish so best not let them start.

As team leaders we pick our teams with the level of rigour we do everything else. We choose people who are conscientious and committed, who are motivated through ownership of their part of the project rather than simply performing tasks. Those people extend themselves, support each other and look after each other. They also learn from those older and wiser than they are and a natural form of coaching and mentoring evolves. There is a corporate win too as both the quality and the quantity of work improves as a result.

Love at Work also develops through clarity of purpose, particularly when it is defined on all four levels; physical, emotional, mental and spiritual. It's interesting to look at how well we are performing as individuals and as a team from this point of view. Photocopy the exercise on the following page twice. First answer the questions for yourself and then again for your team:

See the exercise on the following page.

exercise

Answer the questions by circling the number on each row that best represents your feeling or intuition in relation to the question, where 1 is poor and 5 excellent.

Physical/survival level

How good is my/our environment?	1 2 3 4 5
How strong is our infrastructure?	1 2 3 4 5
How heavy is my/our work load?	1 2 3 4 5
How profitable am I/are we?	1 2 3 4 5

Emotional/relationship level

How well do I/we communicate with each other?	1 2 3 4 5
How strong is the quality of interaction between us?	1 2 3 4 5
How high is the level of trust?	1 2 3 4 5
How highly do I rate our level of teamwork?	1 2 3 4 5
How diverse is our team?	1 2 3 4 5
How strong is the ethos?	1 2 3 4 5

Stimulation/mental level

How creative do I/we feel?	1 2 3 4 5
How stretched do I/we feel?	1 2 3 4 5
How ambitious do I/we feel?	1 2 3 4 5
How driven towards success do I/we feel?	1 2 3 4 5

Contribution/spiritual level

How fulfilled do I feel?	1 2 3 4 5
How much value do I feel I/we give to each other?	1 2 3 4 5
How much value do I feel I/we give to the company?	1 2 3 4 5

How much value do I feel I/we give to the wider world?	1	2	3	4	5
How much meaning is there for me in this role?	1	2	3	4	5
How valued do I/we feel?	1	2	3	4	5
TOTAL					

When you have finished, add up the numbers in each column then add up the bottom row. Your maximum possible score is 100 but what matters is not really the number. The purpose is to get you to take the time to think about how you feel about what it represents to you. Thinking about it and talking about it with others in your team or even as a whole team can be very revealing. It also gives people the opportunity to understand each other better. ♥

Controlling our egos

The essence of Buddhism: no self, no problem!"
Jack Kornfield

The biggest threat to any team is the intrusion of people's inflated or exaggerated ego. That is why I spent so much time in earlier chapters talking about our personalities, how we build them, how we can understand them and work on the parts that aren't useful to us. Combining regular meditation with understanding and working with the concept of letting go of the ego will help to develop a strong team faster than anything you can imagine.

Whilst the skills we learn and develop in doing the job for which we and the company get paid (our intellectual skills) cannot be separated from the skills we learn and develop around people (our emotional skills), they are different. Generally we are formally taught our job skills and rarely if ever formally taught our people skills. Yet it is our hearts which make the real difference. It is this that gives a company integrity and congruity in all its dealings, internally and externally. It is this underlying philosophy, this essence that gives a company's brand real strength. Who we are is always so much more interesting than what we do. I would constantly encourage you to get out of your heads and into your hearts. This is the place from which we can allow others to see who we really are. From here we can create Love at Work. Of course there will be rare occasions when heart people need to get into their heads!

If you are of a more analytic bent then you might also want to take a look at the work of Marcum and Smith. They have taken the assertions that Jim Collins makes in "Good To Great" about the benefits of lack of ego and built a whole business around it and their jointly written book, "Egonomics". Read the book first and then, if you like the idea and it's within your budget then consider having them carry out a survey. The methodology they use is easily understood, highly accurate and well worth using. Based on seven core capabilities, which they identify, it makes a great starting point for improving the strengths of any team. It's worth remembering though why lack of ego will improve the bottom line. It does so because of the improved team performance brought about through people's willingness to understand themselves and each other.

When we work in a team of this quality why wouldn't we feel recognised and cared for; encouraged and listened to; supported and understood, fulfilled and growing? Why wouldn't we feel like we were not only part of a team but among friends? Why wouldn't we then always give of our best? With all of these things aligned we know we are in the right place, doing what we want to do. We become truly passionate. Whether that is because we are in touch with our power, have the guts to do what it takes, feel our sense of ambition, grab responsibility, have great clarity and step up to leadership or we become these things because we are passionate doesn't really matter. It is simply an amazing feeling and one worth working hard for and then hanging on to.

Ego isn't all bad of course. Without it we would all probably still be amoebae – a slightly bizarre idea I admit. With a strong (and well balanced) ego comes confidence, something which we all need as leaders and/or entrepreneurs. In fact, research has shown that although entrepreneurs are no less risk sensitive than anyone else, their confidence level over-rides their view of risk. Put simply, they believe that they can achieve what they set out to. You could equally call it over-optimism but the result is the same – they simply don't see themselves failing. Some do of course

– those whose ability is not up to their level of drive, but the overall result is that it drives businesses and society in general forward. Taking risks has always been the way in which humanity has developed.

Celebrating diversity

Entrepreneurs come in all shapes, sizes and temperaments. It's not something you can automatically discern just by listening to or talking to someone. What's more we need that level of diversity, not just in our entrepreneurs but right across our lives. Recognition and acknowledgement of diversity makes the world go round, helps people grow and releases new ideas. Culture and ethnicity are obvious points of diversity but the fact is we are all unique.

To illustrate the point, I was making coffee one Sunday morning when Jay, one of our grandchildren, who was nine at the time, suddenly said, "I've just set a record." Absentmindedly I replied, "Oh yes, what's that?" His response was "Every time I move I set a record, every time I breathe." Body-popping with his arms he said, "No one has ever moved in that exact way before. No one will again. I've been doing it ever since I was born. Everything in my body is unique. Everything it does to keep me alive. Everything I have ever done is unique and so is everyone else." I wasn't half awake any more. I was fully present. What a mind blowing and absolutely true thought! But how many of us still have the space and time that a nine year old does to think such thoughts?

This little story graphically illustrates our individual uniqueness. Let's make sure we acknowledge and celebrate this uniqueness every single day. Not just our culture and gender but our creativity, our thought processes, our learning styles – and our communication and leadership styles.

Diversity is about adding quality because of the difference between us. I don't know about you but I see the world around me and everything in it as, on some level, a reflection of the diversity of who I am and what I am. Here on this planet in the 21st Century in western society everything around me is here to teach me what it is I have come to learn this time around. Regularly in the past, I have looked around my office and seen facets of myself reflected in the team I work with. Declan represents my loyalty and also my unwillingness to face conflict; Alex my sharp intellect and also my irritation at the slowness in others; Harriet the wild side of my creativity; Suzanne my caring self; Rick my love of people and my Yorkshire-ness. The man in his car who cuts me up shows me my anger and my ruthlessness and on and on and on. Nowhere is this principle better expressed than in Tich Nhat Hanh's beautiful yet disturbing poem, "Please Call me by my True Names". It speaks so articulately of birth, life and death, of how he sees himself in trees and birds and mayflies, of how he sees himself as a child in Uganda, a pirate, a young refugee and a murderer. I wish I could reprint it in full here but sadly poetry is subject to stringent copyright rules, so do go to your nearest search engine and type in its name.

It is in and through this level of diversity that we experience growth. It is through diversity of colour, race, creed, sex, religion, opinion, identity, size, weight, shape and thought that we get the opportunity to both look at who we are and see ourselves and everything else through the eyes of others. For me, whatever the time or place in history, nothing is more important than peace and harmony and love of one's fellow man, every living creature and our planet. Not that I feel for one second that I achieve that to any great extent. Nor is it an evangelical thought about saving the world. It is simply that if, in my small way, within my circle of influence I can offer some love, some peace and some true friendship to those around me, then I want to do it, I want to make that difference. The way I can make that difference, we can all make that difference, is by recognising and welcoming the differences in all those around us.

Our creativity is essential to our life on this planet and it is our diversity which enhances it beyond measure. I use "creativity" in its broadest sense – rather than in the sense of the arts – painting, sculpture, ballet, theatre and so on – because I believe that all of us are constantly being creative and have a capacity to be so beyond measure. Couple our diversity of thought with our underlying but often suppressed willingness to accept diversity in those around us, and we have the single most powerful creative force for good that there is. With it we can move mountains. Diversity, when seen in this way has the capacity to heal relationships, kick-start amazing projects and even end wars or stop them from happening in the first place. Accepting diversity can do nothing but good, in every situation; be it social, family, work, political, charity, community or any other.

Staying awake

We always need to be awake to and aware of people's uniqueness. Not being so once nearly cost me one of the best people that has ever worked with me. James was a Contracts Manager, quite young but both bright and savvy. He was coming along well and his projects were making very good profits. He was particularly good at understanding numbers and putting a cost plan together as well as finishing his projects on time - great assets in any organisation.

The business had grown and we really needed to strengthen the Contracts Department by adding more specialist skills, so I had a meeting with the whole of that team to talk about the way forward and what they felt their individual strengths and weaknesses were. There was nothing unusual in this and my intention was to see who wanted to pick up which particular balls. What I really wanted was someone capable of sitting in front of a client and articulating the project costs. You have probably guessed it was James's strength but even so no-one put their hand up.

I was devastated some three weeks later to find his letter of resignation on my desk, particularly as I prided myself in the amount of time I spent with people getting to know them and their hopes and dreams. What had gone wrong? Somewhere in this period of rapid growth we had failed to notice that he wasn't being properly taken care of. I say we because he wasn't one of my direct reports. He had been head-hunted to do the very role we had been talking about. I'm glad to say that after a week of very intense discussion he decided to stay. Some three years later he is still in that job and loving it.

Somewhere I slipped up and nearly lost a great asset and a great team player in the process. The lesson in all of this for me was just how important it is to look after everyone in our teams and look after our best people. To make sure that their career path is clearly stated and properly mapped out for them. This means that, no matter what their role is in the company, we need to focus on an individual's strengths – and of course help them with their weaknesses. It is this focussing on their strengths that is most important. Do you remember when that great golfer, Tiger Woods, got a new coach back in 1997? When Woods said to him he wanted to focus on a niggling problem in his short game, the coach said, "Yes, we could and we will, but what I really want to do is focus on your greatest asset – your swing." We all know the rest is, as they say, history but it illustrates the point very well.

Commitment is a two-way street

Commitment to its people is something that every organisation needs to take seriously. For years now many companies have recognised the need to take care of people's financial and environmental needs. What they are now rightly beginning to focus on is issues such as job satisfaction. How they are doing this is through creating challenging projects with like-minded professionals, underpinned by open communication, personal development opportunities and skills training. Not forgetting appreciation of effort or work/life balance of course!

These are areas where clear communication helps enormously and it pays formally to set out the espoused values, but only after they have been established through genuine teamwork in open meetings. There's no getting away from the hard work involved but, unless you are prepared to thrash out every single statement so that it has total backing, you will be wasting everyone's time. In fact, worse than that, you will lose your personal credibility and the trust of your team. It is well worth the effort and it only needs to be done once. When it's in place it will be accepted as the foundation upon which all the relationships in the organisation are built. It becomes your statement of Love at Work. Here is just one simple example (as opposed to the one in Chapter 2) of what it might say:

We are committed to:

- *Ensuring our business success through enhancing our competitive advantage*

- *Encouraging change and learning in ourselves and others, embracing new ideas and being the very best we can*

- *Creating integrity and trust through constancy, attentive listening, speaking up, truth-telling and creating a safe place for this to happen*

- *Identifying the needs of those we have external relationships with and responding effectively and appropriately*

- *Respecting our individual and mutual needs and achievements with positivity, passion and energy*
- *Cooperating with each other, sharing work and knowledge and contributing to problem solving*
- *Taking responsibility for our performance and meeting all our goals*

Written like this, in the form of Sutras or aphorisms, it has a level of implied meaning that people can make their own.

Quality is everything

All of these aspirations will of course come to nought unless, as Jim Collins puts it in "Good To Great", you "Get the right people on the bus". A very dear friend of mine always says, "Spend your time with your best people." And of course your team needs to be made up only of those. You cannot afford anything else. There is no room for people who aren't up to scratch, for those you can blame either for their own shortcomings or your own. When I asked that same friend what he would do with the others, he said, "Fire them!" That's tough love indeed but they will learn from it too and go on to find a role somewhere else where both sets of values, theirs and the company's coincide.

Blame and shame have no place in business, or indeed in any part of our lives. They are nothing more than forms of victim consciousness. In this enlightened world we are helping to build, one of the underlying ethics is that of speaking up and listening to each other – and I don't just mean when things are going well. One of the biggest causes of breakdown in any team or any relationship is when people don't tell each other the way it is or the way they see it, good or bad. Whenever we have a problem or an issue with someone we need to take it to that person. There is nothing anyone else can do to resolve it. It's not their problem. If they try and resolve it, they are guaranteed to make matters worse.

Many people find this hard – either as the person with the issue or as the listener – so we need to have ways to deal with this. Some of us can do it naturally, others need to learn how. However, back-biting and back-stabbing are totally unacceptable in any circumstances. When I talk later about conflict resolution you will find the resources you need.

None of this means that we can't talk about each other. Of course we can if we do it with love and for the right reason – to gain understanding, not support for our case.

Out beyond the realm of right and wrong there is a field; I'll meet you there."
Rumi

Teamwork is also about the small things, about making small changes whenever they are needed. When we do this we rarely need to make large ones, particularly if we have got the right people on board. Once again, these small shifts are the platelets in the tectonic plates moving in response to the latest information, the latest techniques and the latest people. It may be something as simple as putting two people next to each other for the duration of a project, but it can make a difference beyond measure.

Such changes are cumulative and some businesses have this idea strongly embedded in their culture. Toyota outstripped all the US born motor companies prior to the 2008 recession partly by its employees understanding the benefits small changes bring. Whereas Ford and GM shed 46,000 employees and closed 26 North American plants Toyota continued to open them.

Just one among many examples of incremental change at Toyota was in the paint shop. Switching from central paint tanks with long hoses to paint cartridges in the spray booths saved 30% of the paint, cars took 20% less time to paint and there were 25% less cars in the paint shop at any one time. Overall they have cut the number of paint booths by a third. Added to that they use much less solvent and have to dispose of much less waste, which makes it an environmental success too.

What's more, such changes aren't seen as projects or initiatives but as simply part of the way people work. Efficiency and effectiveness become part of who everyone is. Doing things better, making things better, is a way of life. So is having the time and space to think things through. Mindless repetition numbs the brain and, whenever this happens, every part of our life is affected and we certainly can't be in a state of Love at Work.

Know what not to do

Leading a team takes many things. It takes knowing what not to do too. None of us start off as leaders, so on our way up we bring with us a whole set of habits and assumptions no different in a way from those that form our personality. In fact they are part of our personality. So often what happens then, is that we end up doing all sorts of things that we don't need to do, that other people are more capable of. We need to make those small changes that will make a huge difference to our team. Indeed we owe it to them and ourselves. Our job in the team is to aim to do only the things others can't and then sit and think – clearly, long and hard. You will read it again before the end of the book but I totally believe that the quality of our actions is only as good as the quality of our thinking. If we don't give ourselves the optimum opportunity to do this then we are failing not only ourselves but our whole team.

 Wisdom consists not so much in knowing what to do in the ultimate as knowing what to do next."
Herbert Hoover

Culture

Ultimately, leadership is at the core of an organisation's culture. Culture in the workplace is an amalgam of the combined values and wisdom as espoused by its leaders and accepted by everyone within the organisation. This applies whether the organisation is two people or a whole nation. Leadership is best expressed as a combination of example, listening and feedback. Therefore all we can do in this world is to be peace, be leadership and be love in action. It is the only way we can make a lasting difference, the only way to create Love at Work. We are all leaders in our own way.

No matter how hard we work there will be times when our leadership skills will be sorely tested. There will be people, particularly in companies working at the cutting edge of new technologies and services, who are so intellectually bright and so focussed on innovation that they aren't interested in rules. Unless, that is, it helps them get what they want in terms of resources. What they want is to be challenged creatively and to be recognised for their success by their peer group even when that is outside their own workplace. In fact perhaps more so by this group because it means a higher level of validation. In this case the leader's job is to make sure they know that you know what their needs are and then fulfil them. It's also to take away anything of the day to day routine that gets in the way of their creativity. Yes, they can be special and different and yes that cuts across the grain of building a collegiate organisation but if you need them to make the business fly then you need to learn how to handle them.

A quality coaching and mentoring system will help facilitate this. Remember that coaches and mentors aren't only for those on our team, they are for leaders too. Make sure the funds are available for this and make sure you get your share because nothing is more important than the leader thinking at his/her very best. Go out and find someone you feel you can work with, someone who will listen to you, someone with real business experience. Their experience doesn't need to be in your field. In fact it may be better if it isn't. Currently, coaching is a minefield. It is full of people young and not so young who seem to think that taking a couple of weekend courses entitles them to call themselves a coach. Nothing is further from the truth of course. The latest research shows that you need to spend in excess of 10,000 hours to become expert in something, even when you have an aptitude. The very best coaches and mentors will have this level of experience of life and business. They are out there and worth searching for. All you have to do is find one.

What to take with you from this chapter

- **Keep a clear head**
- **Lead by example**
- **People follow those they trust**
- **Personal rigour is essential**
- **Focus or fail!**
- **Keep your ego well in check**
- **Celebrate diversity**
- **Commitment and quality are everything**
- **Do the things that only you can**
- **Demonstrate peace and leadership**

and to remind you to...

- *Make sure you do the exercise in this chapter before you move on*
- *Type "Tich Naht Hanh - Please Call Me By My True Names" into your web browser*

Notes

....

....

....

....

....

....

....

Chapter 7

What's in this chapter:

- Defining the differences and the difference we can make
- What makes a great coach or a great mentor
- Getting the best results with the best people
- The need to change our perspective

Coaching and mentoring

" Knowledge is love and light and vision."
Helen Keller

The case for creativity

Constantly growing our people and ourselves is at the very core of Love at Work. Nothing is more important, for it underpins the level of creativity we are able to generate. Creative people adapt to change much more readily. They have a willingness to try and accept new ideas and then think of something else if those didn't work. Openness and frankness are vital in a world where the education systems are still generally based on suppressing our creativity and individuality. In our 21st century world, the 3 Rs of reading, writing and 'rithmetic need adding to if we are to solve the many problems facing our planet. Creativity comes out of our ability to think independently. The problem is that the vast majority of us aren't taught to think independently, because those holding political power (in many senses of the phrase) on every level are afraid of what might happen if we did. What they should really be afraid of is what might happen if we don't!

The huge shift that took place during the latter half of the 20th century from manual to intellectual work is having huge effects on our world economy. Earning a good degree used to be a passport to a decent living for the rest of one's life, but we all know this isn't so any more. At best it might get us an interview for our first job, but what happens when we want to move on or up a few years later? I suggest we need, in addition to teamwork which I talked about in the last chapter, two things: creativity and communication. In fact all three – creativity, communication and teamwork - are so closely interlinked as to be inseparable.

I have spent most of my career in a "creative" profession and it's a total misconception. Most of the work that goes on in so-called creative professions is in fact routine and repetitive. I believe that there is at least as much creativity in those professions such as accountancy and law as there is in architecture or design. They have all taken on false identities.

We have created a myth based on lies. We are all highly creative – it's in our genes. On the level of matter our bodies are being constantly creative in ensuring our wellness and regeneration. Getting out there and dispelling the myth is fundamental to creating Love at Work. You could say the same of the so-called caring professions. Whilst they are indeed that, caring is to be found in every workplace.

So often I watch with wonder the level of creativity we now see every day in so many areas of our lives. If it weren't so how did we end up with electricity, natural gas, aeroplanes, motor cars, washing machines, power tools or super computers? How did we end up with the Internet, with Google and with Skype? How is it that the lap top I am writing on is more powerful than the physically vast computers that took man to the moon and back? It is because of our innate creativity. Whilst creativity is the seed we plant in fertile soil, innovation is the act of nurturing it to maturity.

When Edison said, "Genius is one percent inspiration, ninety-nine percent perspiration." he was so right. We cannot afford for it to take generations to build our level of creative confidence to where it needs to be. We need a two pronged attack – one prong for those of us who have already had much of our creativity suppressed or beaten out of us and another to make sure that our children and our children's children see creativity as a matter of birthright. The focus of this book has to be on the former, on helping all of us release our creativity. To quote Marianne Williamson again, "Who are we not to be brilliant, talented, fabulous, gorgeous?" When we are the powerful, vital, magnificent, creative, fun loving human beings we were meant to be, we make a real difference in the lives of not just those around us but in the whole world. Our joy is infectious.

Ability is what you are capable of doing. Motivation determines what you do. Attitude determines how well you do it."
Raymond Chandler

Getting better at getting it right

We have all been brought up to aim higher, to raise our standards, get better grades and so we should. It is this drive that has led man to where he is now and whilst I wouldn't for one minute suggest we got it all right, it's a lot better than sitting in a cave wrapped in animal skins in the middle of a freezing winter. There is no point though in getting better at the wrong things. We need to be focused on those things that will make a real difference and to recognise that business, education and society are not separate or opposing interests. They all have so much to give to each other.

It's not just creativity that we have within us. We all have all of the potential we need to become highly successful. What we often lack is the appropriate support, coaching, mentoring or training to become so. Coaching for example is not a management skill but a way of life, a method of communication. Mentoring is all that and more. So what is coaching and what is mentoring and why are they so important? The dictionary definitions state:

Defining the role

coach^2
- *noun 1 an instructor or trainer in sport. 2 a tutor who gives private or specialised teaching*
- *verb train or teach as a coach.*

mentor
- *noun 1 an experienced and trusted adviser. 2 an experienced person in an organisation or institution who trains and counsels new employees or students.*
  ORIGIN from the name of Mentor, the adviser of the young Telemachus in Homer's Odyssey.

I would add to that. A coach supports your professional skills. A mentor may well do that but will also support you in your personal growth. A coach may be someone who is given to you to help learn something specific. A mentor should never be given but always chosen.

One of the most important qualities of any coach or mentor is experience. Confidentiality is another. Add to this a profound interest in people, a high level of empathy and finely honed professional skills, stir in a good sense of humour and you will have found someone both willing and able to support you on your path to success. The real key to helping people unlock their leadership potential is to teach them how to really listen to one another and in so doing create the space for them to genuinely think for themselves. No one knows better how to solve a problem or a challenge than the person facing it. No one has more information about the problem and, given the right circumstances, no one has more ability to solve it. Sadly, creating the time and space for someone to do that is an incredibly rare and valuable commodity. When it happens, people gracefully form their own opinions, come to their own judgements and jump to take action.

We all know quality is important but never more so than in that of coach or mentor. Working with someone at this level demands from both sides all the things we have already determined about trust. Knowing what effect they can have on their mentee is an essential part of the mentor's role. As is the need for them to understand how they can affect that person's self image and self belief, how to help them set and develop their goals and be a master at asking open ended questions.

Appreciation, appreciation, appreciation

I guess we would all recognise that in the UK we have a national disease called deprecation and another one called criticism. Neither of which serve us. Why this should be I have no idea, because it certainly doesn't serve us as individuals or as a nation. I have always wondered what it was in our group psyche that makes us that way. Back in my college days we actually had regular "crit" sessions of all our work, where tutors and students alike could pull your work to pieces regardless of its merit. Maybe this is why I believe so strongly in the principle of appreciation in everything we do. I can't think of a single person who doesn't grow or perform better when they receive regular and genuine appreciation of who they are and what they do. That's not to say we shouldn't help them grow through appropriate appraisal and evaluation. We all need that if we are to learn and improve, but it's the ratio in which we receive it that is important. Praise and appreciate people at least five times as often as we offer constructive feedback, no matter how kindly put, and we all blossom and grow. Reduce that ratio and we respond like a plant without sunlight. Increase the ratio above ten or twelve times and its effectiveness disappears because we drop into disbelief as our ideas of honesty and integrity are challenged. Like so many things in life it's all about balance – but these are facts well worth bearing in mind whatever the relationship, whether it's with a loved one or with a waiter in a restaurant we may never visit again. A smile and a compliment go a long way.

My mentor

I have had many coaches in my life; in my profession, in sport and in my personal life, but very few mentors – in fact only two. One of these, George Freeman, I met when I was a struggling design student just going into my third year. That autumn, the Head of Department had taken on two external tutors for the next year and George was one of them. It was an inspired move because he (and his business partner, Harry Bartram) brought a sense of reality, a breath of fresh air into the dusty studio. They knew what it was like to have deadlines and to have to solve real problems and it was just what I needed. Nothing was ever too much trouble or took too much time. We went on site visits to real jobs. We went to the pub. They came to our parties. Over time George and I developed a genuine friendship based on respect, trust and probably early on a little hero worship. Not surprisingly, these are all things I believe you need in a good mentoring relationship.

When I left college we stayed in touch. He was always there at the end of the phone and never in a hurry. Almost laconic in style, nothing was ever too much trouble and I'm sure his clients felt that too. He found me my second job, after which I went to work for him for a while. When I left and went to work for someone else again we kept in touch, having a coffee or a drink or lunch once in a while. About ten years on he pointed me in a direction that I pursued one way or another for the rest of my career. It wasn't all one way by any means. We worked together on major projects a couple of times and I introduced him to a hotel designer with whom he was to work for many years. To this day, some 45 years later, we are still friends and we still meet up. I ring him if I think he might be able to help and equally he'll ring me if he thinks I might know the answer. All in all it's been a career long mutually supportive relationship but at heart he will always be my mentor and I will always be grateful to him for what he gently did at the start of term in September 1964. He is the reason I have written this book and dedicated it to him. If I can do half as much for others as he has done for me then I will be content.

Our ever changing nature

When we are starting out on our career path, we need over time an ever changing and increasing range of skills, not least of which are those of an interpersonal nature. In this regard, I can't stress highly enough the importance of both coaching and mentoring. It provides us with a level of motivational support that helps us identify our beliefs and values and through this our mission and purpose in life. As this happens, we get the opportunity to witness our behaviours and change them as necessary. Our stress levels are lower and our general sense of well-being improves. Coaches and mentors are different and have different roles to play in our lives. A great mentor has the ability to support us emotionally, mentally and spiritually. Others may not agree, but my view is that a great mentor is always chosen by us and never foisted upon us. Great coaches may have these qualities too, but they often aren't as essential.

Enlightenment and personal advancement are not dissimilar in some ways. They both involve a great deal of rigour and application. They are both always slightly out of reach but they both demand the same philosophy. A couple of Zen sayings reflect this:

> **Before enlightenment, a tree is a tree, a river a river and a mountain a mountain. After enlightenment, a tree is a tree, a river a river and a mountain a mountain."**

> **Before enlightenment, chop wood, carry water. After enlightenment, chop wood, carry water."**

Everything is different and yet everything is the same. Socrates interpreted Heraclitus's view of this as "…all things are in motion and nothing at rest; he compares them to the stream of a river, and says that you cannot go into the same water twice." So too is it in business. As we move through our lives and careers many things stay the same and many change. Sadly one thing that can and does change whether we like it or not as we take up a leadership mantle is the attitude of others towards us. Because none of us are actually enlightened, what we say to and how we behave towards others is coloured by our ever changing world view. This is why above all we need to keep integrity within the team by letting those people go who don't fit and by supporting unconditionally those who do.

Leaders have needs too

As a leader at any level we have both coaching and mentoring responsibilities. There is one person of course who cannot get that support within the organisation and that is the CEO. You could say that this support is the role of the Chairman and in some respects it is. In some cases of course, he is shareholder imposed and therefore cannot be called a mentor because the mentee has had no part in choosing him. In other cases the organisation is too small to warrant a chairman. My view is that in either case, if you are the CEO, you need to find someone (or more than one person) outside the organisation to support you. It's worth reading again the qualities that George exemplifies and bearing them in mind as you search for the right person for you. Remember, only you will sense who that is so trust your instinct, your gut or your heart and pick someone who will both support and challenge you. Tough love is an important part of Love at Work.

Mentoring works

Mentoring works whatever sort of organisation you are building. My wife and I have been involved in Toastmasters International, the not for profit, worldwide public speaking and leadership organisation for many years now. When we set up a club called London Cardinals in 2004, one of our aims was for every member to choose a mentor for themselves within the first few weeks. We did it and it works. How do we know? Not just because we have produced no less than five UK and All Ireland winners in as many years but also because week after week our members produce speeches at a masterful level of daring, sharing and fun. All our visitors (and there are many) remark not only on this but on the level of support, friendship and camaraderie within the club.

One often overlooked role of coaches and mentors is that of ensuring that the person being coached or mentored fully understands their job role. This breakdown in understanding often occurs at the same time as a promotion. They fail to let go of parts of their old job and therefore don't have the time or space to fully embrace the new one. All of us live our lives based on assumptions and there's not a lot of point in that. Why on earth would we want to base our actions on things we don't know to be true? If we all work at helping those we interact with (at whatever level) recognise this, many positive events will follow naturally. When we do it with an open heart, with the principles of Love at Work in mind, we create a powerful 360 degree review tool that enhances any formal review process. So much so, that annual appraisals should never hold surprises – good or bad.

A way of being

When we see coaching and mentoring as a way of being rather than a way of doing, people have the opportunity to grow exponentially. Incremental shifts become fundamental shifts and fundamental ones become transformational. As we set the bar for our achievement higher we have no alternative, if we are to succeed, but to look deep into ourselves, to increase our self awareness. In developing a more accurate self image, we become less fearful of failure and therefore, paradoxically, less likely to fail. Early childhood fears and assumptions fall away with our new found confidence in Self. We discover our Will – the real power that lies within all of us.

Looked at like this it seems to me we have an absolute duty to do all we can to help and support others. What we can accomplish on our own is so much less than we can accomplish together. This apocryphal, if unlikely story illustrates our power to help and influence others:

When the house lights dimmed and the concert was about to begin, the mother returned to her seat and discovered that her child was missing. Suddenly, the curtains parted and spotlights focused on the impressive Steinway on stage. In horror, the mother saw her little boy sitting at the keyboard, innocently picking out "Twinkle, Twinkle Little Star".

At that moment Paderewski, the great piano master, made his entrance, quickly moved to the piano and whispered in the boy's ear, "Don't stop, keep playing". Then, leaning over, Paderewski reached around to the other side of the child, and he added a running obbligato.

Together, the old master and the young novice transformed what could have been a frightening situation into a wonderfully creative experience. The audience was so mesmerized that they couldn't recall what else the great master played. Only the classic "Twinkle, Twinkle Little Star".

This is the real meaning of empowerment: to help others recognise their own strength and confidence, their own authority so that they get into their personal power and take right action.

Saying what we mean

Very often it's not what we say, it's in the way that we say it. How often have you heard children (or anyone else for that matter) say, after they have fallen out with a friend, "I only said…" It is probably the biggest single contributor to the death of any relationship. The converse is true of course; that when we really express clearly and concisely what we mean people cannot fail to understand us and the feelings behind what we say. Let me give you a slightly abstract illustration. I was mentoring a young man during his preparation of a competition speech. At one point in it he had written "…the first girl I ever fell for." At first sight this might seem fine but when he gave the line it fell flat, lacking emotion. After we discussed it and he realised he was speaking of his first love, I suggested he change it to "…the first girl I ever loved". The result was amazing and for him quite unexpected. He suddenly felt all the strength of that first love and what it meant come flooding back to him, making it difficult for him to hold back the tear in his eye and the tremble in his voice. This one simple change altered the delivery of the speech and turned it from the ordinary into the extraordinary. In short it made it a winner. At every level of the competition he felt the power of it and his audience felt it too. Why? – Simply because he was telling (and feeling) not just part of the truth but the whole truth. He was being authentic and there is no more powerful form of communication.

What's the difference?

So, how do we know when to coach and when to mentor and what's the difference? It's a good question. In principle, coaching could be described as something that happens at the lower levels of Maslow's hierarchy diagram. It can achieve much at levels one and two (physical and emotional), with some element of level three. It is possible to coach someone while knowing very little about them other than issues pertinent to the skill concerned. On the other hand mentoring requires more intimate knowledge of the mentee to make it successful. In fact the more you know about the mentee and the more they know and understand of you as the mentor, the more successful the relationship and therefore the outcome becomes. Through the alignment of their values, particularly at levels three and four (mental and spiritual), both sides gain greater understanding and greater insight not just of each other but of the issues they are dealing with. The result is a relationship that grows in an ever increasing upward spiral. Just remember the story of me and George.

It's so important

Whether we consider ourselves a Coach or Mentor, a Champion or Advisor we play an important role in the lives of those we support, enable and develop. Our actions become inseparable from our leadership and produce results high on Maslow's hierarchy. It is a concept that comes from our conscience, is envisioned in our minds, feels right in our hearts and is actioned through this whole process of active support. In other words, we grow together. We are in win/win/win – you and I win, the organisation wins and our customers and clients win.

Persistence eliminates resistance."
Nigel Cutts

These are all principles which we can help each other with whatever our level of experience. Those of us who have benefited from a mentor in our lives can give that to others. Those of us who have not can learn through the opportunity of experiencing this level of support, enablement and development. Eventually we too will get the pleasure of giving to others in this way. Aligning these principles with the goals we need to reach and the actions we need to take to get there produces outstanding levels of success and satisfaction. Always remember that coaching and mentoring is a two way street; the more you put in to these relationships the more you will get out.

Whenever we enter into a coaching or mentoring relationship these are the things I believe we have a right to expect:

Principle	Goal	Action
Supporting	• Helping each of us to understand that the best coach for our self is our self • Working with great and knowledgeable people	• Championing our cause • Supporting us in pushing our boundaries • Sharing in our success • Encouraging us with unbridled enthusiasm • Encouraging our unbridled enthusiasm • Being there to talk to • Listening without interruption • Recognising our true worth • Believing in us
Enabling	• Encouraging us to constantly improve our abilities • Creating a two way commitment	• Being our champion • Being the best they can • Getting us to believe in ourselves • Instilling a "can do" attitude in us
Developing	• Helping us learn on the job and stretching our talents and abilities • Nurturing our independent thinking	• Allowing us to make mistakes • Allowing us to make difficult decisions • Allowing us to get on with it • Creating a place for us to learn • Encouraging us to be the best we can • Giving us opportunities

Everyone needs coaching sometime

Within this coaching and mentoring environment there will of course be a need for specific training right from the day someone joins the organisation. Some of it will be internal and even informal; some of it may need to be external but it will be different for every single person. Whatever its form, there will always need to be a balance between the benefit to the individual and the benefit to the organisation. It's what a colleague of mine once called enlightened self-interest.

The first thing anyone needs when joining a new organisation or even a new role is a thorough orientation. In embryo organisations this is relatively simple, although by the time a company has grown to 15 or 20 people there is an awful lot of day-to-day information that we take for granted so it's wise to formalise it early. Making sure the new recruit gets to talk to at least the heads of all the departments and understands the relationships and functions is essential. Even more important, in a company being built on Love at Work principles, is them being given a clear presentation of the vision and values you hold. Without this there is absolutely no point in them being there.

Getting results

There is no doubt that there are many occasions when group training is useful, for example in disseminating standard procedures and methods of working. Outside this, I'm not personally a big fan of it. I think people have to want to learn, to advance their knowledge and push their boundaries and then take the initiative in getting that training for themselves. Let me give you just a couple of examples. In one business I ran, Georgia came as temporary help on marketing. It was soon evident that she was a very capable administrator so she was offered a permanent role. After several years we had grown to a size where she felt her HR skills didn't match the company's needs any more so she asked me if she could take a two year, part time HR course with the Chartered Institute of Professional Development (CIPD). I was more than happy to agree and pay the costs. She worked incredibly hard and at the same time always kept on top of her "day job". The end result was that she is now the full time HR Manager there and doing a great job.

Here's another example. Peter was leader of a small team and felt his skill base would be greatly enhanced by his doing a Masters in Facilities Management. I happily agreed to pay the fees. Doing this meant he felt incredibly supported by us, that he mattered to the business. The knock on effect of which not only meant he felt more committed to the company but that he also gave more of himself in speaking up, offering his opinion and spreading not only his new found knowledge but his existing knowledge too. You can imagine that long before the two years of his degree were up his increased knowledge was paying dividends right across the business and washed through to his clients.

His career progressed more rapidly as a result of it of course. A real example of win/win/win!

All of these things help create an ever increasing level of self awareness in us. Without self awareness we cannot have awareness of others, at least not in the way that it can be expressed in an environment of love and care and understanding. It takes self awareness for us to recognise when we are doing something because we want to or because we feel we ought to. Whenever we feel we are doing something out of obligation we are doing it because we have "agreed" to do it down at the level of victim consciousness and the cost to ourselves is enormous. Our underlying resentment and anger will eat away at us or spurt out inappropriately – or both. Food spilt over guests doesn't happen by accident, it happens through anger. The mechanic who leaves a tool loose inside your engine compartment, the surgeon who leaves a clamp inside your body after an operation, the delivery guy who drops your brand new television – they are all examples of what happens when someone doesn't feel valued enough, cared for enough, loved enough.

Our job as leaders

As leaders it's our job to make sure everyone on our team feels they really are valued, cared for and loved because not everyone else they meet will do that for them. I can instantly recall one client, Andrew (another pseudonym), who is the antithesis of this philosophy. He thinks he knows everything about everything and treats everyone else as if they know nothing about anything and treats his staff exactly the same way too. I remember him calling me and another director into his office one day and telling us very clearly that what anyone else on his team thought was of no consequence and the only person to listen to was him. All of this took half an hour while the rest of his team and ours cooled their heels in the boardroom. He has a short temper bordering on volatility and he talks to his people as if they are dirt or mediaeval serfs. On the other hand he can be utterly charming. What's more, his employees follow his example and behave in the same way. The trouble is they can't pull it off because they don't have the authority, so much of the time life becomes hell for everyone involved.

I was talking about this with a good friend one day and he asked me if there was a way I could get close enough to Peter to train him – a bit like a cat trains its owner! It was a rather strange question but I did know what he meant. Getting close to people is always important for me - and sometimes you just can't. All you can do is stick to your own principles and way of being every time you meet them, be courteous, kind, non-abusive and non-reactive. I like to think that in this case even if it didn't rub off on him it rubbed off on his staff and they could see that there was another way of being. Not allowing fear to enter into the culture of an organisation in the first place should always be our goal. Sadly it's not always possible because as human beings it is highly likely that we will have experienced it and be carrying it around with us - and therefore react badly in certain situations. I know I do.

Sometimes it is easy to jump to conclusions about people and it must be something we all have done or do, yet it doesn't serve us or them. After the world financial crisis we could roll up all the city bankers and financial people and categorise them as sharp with overt business acumen, deal makers; duckers and divers; or even well dressed market traders. Apart from the fact that every one of them is an individual those words are all rather negative. How differently might we feel about them if we described them and saw them as having a broad awareness, finely honed business acumen, skilled negotiators, masters of the segue and working hard to be successful rather than negatively lumping them all together?

Love at work

There is no doubt that there is a strong case to be made for coaching in the business world. It certainly improves learning, development, performance, productivity, flexibility and therefore the bottom line. How often does it improve people's quality of life though? How often does it help people relate better to one another? How often does it generate acceptance and diversity? At its best it certainly does - and it is then that it has that added ingredient of Love at Work, which is the constant theme of this book. Sprinkle in some of that and everything else will fall into place. That much vaunted theme, Corporate Social Responsibility (CSR) will become something people do naturally rather than paying lip-service to. Holistic coaching or ongoing personal development is fundamental to building a business for the 21st Century, the information age; the age where people are paramount.

A new phenomenon...

Whilst the principles of coaching are as old as man himself, coaching as a profession is a relatively new phenomenon and covers such a broad spectrum of disciplines. There are Business Coaches, Life Coaches, Executive Coaches, Sports Coaches and Health Coaches – and I'm sure you can think of many more. Coaching is not the first profession to face the problems of its diversity and growth while trying to find its feet. Fortunately, there are many wise and experienced people involved who are intent on establishing and raising standards. No doubt an adequate accreditation system will eventually emerge – but that alone will provide only a minimum benchmark.

You would be wise to think carefully about whom you might choose as your coach or who you allow to coach others within your organisation. Seek out those both inside and outside your workplace who are brilliant coaches because of their level of expertise and understanding. Look diligently for a combination of experience, expertise and communication skills. Best of all, of course, is to find your coach (or coaches) through recommendation or referral, so ask your friends, ask your colleagues and your clients, and then create a shortlist. Don't be afraid to ask questions and get references, after all it's your life or organisation that will be affected and your hard earned money you will be spending. No one worth their salt will mind – in fact they will welcome it.

... and an ancient one

Mentoring is equally as old as man himself. It demands many of the qualities one has a right to expect in a coach and then much more. Not everyone has the ability to know what to do with the knowledge collected over their lifetime but a good mentor does. They need sagacity, wisdom and a life well lived. Wisdom, someone once said, is knowledge applied through experience. Only then can we pass on to others what we have learned and help them achieve even greater goals than they already have. Your search for someone you can trust on this level may be long or that person may already be in your life. If it's the latter, grab every opportunity you can to be in their presence and then simply listen. If they aren't, then the same rules I spoke of above for choosing your coach can equally be applied to choosing your mentor.

Breaking the mould

Coaches coach because they are committed to making a difference in their clients' lives. If they are business, executive or leadership coaches, one of their aims is to help their clients to be successful inside the organisation they work for and on its terms. Here lies the dilemma. At first sight this appears perfectly reasonable. Consider though what might actually be happening. The potential conflict of interest between the individual's and the organisation's needs could keep them from developing to their full potential. There is the possibility that they could be helping embed in their client a level of compliance and obedience to a style I used to work so hard to create in my obedience competition dogs. In that situation, unquestioning obedience was exactly what was needed to win – you certainly wouldn't if your dog decided to do its own thing and go back to the car and lie down! In that situation, that level of independent thinking doesn't win prizes. There are still organisations where it doesn't either. As coaches and mentors, it is incumbent on us, first and foremost, to help our clients create their best thinking and in so doing help their organisations rise above the norm.

Great coaches and mentors know that the real expert is you. They know intuitively that no one has more information and knowledge about a specific issue than you do. No one, but no one else knows what the answer is. With this knowledge always to the forefront, they work tirelessly in support of you, listening profoundly to all you think and have to say, to all your outpourings, until you arrive at your own magnificent answers. Your mind is unique. Your mind is truly magnificent, as all our minds are. Your coach's job is to water it, feed it, nurture it and then let it grow in an environment of profound respect. Now that really will create independent thinking!

Such people will not do your thinking for you. They will put a stop to the myth that they are the ones with all the answers. They will not set themselves up as the experts. They will not allow you to think of themselves as the fount of all knowledge. When they speak it will very often be in the form of questions. When you ask them what they think they will couch their answers in terms of experience not advice. They will tell parables, not give instructions

An experienced mentor knows all of this intuitively. It is the very reason he (or she) is that good. His (or her) combination of time and patience will reap huge dividends. This is the nature of genuine wisdom. This is the place from which our personal growth actually starts – and when that happens, the sky really is the limit. We learn to connect our head and our heart and naturally create Love at Work.

What to take with you from this chapter

- Creativity is everywhere
- Coaches and mentors fulfill different but not conflicting roles
- We need to coach and be coached
- We need to mentor and be mentored
- Take time to support, enable and mentor others
- Support others with care and love
- Break the mould of compliance

Notes

....

....

....

....

....

....

....

....

Chapter 8

What's in this chapter:

- Understanding the greatest skill of all
- Why attention improves attention
- Learning to think independently
- Guaranteeing our potential
- Dealing with conflict

Listening, thinking, speaking

" A wise old owl lived in an oak.
The more he saw the less he spoke,
The less he spoke the more he heard.
Why can't we all be like that wise old bird?"
Nursery Rhyme

The importance of listening...

The quality of all our actions is a direct result of the quality of our thinking. The quality of our thinking is a direct result of the quality of the environment in which we think. Or put another way – the way in which we treat each other while we are thinking, hence the heading for this chapter.

In simple terms there are five levels on which we can listen to someone:

1 **Ignore them completely**
   Not listen to someone (and be thinking about something else, openly showing that to be so)

2 **Pretend to listen to them**
   Try to look as though we are listening even though we aren't paying attention and couldn't repeat a word they said

3 **Listen to them selectively**
   Listen only to the parts of what they are saying that interest us.
   This is what most of us do most of the time

4 **Listen to them attentively**
   When we are interested in the logic and information they have to offer

5 **Listen empathetically to them**
   To truly want to understand what they are saying, what that tells us about them and are genuinely interested in what they are going to say next

Almost until the turn of the century the most advanced listening technique available to us was that of Active Listening (close to level 5 in the diagram above), wherein the listener would pay attention not only to what the other person was saying but also to their behaviour and body language. They would then feed back to the other person their interpretation of what the speaker had said. No doubt you can imagine the variety of situations where it was useful, particularly where it was important for the person to feel heard or understood, such as in conflict resolution.

Rogen International calls the silence of the listener "digging for gold". What I think it means by that is that closed questions create brief answers; open questions create longer answers and therefore more information. The gold comes from asking open questions and then sitting in silence and simply allowing the pause. It is at this point that people get to hear their own thoughts and feel their own feelings – and that is when things begin to change for them.

... you know," she said slowly "I like you, Lin."...
" You do?" I asked...
" Yes, you're a good listener. That's dangerous, because it's so hard to resist. Being listened to – being really listened to – is the second best thing in the world."
Gregory Roberts, from Shantaram

...and attention

Attention is at the heart of everything. When someone places their attention on us, then we are able to place our attention on our own thoughts. Therefore the more fully someone places their attention on us the more fully we are able to place our attention on our own thoughts. The results are exponential.

This is why giving someone "a good listening to" is the ultimate gift we can bestow on them. It is something we should encourage in ourselves and others every day. Without it we simply cannot create Love at Work. An organisation based on trust, integrity, love and understanding will help people to learn how to listen. The stillness it provides is a key ingredient of inner peace and therefore external peace. This is why the work of Nancy Kline and her organisation Time To Think is not an invention but a discovery; a constantly unfolding understanding of what happens when the mind thinks clearly and without intervention. If you haven't read her book "Time To Think" or its sequel "More Time To Think", I strongly urge you to order it now and read it as soon as you have finished this one.

You can't get to the good stuff if you already know the answers."
Anon

A thinking environment

What a Thinking Environment does is turn up the brilliance in people (Marianne Williamson again!). It is a sort of spiritual spa, a clarity consultant that creates exponential growth for inexplicable reasons. The ways in which it can improve the quality of our thinking aren't normal on the one hand but on the other are common sense yet not commonplace.

Some years ago I was given a copy of Nancy's book by a business colleague. Once I started to read it I couldn't put it down; it just made so much sense. By the time I'd finished reading I knew I just had to meet her to find out more. Eventually I tracked her down (the internet wasn't what it is today nearly ten years ago!) and was delighted to find that although she was American she was married to an Englishman and lived over here. I booked on one of her courses – 4 days of "Thinking With Other Leaders" and that was it. By the time it was over I was totally hooked. I knew in the deepest part of my being that this was one of the keys to what I have come to call Love at Work; a simple but elegant process which anyone could understand; a system that didn't purport to be therapy but was therapeutic. As I said in an earlier chapter I also knew that it was the key to my dream for the business I was running to continue with the values I held way beyond my ten year tenure. I racked my brains to find a way to achieve it and eventually found the solution. It came to me in a thinking session and was mind-blowingly simple. All I had to do was have the leadership team trained in Time To Think – and I'll talk more about that in Chapter 9.

All the while, I was using it myself and seeing more and more of its nuances. At its heart is a six step process that is both simple and complex.

The majority of thinking sessions (probably upwards of 95%) that any of us ever have are straightforward and only involve us in step one. In a space of being fully listened to our mind rapidly works its way through what we want to think about and reaches the conclusions or actions we need. This space is what Nancy has named The Ten Components. They are: attention, equality, ease, appreciation, encouragement, feelings, information, diversity, incisive questions and place. More of this later and of course, in Nancy's book. Most important of all though is the principle of non interruption – under any circumstances – ever! It is this principle that we as individuals, whenever we are thinking, know better than anyone else what the answer is to what we need to do, what actions we need to take, that makes Time To Think so powerful. Interrupt someone at your peril, for you risk damaging the relationship irretrievably – and yet we all do it nearly all of the time!

Removing the block

There are occasions however when we get stuck, when we can't seem to see our way through to the other side, when we reach a block. This is the point at which we are most likely making a limiting assumption about whatever it is we are thinking about. It is then that we turn to step three of the process: looking at the assumptions we might be making (which are different to beliefs because they are questionable), deciding whether they are true or untrue and, when appropriate, turning them into what are called Incisive Questions.

I have come to recognise that these Incisive Questions, asked in the space of a Thinking Environment, are the most powerful of tools in support of our independent thinking so, let me give you a worked example to help explain the principle more clearly. I spent seven or eight years thinking about writing this book, making notes and gathering information, hoping all the while that I would find the time and space to be able to realise my goal. Eventually it happened, I spent a full month organising the material, creating a mind map and then for no apparent reason I was stuck. You could call it writer's block but then I'd never written anything like this before – thousands of reports, proposals, presentations and speeches but never something on this scale. So at the next session with my Thinking Partner, Jamie, we went straight for an Incisive Question, setting the challenging step as "The Physical Act of Writing my Book".

After a brief discussion, in order to find the limiting assumptions behind the block he asked me this question:

"What might you be assuming that is stopping you from writing your book?"

My thoughts went through things like:

"I don't know how to do it."
"I've never done anything like it before."
"The material and thoughts aren't all mine."
"I can't remember what I need to."
"I don't know how to articulate them well."

When I couldn't think of anything else Jamie simply asked:

"What else might you be assuming?"

A simple question but more than enough to get me started again,

"It's too big a task."
"I don't have enough examples."
"Everybody has already said what I want to say."
No one will want to publish it."
"Who will want to read it?"

When I stopped speaking the next time he asked:

"What are you assuming that is most stopping you from taking that step?"

The key assumption was very simple:

"I am assuming that I can't remember or articulate what I need to."

Next Jamie asked:

"Do you think it is true that you can't remember or articulate what you need to and what are your reasons for thinking so?"

My response was fast and direct:

*"No! Because I remember many things. I have a good, strong
and intelligent mind that constantly organises and articulates my
thoughts."*

To find the credible true liberating alternative assumption he asked next:

*"What would you credibly have to assume instead to be able to
write your book?"*

Again my answer came quickly:

"My mind always organises and articulates my thoughts perfectly."
"I can always find and articulate my thoughts clearly."

From which we were able to create the incisive question that in my
experience always leads to break through:

*"If you knew that you always find and articulate your thoughts clearly,
how would you write your book?"*

Answers popped instantly into my head:

"Stick this question on the wall."
"Do an NLP six-step reframe on this assumption."
"Put time in my diary every day."
"Just do it!"
"Be direct."

These were some but not all of the answers, so I did what I always
do. I printed the question out in big letters and put it in various places
around the house. In this way these wonderfully freeing questions go
on working and working. I simply take them down when I notice I have
stopped looking at them. What is most interesting in all of this is that the
mind thinks better in the presence of questions. It's almost as though
we are giving it permission to go off in whatever direction it likes, to have
wild ideas, to be creative.

It was this part of the whole process that made me take the final step to complete the coaching and consultancy aspects of this work, even though I thought (and Nancy thought) I might never use it directly as a coach or consultant. Not something to undertake lightly when you are holding down a senior role in an international company, but I have never regretted one moment of the time it took.

The speed of thought

Here's another example: one that happened spontaneously at a Toastmasters' meeting. A young woman came up front to give what we call a Table Topic – a brief impromptu speech. With 35 pairs of eyes focussed on her and ears listening intently to what she had to say, this is what she said:

"I don't know about that, but I was in my annual review this morning and they said I was great at completing projects but not at starting them. It really upset me. I didn't know what they meant ..."

And then in no more than a minute and a half she completed the whole thinking process, knew exactly what her reviewers meant and exactly what to do about it! What was astounding was the speed and clarity with which she did it. I watched as her thoughts started in a random, meandering, unstructured way. Then as they came more rapidly they became more and more structured until she reached a conclusion which no one but she could have come to. It was stunning – an absolutely perfect example of the Time To Think process without her even realising it. I believe she achieved it because of the environment she was in which contained nearly if not all of the Ten Components. I believe she achieved it also because of the factor of 35 people completely focussed on her, listening with respect, interest and fascination to what she thought. It was this that accelerated her thinking.

All of this is like digging for gold, as Rogen would call it. It takes Active Listening apart and creates a new and more powerful listening model. Such a model will be called anarchic and revolutionary (in the political sense of the word) in a lot of organisations. This is because Time To Think creates Independent Thinking and, if the truth be known, there are plenty of organisations which don't want their people thinking independently. They are stuck in a time warp, in a Victorian way of thinking. The bigger the business the more likely this is to be true because the company is driven not by its own goals but by those of its shareholders and that goal is money – more and more of it. The public sector, seats of learning, Not For Profit organisations, Quangos and charities are no different except the word profit is substituted for staying in power. Ironically the closer to the top you are, the more vulnerable you are to losing your autonomy because you are expected to espouse the corporate view.

Thinking independently

Most of us have friends or know of people working for huge international corporations. We know therefore that, whilst these companies may pay disproportionate salaries and bonuses, they expect and get absolute loyalty and your time becomes their time. They expect that you see them as your top priority and that you align yourself with their views. In these circumstances, thinking for your self and thinking independently will not be seen as in the interests of the company. If it were then we may well not have seen the global financial mess of the latter part of the first decade of this century, nor the Iraq and Afghan wars amongst other things.

I can't think of a better cause to take up in this world of ours than that of independent thinking or as Thoreau put it, to "step to the music which he hears, however measured or far away". Indeed I believe that not thinking for ourselves is a trap that we all fall into time and again. The more aware of that fact we become, the more attention we are able to pay to it, the less we will do it.

Look again at the diagram I used in Chapter 5 to explain Jack Welch's description of the sorts of people he believes you keep or get rid of within an organisation? To recap, he categorises people into a combination of eight boxes around those people who do or don't hold his values and do or don't make him money. From that he easily decides who to keep and who to fire. It occurs to me that this is a principle that works both ways – for the employer and for the employee. I just don't recall anyone ever using it like that. It's all very well the big cheese saying, "This is how we run our business. Obviously, we do everything we can to keep those people who hold our values and make us money. Those people who don't hold our values and don't make us money we fire instantly." But what about the people who are subject to this? In a lot of ways I can empathise with this view and I've felt for a long time that people who don't fit in one organisation will find their fit elsewhere. Only in the trauma of being let go, they just don't know it.

A flaw in the theory

However there appears to me to be two things missing from Welch's theory. The first is: "What are the values being assumed by the boss in this situation? Are they ones of high integrity where people really matter, where they are really cared for within the organisation and where making money is not the absolute be all and end all? Obviously money and profit are part of the need of any organisation, because without them the business will collapse and die – it's no different from the need for food in a human being on level one, the physical, of Maslow's hierarchy.

The second is that there is another side to the argument and that is the reverse of the boss's view. What about looking at it not from the company's point of view but from the individual's point of view? If I'm working in an organisation or I'm thinking about going to work in an organisation do I not need to ask: "Does that organisation hold my values?" I don't think many people do that. I don't think I've ever consciously done it and I certainly don't think I've ever done it on a regular basis. I can think of at least one job I did where I didn't bring it fully into my conscious mind. I didn't think about it and, even if I knew the answer subconsciously, I didn't do anything about it. I think if I had paid attention to it – and here's another of my favourite words in respect of Love at Work – if I had been fully awake and aware I think I would have moved on a long time before I did.

When I look back over that time I see an enormous lack of integrity reflected in the sorts of people pushed forward and promoted. What I also saw in that instance was some form of corollary between lack of integrity and making money (which is their principle value). I'm not saying for an instant that the owners would see it that way. In fact I am sure they would say they are very caring about their people. Hindsight might teach that they are very selective in whom they are caring of.

Can you see how this principle might apply to many big commercial organisations and how it could apply to other types of organisation too –

it doesn't matter if it's a Not for Profit organisation or a charity? The truth is that the person who sits at the top of the organisation picks the people below them, subconsciously recognising traits that fit their belief system and then in one way or another tells them what to do. Sometimes they get it wrong and the subordinate then challenges them. When that happens they may be slapped down or life made so difficult and uncomfortable that they feel they should leave or are eventually fired.

Let me illustrate it with a story about one of my clients, Julian. Never afraid to express his personal values and speak up when he saw what he felt were unacceptable things going on, he brought to the chairman's attention a particularly outrageous issue – around the way more junior staff were being treated – which was happening in another office. No one at group level was going to do anything about it because, I guess unconsciously, either it met their values or they knew what would happen if they did. This was the dilemma for the owners: they knew it was wrong but it made them money. In raising it, my client laid down a marker somewhere in the minds of his bosses that his values were in conflict with theirs and it became only a matter of time until they found a way to get rid of him.

As Lewis, Amini and Lannon say in "A General Theory Of Love" our limbic brain is pre-programmed genetically to make sure we become attached, from birth, through our Attractors (such as our mother's milk) to someone or something who can provide for us when we are unable to provide for ourselves. If it's that strongly laid down in us (and I believe it is) it's not a huge step from the imprinting of our primary relationships to those behaviours being transferred to every other relationship – family, friendship or business. It is probably at its most dangerous in business.

Repeating patterns

When I was a child of around twelve, I was given Konrad Lorenz's wonderful book on animal behaviour, "King Solomon's Ring" as a form prize and remember being enthralled by the idea that if he was the only thing that his goslings saw when they were born and if he fed them, walked with them, swam with them, they treated him just like their real mother goose. We now know that imprinting goes far beyond that in human beings so that, without rigorous attention and years of hard work, it's extremely difficult to change our behaviour. It's why so many times in relationship, when we create what looks like an ideal partner, within weeks or months the other person is doing to us exactly what happened in our previous relationship and most likely happened with our mother or father in terms of criticism or nit picking or nagging. Then suddenly, once again, we can't bear to be in relationship. A lot of people do stay in those sorts of relationships rather than leave them and I am sure it accounts for much of the physical, emotional and mental abuse that goes on. Something I believe happens as much female to male as male to female. What, so far, nearly all of those people haven't realised is that, because they are simply going with their pre-programming rather than thinking for themselves, they are just as much a part of the problem as the abuser.

Even when we can't stand it any more we often can't live without relationship so what do we do but go out looking for another one which looks on the surface like everything we wanted? Within a few weeks or months we are on exactly the same merry-go round which is an exact parallel of what we were learning from our mother for example, when we were at her knee. Bearing in mind that we spend more time at work than anywhere else, why should any of those sorts of relationships be different?

Taking this back now to my client, his boss's behaviour is completely predictable because it is totally ingrained. The boss learnt it from his mother or his father and in his family and his society and his country. So he unwittingly gathers around him the sorts of people who hold his values and when there are people who don't he will, overtly or covertly, get rid of them. Put more succinctly, my point is that I think a great many of us don't actively contemplate how well the company we work for holds our values in the same way as the company thinks about how well we uphold theirs. In other words, most of us most of the time don't think independently.

All of which brings me back to level three of the listening diagram at the start of this chapter:

3 Listen to them selectively
Listen only to the parts of what they are saying that interest us.
This is what most of us do most of the time

Paying attention – or not

We might believe that we think independently but is that true – or is it an assumption? There is a current theory called Continuous Partial Attention (CPA) and I have a feeling that it may be more prevalent and pervasive in our world than we realise. Perhaps to survive in our world we actually need CPA. For example, if you really only did focus on one thing at a time you couldn't actually get up from where you are reading and walk to make yourself a cup of tea. I know I certainly couldn't drive my car from my house to the next village without having an horrendous accident.

Maybe in that sense it is a very useful thing for us to have. So where is it not useful? It's certainly not useful, as in the example above, if we want to move from where we are now to somewhere else or if we really want to think a problem through in whatever form. It's not useful in terms of all the "stuff" distraction is made of, that really doesn't make a difference in our lives – in advertising, fashion, style, theatre and cinema. TV in particular plays on our butterfly minds and if we really want to make a difference in the world our minds need to be less and less butterfly, less and less cluttered.

My sense is that we are short changing ourselves and I feel really mad about that; really, really mad about it. We so need to find a way of teaching all of us how to be here, fully present in the moment. We need to imbue all of this and thinking for themselves in our babies, our toddlers, our children. I have no idea how we can ensure that happens. It is indeed what Montesorri and Steiner teaching is all about. However, the new government Early Years Foundation Stage legislation sets 69 targets for under fives, all of which will undermine and erode any chance of independent thought. What on earth are we all (not) thinking about when heads of Steiner schools contemplate closing their nurseries rather than comply with such ridiculous legislation? What are we all doing when we allow these things to perpetuate in our State schools?

I know you believe you understand what you think I said, but I am not sure you realise that what you heard is not what I meant."
Jack Dusty

There are green shoots appearing though and those bring much hope for the future of our children. One of these is in the form of the KIPP

(Knowledge Is Power Program) Academies started in the US by Mike Feinberg and David Levin in 1994. By 2000 the not for profit KIPP Foundation was started with the support of Doris and Don Fisher, co-founders of Gap, to replicate the success of the two original academies. In less than ten years it has grown to more than 80 schools. Its relevance to the concept of independent thinking is that the first class of each day for every student is in thinking skills. If this idea were to reach a tipping point and reach epidemic proportions we would be confronted with the very real possibility of major positive changes to our world in less than a generation. Thank goodness for people like Feinberg, Levin and the Fishers.

Even if we could implement a worldwide plan right now that gave our children the ability to think independently we cannot wait until that generation can take up the reins of the world. We have to do whatever we can with our own generations. They are the material we have to work with and that's what makes it so important to take a thinking environment out to as many people as possible. When individuals start thinking independently, even in the tiniest ways, it will collectively make a huge difference. Every grain of sand goes towards filling a jar; every jar of sand adds to a pile; every pile adds to a beach and to every beach in the world. Every single step we can make to bring people to conscious awareness of how they operate is worth while. Every opportunity we can create to give them the time and the space to think for themselves is worthwhile.

Playing our part

Whilst we can't solve all of this all at once, we can play our part as individuals and that simply means being prepared to step up to the mark. We need to let as many people as possible know that all the poor decisions in the world are a result of poor thinking. All the poor or wrong decisions, all the conflict, all the famine, all the lack of education, all the health problems, all the wars are a result of bad collective thinking. It's the stuff of not listening too; not really listening; not really putting yourself in the other person's shoes and of wanting it your way rather than their way.

Nancy Kline and people like her have a huge task ahead of them, daunting but not impossible. We must not let ourselves be put off by the scale of it. We must talk about it at every opportunity and what is more, we must live it. Finding and working with like-minded people, creating communities and loose associations both face to face and via the internet has the potential to make a tremendous difference. The world can change but that change has to start with ourselves.

Fundamental to this methodology is the idea of non-interruption. How many meetings have you sat in, in your life, where you have just started to speak and someone has interrupted you, or the whole essence of the meeting has been overshadowed by those who talk loudest and longest? Using some simple techniques anyone can, with a little practice and guidance, hold meetings that are powerful and inspiring. How often can one say that? Creating an environment in which everyone matters, in which everyone knows they will get a chance to speak and gets 100% uninterrupted attention when they are speaking literally transforms the way people think and therefore the whole meeting.

I could describe the whole process in more detail here but of course Nancy describes it so well herself in her books Time To Think and More Time To Think. So perhaps it comes better from the horse's mouth. Even then there is nothing quite like experiencing it for oneself. The way to do that is to book or organise a Foundation Course for up to ten people. Just go to the website www.timetothink.com for more details. I guarantee you will have a really special two days.

 Listening itself is an art. When we listen with a still and concentrated mind, it's possible to actually be responsive to what the words are saying. Sometimes deep insights come in a flash, unexpectedly."
Joseph Goldstein

On the other hand, how many times have we been on courses that have made us sceptical of training days and away days? How many of us have had thoughts similar to these:

"Nice hotel, nice lunch but not much else"

"I really can't afford the time I'm losing away from my desk and all that email"

"There are a thousand things I'd rather be doing"

"Even the good ideas won't get implemented"

"Do I really want to spend a day here?"

"Was that really worth my hard earned cash?"

I know I have and if you have too, don't you think it is so important not to feel like that but to come back inspired and energised? Wouldn't it be great to do that on a regular basis – say twice a month? Well – you can, as you will see!

Presentation skills matter

There is another area where we nearly all, nearly always, need more training and that is in our presentation skills. Whoever we are in any organisation or whatever we do in our lives, personally or professionally, we will give more the better we are able to articulate our thoughts and ideas. It is the one area though where I feel group training works least well. Now, not for one second am I saying that the people I have come across aren't excellent trainers – they most certainly are. They give freely of their knowledge and pack a lot in and that is part of the underlying problem. We come back from such courses brimming with energy and good intentions and then, because of day-to-day pressure, over the next few weeks, we forget so much of what we were given. It's like cramming for exams – it simply doesn't stick long term.

Like most things worthwhile there is so much to learn and at such a subtle level. In addition, it is an area of intense interpersonal skill where it is essential to get rid of old habits and embed new ones. Whilst you can teach many things in two or three days, whatever techniques you use you just can't eliminate old habits and replace them with new ones. It takes time and repetition way beyond the end of any course. There is however an organisation I have already mentioned which gives the best presentation skills training there is and that is Toastmasters International. With over ten thousand clubs world wide, wherever you live or work you aren't far from one.

The reasons it is so successful are several and varied. As with all things to do with people, some clubs are better than others but the strength is in the manual system it provides to every member. From the first one leading to Competent Communicator right through to a whole host of advanced ones leading to Distinguished Toastmaster, the quality of information and advice is unsurpassed. In the first manual are ten speech projects, carefully thought out to build your skills in everything from speech construction to body language, to vocal variety through to the use of props and PowerPoint. Drop that into a supportive club environment where everyone wants and wills you to succeed and the scene is set. Receive feedback where the appreciation is three times greater than any suggestions for improvement and you can begin to see how powerful it can be. When you listen to the feedback others are getting and combine that with your own improving ability to give feedback your critical skills improve and this benefits you too. With the opportunity to practise at every meeting with either a formal speech or a shorter impromptu one, over time all the new habits you are learning will become thoroughly embedded. I wrote earlier of how in my own club everyone chooses a mentor – and this is the icing on the cake. It emphasises once more the part that coaching, mentoring and training plays in creating Love at Work.

Success guaranteed

Toastmasters teaches us that great presentation skills and speaking performances come from confidence and it then goes on to instil that. Confidence is the skin which holds everything else together. In developing it we get to understand that what really matters is our connection with our audience, be it a small group or a full conference hall. Confidence gives us the strength to be fully present in the space and then really connect with and pick up on the energy in the room. The more relaxed, centred and present we are the stronger connection we can make with our audience. We all know what it feels like when someone makes that genuine connection and it is this which makes the difference between a great presenter and an average one. The best news of all is that we can all learn how to do it given time and willingness to learn.

I have watched in amazement as people do the craziest things in their speech focussing on body language. I have listened incredulously at the power of their voice in their speech on vocal variety. I have laughed hysterically at some of the props they have used to illustrate a particular speech. I can't count the number of times I have seen people come to a meeting to give their first speech, terrified out of their wits, only to give their graduation speech, a year or two later, full of power, persuasion and confidence.

All of which does take time and so, in the meantime, here is one very useful exercise for you to try and which you can use whenever you have to make a presentation or speech:

exercise

Find a quiet place somewhere away from the room or hall you are going to speak in. Sit down if you can but otherwise simply close your eyes and, remembering your meditation technique from Chapter 4…

Close your eyes and take a few deep breaths. Inhale through your nose and exhale through your mouth. Allow yourself to relax, letting all the stale energy go as you breathe out. Settle into your body and imagine this…

You are a giant tree reaching to the sky – an oak, a beech, a cedar or whatever is your favourite tree. Feel the trunk and the branches stretching skyward and then imagine your roots growing deep into the earth, drawing all the qualities you need upwards – memory, connection, clarity, oratory and any others you feel you want…

Now drop your energy down from your breath and focus on your power centre somewhere near your navel. Slowly breathe into it and then just as slowly breathe out, each time drawing in all the energy, courage and strength you need to give your presentation. The energy gets more and more concentrated the more you breathe…

As you imagine yourself in front of your audience the energy you have built expands to surround the whole audience and you notice that every single one of them is willing you to succeed, to do better than you have ever done before. They are eager for your knowledge and wisdom and wanting you to impart it with fun and laughter, with skill and dexterity…

Take a few deep breaths and gently let the image fade, knowing that what you have seen is the truth and will stay with you as you walk into the room or onto the stage. Know too that you can draw on your audience's energy and build on it...

Take a few more deep breaths and slowly bring yourself back into the space, bringing all of your visualisation with you. Open your eyes and get out there and wow them! ♥

Being understood

Earlier in the book we took time to look at the importance of relationships, most particularly the one with our self and how everyone around us is a reflection of that self. Our ability to communicate is at the heart of understanding that relationship and so the time we spend improving our speaking and presentation skills will never be wasted. After all, we use them every day and the better we are the more persuasive we are, the more persuasive we are the more able we are to get our thoughts, ideas and desires across to others and therefore properly understood. It certainly doesn't only apply to business – it applies just as much with our partners, spouses, children, friends and family.

When we think well and then speak well as a consequence, our powers of persuasion multiply. There is nothing new in this; our ancestors and we have been doing it for thousands of years particularly in our romantic lives and through plays and poetry. How did Shakespeare's Juliet win her Romeo? How did Anthony woo Cleopatra or Edward Windsor, Wallace Simpson? If we want something badly enough we think of a way and so often that way is through the power of words. We choose to woo people in different circumstances too – in fact whenever we want someone to support our opinion, we woo them. We do it in business, we do it for charitable causes, we do it every day. How successful we are depends on a variety of things. Yes, the better we think, the better will be our logic and reasoned argument. Yes, the better we speak the more likely people are to listen, but there are other factors too. It comes back to issues we have previously talked about – integrity, congruence, trust and passion. Without them we are doomed to failure. There is another ingredient though and that is a genuine interest in the person we are courting or to be blunt, selling to. Understanding their point of view, their issues and their problems and how what we are suggesting might affect those is the final vital ingredient. Looking at something from another's point of view isn't easy but it is essential if we are to both serve their best interests and get our point across. Preparing your speech or presentation may well not be enough. You may also need to develop a whole strategy towards achieving your goal, of which your presentation is but a part.

The potential for conflict

It is only when people stop listening to one another and in return speaking their truth that communication breaks down and we get into conflict. Whether we like it or not conflict is a part of life and whilst we can do everything in our power not to create it we are unlikely to be able to avoid it. There is much good work being done and written about conflict resolution on every level from families and within business to between countries and at the extreme end of the scale, wars. Whatever the problem the same principles will always apply – listening first then thinking before we speak. Now that we understand these principles, combining our improved thinking ability with our new found speaking skills presents us with all sorts of possibilities, not least of which is supporting others and ourselves in conflict resolution.

One of the leaders in the field of understanding conflict (and there are many wonderful ones) is the Arbinger Institute. The basic tenet of its work is that conflict does not start when we have a row with someone, fail to see their point of view or get into a fight but much earlier than that. They propose that conflict or at least the potential for conflict starts at the point where we give our power away, or in their words "betray ourselves". This can be and often is so subtle that we don't even notice it. It creates a level of self deception or, again in their words, an "insistent blindness" that colours everything we do. As soon as this happens we start to justify our behaviour, most usually by making others wrong. It's easy to understand how in this state we can't possibly see others as they really are or the affect we have on them because of it. We are most definitely wearing coloured glasses, although the view we see may not be as pretty as this suggests. What's really fascinating is that our bodies always tell us when it happens. As with everything we do, say or feel there is a metaphysical connection.

Its relevance is profound in creating Love at Work. Let me give you an example. Imagine I have had someone working for me for a long time (let's call her Janice) and she has never asked for a pay increase so I never raise the issue with her either. I go on seeing just how little I can get away with until she either explodes or leaves or both. Both of us have given our power away, betrayed ourselves, and so there is a double level of conflict. However, neither of us has done it at the point you might think. In the case of Janice it's possible (although unlikely) that the first time she unconsciously felt it happen was when it crossed her mind to ask but didn't for whatever reason – she was too scared, I was always too busy and so on. In my case it most likely goes back much further, even into childhood and is a pattern I built up because I learned that there was never enough (just for the record, this is no longer one of my patterns although I confess to many!). The result is always the same though – conflict.

Resolving conflict

In theory it's easy for all of us to resolve conflict – all we have to do is speak our truth all of the time. Do I think it's actually easy? Do you? Absolutely not! When we have spent the majority of our lives looking out from behind those glasses, change becomes extremely difficult but we can and must do it if we are to become the leaders we want to be based on connecting our head with our heart. We come right back to the idea of witness consciousness I spoke of in Chapter 3. Of course recognising our behaviour is one thing and doing something about it another, neither of which is easy. This is where our head really can help our heart. If we are both rigorous and determined in our thinking we can, whenever we get the feeling that something isn't right, that we aren't behaving congruently, look back and back over the situation to find that point where we gave our power away. It will take time and we are almost certainly going to have to look further back than we first thought. We are also going to need to be scrupulously honest with ourselves. Eventually we will get to a place where we don't walk away from difficult situations or use coping strategies or worst of all, try to change other people.

Much of my thinking around conflict resolution is influenced by my early training with The Conflict Resolution Network of Sydney, Australia and heavily seasoned by the latest listening techniques described earlier in this chapter. Both of which clearly align with the thoughts and ideas of Walter and Gita Bellin which contributed much to my thinking in Chapter 3. At this point I think it's worth dwelling a little more on the concept of mask, projection and shadow as described by Jung. In brief; mask is the image we present to the world; projection is those attributes of self that we put on others, usually because we find them unacceptable in our self; shadow is those parts of our self that we either are and don't want to be seen as, or aspects of others that we fear being.

Perfection is a state in which things are the way they are and not the way they are not. As you can see, the universe is perfect. Don't lie about it!"
Werner Erhard

Every day we get the opportunity to work on and understand the consequences of our projections. Whenever someone angers or upsets us there is something for us to learn from them. We need to learn what and where we are projecting of our selves onto others. Hopefully this brief explanation will help. Demonstrating extremes of behaviour (and we do know when we do this) in wanting too much of someone or alternatively not being able to stand the sight of someone are clear cases of our shadow rearing its head. If for example a person's shadow were to manifest itself in them being deeply hurt when a friend cancels seeing them, what is actually happening is them not consciously recognising their need for companionship. As soon as they do and are able to express this truth, the hurt and anger simply evaporate. Another explanation may be that they were constantly let down on promises as a child and their un-integrated self reacts by having a tantrum. Once again, understanding and expressing this dissolves the issue.

When we understand this principle we are ready and able to work with others in resolving conflict. There is no more important role in doing so than that of mediator. It is a highly skilled job and demands lots of practice using role play before anyone is ready to take on a serious if small conflict situation. The keys to successful mediation are being objective, supportive, non-judgmental and encouraging combined with a win/win approach. Whatever you do, always mediate from a totally neutral position and only if you are confident of your skills. Otherwise find someone who is used to this work or, if it becomes a real interest in you, follow the necessary training path.

Some helpful tips

There will be times in our working lives when we find ourselves in a situation where the other person is unwilling to resolve a specific issue we have with them. When this happens there is much we can do without either side losing face. Here are some tips you might like to try, whilst at all times owning the part that you might be playing:

exercise

- Ask them if they are willing to try resolving the issue and get their agreement
- Get their agreement to equal turns and non-interruption
- Set an overall time limit for the session

- Discuss the benefits of resolving the issue such as less stress, more harmony and better effectiveness. Stay away from negative values at all cost
- Identify the issue(s) between you clearly – logistically in terms of requirements, outcomes and objectives; emotionally in terms of feelings, views, values and concerns
- Agree the veracity of the information underneath the reasons for the conflict
- Think about whether over time you can build a level of trust between you and how you might do that

- Break the process down into manageable steps
- Explore both their needs and concerns and yours
- After the other person has stopped speaking and before you start, let them hear what you heard them say and ask them to confirm it is what they said

- Move slowly and gently towards common ground
- Don't expect miracles, remember that they (and you) may be making emotional capital out of the issue ♥

Resolving rackets

So often, what starts as a mild disagreement develops into a racket, a very uncomfortable game. It works like this: In the world of win/lose John and Jane stand either side of an invisible gap called choice. She serves first and the ball crosses the gap. John of course sends it back but he can do this out of reaction or response. If he reacts the ball goes back faster. Jane does the same and the ball just gets faster and faster until everything crashes. However if he responds the pace is steady and manageable and they can go on without crashing until they feel the game is complete. Now think about this not in terms of a ball game but as Jane (or John) saying something that the other one mishears. If John reacts they are immediately in an emotional racket and the gap of choice gets narrower and narrower. If John responds the gap gets larger, creating more time for him to hear what she really said and to choose his reply. Now that the gap is wider Jane has a chance to hear too and then respond rather than react. Playing it in this way means that each of them has the chance to recognise the racket and put it down and – guess what – the game is over and there is nothing to get into conflict over and therefore no conflict to resolve.

All of this is about appropriateness and safety. When we express ourselves appropriately people feel safe, they have no reason to take offence or get on their high horse. Of course, very few of us can do this all of the time. It also involves a sense of place, of knowing who we are and how and where we fit in our world – and we will fit differently in every situation; work, home, love, out shopping or playing a sport. Add all three together and we get a sense of comfort which comes through openness and trust and it being OK to say whatever you want to say, safe in the knowledge that we will express it appropriately. It becomes a never ending circle, a sort of Mobius band. Love at Work is like that. We are creating organisation where people feel supported and cared for, even if they can't all bring themselves to use the word love!

In his book, Peace Is The Way, Deepak Chopra states that as long as we are thinking about stopping wars we will never stop them. We need to think not about stopping wars but creating peace. This is because we make manifest everything we think about. As with visualisation, our mind does not recognise negatives indicating opposites but only the noun or verb itself. In addition, negative thoughts create negative feelings and we know what can happen to those – they turn into the metaphysical, they become psychosomatic. Worry long enough about getting a particular illness and there is a high likelihood you will. Worry long enough about crashing your car and there is a higher likelihood you will. So often what we resist is what we get. The same applies to conflict; think about not wanting conflict and, sure as eggs is eggs, it will pop up in your life. So why not think positively and peacefully and let those qualities pop up in your life instead.

What to take with you from this chapter

- **Listening is the greatest gift there is**
- **Give people your full attention**
- **Silence is golden**
- **The mind thinks best in the presence of questions**
- **Learn to think independently**
- **Remove repeating behaviour patterns**
- **Constantly hone your presentation skills**
- **Watch for and resolve conflict early**
- **Think peace**

and to remind you to...

- *Make sure you do and use the exercises in this chapter before you move on*
- *Make sure you order "More Time to Think"*
- *Make sure you visit a Toastmasters club*

Notes

Chapter 9

What's in this chapter:

- Imbuing heart in everything we do
- Passion, empowerment and vision
- Open-heartedness and trust
- The need for reality
- Understanding change
- Building a realistic model

Developing the business

" Work... like you don't need the money
Love... like you've never been hurt
Dance... like nobody's watching
Sing... like nobody's listening
Live... like it's heaven on earth"

Aurora Greenway

From the heart

Of course you can build a business not from the heart. It's just that building one from it makes such a difference to our own lives and to the lives of others. It creates a sharpness to the arrowhead of leadership which is like the difference between the steel of a blacksmith's plough compared to that of the finest sword maker. A business, an organisation or even a family with that strength of heart has such strong core values that it makes it so much easier to change its strategies. Those core values are also there to support us whenever our resolve as a leader is tested by the vagaries of the markets we operate in or the people we deal with.

Even if your business hasn't been built on these foundations it's never too late to start, to implement the necessary changes and create a new culture of leadership. It is worth all the hard work and effort it will take because with it you have at your command a culture that will support continual change. An organisation with strong core values naturally creates the right strategies which will knock on to the developing brand, making it easier for people both sides of the business to really understand what it is the company does and where it is headed. All the market opportunities in the world won't make up for the quality of the leadership. Allen Loren of Dunn & Bradstreet put it this way, "Leadership development is virtually the most important control lever you have for success...If you have leaders who are adaptable and capable of leading just about anything, you will be successful." High quality leadership is not just altruistic, it makes business sense too.

If this is the case, then owning the culture and the strategy is vital for the long term. Constantly being and demonstrating the values we expect of others is a prerequisite for success. When we are willing to look at our own strengths and weaknesses, it makes it possible for others to look at who they are and how they operate too, thus building a platform for future growth both personal and professional. That's not to deny that they won't always do that. This quality of leadership development is like a living organism, growing and changing as we all do every day of our lives. Change becomes a welcomed aspect of our lives to the point where we seek it out through the quality of the feedback we receive.

The first branches

You could assume from this that any Human Resources (HR) person has an important part to play in developing leadership. It does and it doesn't at different stages in the growth of a company. When a company is small most of us find we have to be all-rounders, not just in terms of our business or professional skills but also in terms of the HR function. Small companies can't afford too many specialists. However, on the earlier premise that we need to focus only on what we are good at, the time may come sooner than we think to separate out this particular area of expertise. My belief is that, when we do, the HR team is there to support the leadership by taking off its hands all those administrative tasks that they cannot only do better but which the leadership (at all levels) shouldn't be and isn't interested in. HR can support all the training, coaching and mentoring initiatives but it is down to the leadership team to carry it out.

Marketing falls into this area too. Many of us are incredibly bad at marketing and selling ourselves – although we are probably very good at selling the qualities of others. I know I am. I know too though that once I am in front of a potential client my professional confidence kicks in and the client senses it. Most of us are like this and so it makes sense to think about expanding this area of our business sooner rather than later. You could call it speculating to accumulate. There is no point in kidding yourself that you are going to make those cold calls if it is not in your make up. Read all the books and go on all the courses you like but if your in-built rejection level is too low it just won't happen. Even though one could argue that they are and are not different skill sets I'm not going to differentiate between marketing and selling at this point. Principally they both demand an ability in us to not feel rejected when someone says no to you. One of my daughters is a natural in this field. Looking back, she's been like it all her life. When she was quite young, if she wanted say a pair of new trainers, she would simply come and ask for them. If I said to her, "No, sorry, you really don't need them this week, Harriet." she would shrug and say, "OK Dad." Then promptly forget about it and go off and play. She has taken that into adulthood and her career in the charity world where she is and has always been a highly successful fundraiser. Her ability to hear people say no and then move on is obviously a huge asset. All I am really saying is know your strengths and let others fill in the weaknesses for you.

These early steps in breaking out areas of work and responsibility which others can do as well or better than we can, will be followed by ones closer to our professional or business skills. No one will know what these are as well as you and they will vary according to the business or organisation you are building. The all-rounders (but not jacks of all trades, masters of none) of the early growth years will naturally give way more and more to greater specialisation. My recommendation is, don't fight it but positively enjoy it. After all it is going to give you more time to spend on what you are best at and what you enjoy most. When this time comes make sure you invest in the best – the best people, the best equipment, the best programmes – that you can afford. Don't be profligate though. Make sure you spend wisely and always as if the money was yours personally, even when you are building an organisation for someone else.

Setting sail

Perhaps a good analogy for building a business is that of preparing a sailing ship for sea. Designing it and building it in the first place is one thing (all the work that goes in before we take the plunge) but then we have to rig it (the office infrastructure of computers and systems) and provision it (by winning those first jobs or making those first sales). Then come the sea trials (where we have to deliver on our early promises) and finally we are ready to set sail. We still have to choose the crew carefully – as they have to choose us too. Every ship needs a captain, lieutenants and a crew but not, in our case, in the hierarchical sense.

The captain's job as leader is to keep the ship pointed in the right direction – towards the vision. Back to back with him or her we need one or more people who understand and are committed to that vision and help to orchestrate everything that needs to be done by the crew on every level to make sure that we drive our ship forward towards our goal as fast as possible. On the ship the crew understands this need and are in alignment. This is because they have bought into our vision and purpose – of an exceptional place to work, pushing the boundaries of relationships in the knowledge that people really matter and are our organisations' most important asset. With a crew of this calibre we can sail both calm and rough seas, deal with the odd rotten apple in the barrel and press on to new horizons.

Get passionate

Most of all, though, we are going to need passion; without it we are nothing. Passion and the conviction that comes with it are vital. Passion so deep we know we cannot fail; that very real passion to want to make a real difference in our world. Some time ago I met a young man who wanted me as his mentor and at our first meeting he said to me, "I want to be an entrepreneur". To which I replied, "And what's your passion?" It wasn't meant as a trick question. I wanted him to see that entrepreneurship is not an end in itself and that passion is a huge part of it. We need to be passionate about something to become entrepreneurs. Even if you think your passion is just to make money you need to have a vehicle to be able to do that. You have to know what your real passion is. It might be accountancy or law or mechanics or cancer fighting drugs – but the only thing that matters is that you are passionate. It's passion that creates the willingness to do whatever it takes, to give whatever it takes and then go on even when you are exhausted.

Love is power and passion expressed safely."
Nigel Cutts

Empowerment

The most important thing any of us can do in developing our organisation is to empower everyone in it to deliver total customer satisfaction. By this far into the book you will have either discovered much of what you need to know to do just this or have confirmed what you already knew.

Empowerment requires all of us to buy into not only the values we have established through implementing the ideas on personal and professional values in Chapter 2. It also requires us to buy into the mission and vision we need to have in place. Not surprisingly the best way to do this is in the same way you developed your values statements – by building them with your team. Of course, once they are established you aren't going to want to rewrite them every time someone new joins, but you are going to want to review your values, your mission and your vision with them.

Clear vision

 To grasp and hold a vision, that is the very essence of successful leadership."
Ronald Reagan

Clear vision makes such a difference. I have worked for people with it and without it and even if you haven't, I am sure you won't need a second guess as to which I preferred. Parts of the vision and mission statements you develop will naturally be around what you do or produce as a business which means we can't talk about it in specific detail here. You will want to include a statement about what you produce being of the highest possible quality and standard, regardless of whether it's a computer, a set of accounts or health care provision. Other parts though will be about people, ethics and morality - all of which we can talk about and which overlap with your values statements. What will always matter most in any organisation aiming for Love at Work is its people and how we treat them. I remember once a managing director talking to me at length about it not mattering how good we are technically, but only how good we are with people. It's a fundamental though not exact truth of course. She went on to say that every aspect of the environment in which we work supports and enhances our abilities as people. It must have been something she had recognised consciously or unconsciously when she started the business or it couldn't have been there 25 years later operating worldwide. It must be this belief which allows her particular business to push its boundaries outwards and give a continuing high level of service to its clients.

Vision is so important because what we see out there in our future is what we get. Don't think about your vision or don't really care about it and what you manifest will be an organisation that doesn't think and doesn't care and which in the long run is doomed to failure. For me vision and visualisation are inextricably linked. There is no point in having a vision if we don't continually visualise it in order for it to become real. When I was young I unconsciously dreamed of many things that then happened and became real. At some point much later in my life I realised that we can do all this on a much more conscious level and use it all the time. I'm not saying that it happens without any effort, but when we really focus our attention on the intention the whole process speeds up. I have visualised and then created jobs, bought and sold houses and found relationship through this process. Do not underestimate its power. The very house we live in now is a result of it. My darling wife is a result of it – and she is one of the kindest, most open hearted people I know, giving her time freely in support of others. What's more, everything she does, she does with love. She is a living, breathing example of Love at Work – ask any of her friends and they will tell you the same story. She is my soul mate and my best friend.

 A vision without a task is but a dream, a task without a vision is drudgery, a vision and a task is the hope of the world."

From a church in Sussex, England, ca. 1730

It really works

I also built a whole business using it. First by visualising the job and then when that had appeared I visualised the office, then the clients and the level and type of business. When it grew too big for its space I did the same thing again for the new office and the business it needed to succeed. Eventually I even visualised my exit route from it. Sure enough it happened and, perhaps it might not surprise you by now, at lightening speed.

Here's one vision statement I have used:

Always to be the best we can be by:

- *Nurturing our innate desire to make a difference in the world*

- *Being thoroughly competent, business like, highly professional and profitable*

- *Deeply caring for all the people who work for us or are touched by what we do*

- *Building trust and integrity through honesty and openness*

In this way our work becomes a vehicle through which we can learn about life, relationship and above all ourselves.

And another:

- *As we hold the awareness that everything we do is focussed on producing the best possible product we can, we constantly listen, question, think and draw upon our accumulated skills and knowledge.*

- *We passionately pursue our goal of providing a complete service covering all aspects of our professional skills.*

- *In short, we are a highly professional, creative and profitable company that our clients and suppliers alike are proud to be associated with.*

Stay open hearted

Visions aren't fixed things. They shift and change as we gain more knowledge and information, as markets move and grow or new ones develop. That's why it's important to achieve buy-in not just to that but to your values and mission too. We do need to bear in mind that what we think our values, vision and mission are, is coloured by our personal perspective - something which we talked about at length in the previous chapter. Forget this and we can revert to judging others and closing our hearts. Coming from an open heart and non-judgement allows us to consider the wants and needs of others, be they employee or employer. When we do this we create the space to understand the individual we are dealing with, what their needs might be, suggest rather than dictate solutions and actions, then ask for and get agreement. Once more, this is where our questioning and listening skills from Chapter 8 come to the fore, as does our ability to suggest rather than impose.

Man's capacity for justice makes democracy possible. Man's tendency to injustice makes democracy essential."
John Schlesinger Jr.

Building trust

On the other side of the picture is the need to treat our customers and clients with similar respect. Building a business based on the values in this book means we absolutely have to walk the talk. It's something we can't fake but when we do live our lives with integrity and openness, people get to see who we really are and can make up their own minds about us. Trust is not something someone gives another lightly. It is something built over a varying amount of time depending on the circumstances and on our individual life experience. When we first meet someone we might get a feeling that we like them – and that's important. As we get to know more about them we could get to respect their attitude and opinions. Then finally we may well decide that we can trust them. This sequence of Like – Respect – Trust is something most of us do without thinking (and at the speed of light) but is important to consciously follow from both sides of the fence because it helps us know exactly where we are in our relationship with someone, be it colleague or client. If we are in a relatively new relationship with anyone it is useful to know where we stand in that sequence from the other person's point of view and to be able to think about how we can build firmer foundations. We also need to think about where we are from our point of view. Getting to a place where we feel we can trust the other person we are dealing with is just as vital for us as it is for them to feel they can trust us. It is a mutual feeling and one in which we feel confident of each other. In their fascinating book The Trusted Advisor, David Maister, Robert Galford and Charles Green give much sage advice. In respect of trust they say, "Engage; Listen; Frame; Envision; Commit." Here is my interpretation of what they mean:

"Engage" may seem to be and is obvious, because without engagement there is nothing to listen to, no interaction and nothing to discuss. It is up to us to find that point of engagement and interest in order to open up any conversation. It is a skill we have all learned but it is one that some people are much better at than others. Some of us find networking and parties easy and fun. To others it can be terrifying. Given time and

application we can shift our perspective – I know I have. There was a time, not that many years ago, when I would go to a cocktail party or other networking event and do one circuit of the room (probably without speaking to anyone) and go home. Now I stay for hours and love it. Why? Because I have learned to ask open questions and then…

"Listen" Just reading the first half of Chapter 8 on the importance of listening will give you much help in doing this. In social situations, if you are nervous, it is worth having a few generic questions up your sleeve to get you started. The simple questions are usually the best. "How do you come to be here?" and "Where did you meet our hosts?" will always elicit an interesting response. It's worth remembering two things: the other person is probably struggling as much as you are and everyone loves an opportunity to talk about themselves. At business meetings it can be much easier. Even a little preparation should allow you to have a handful of relevant questions ready. Then, in both situations all you need to do is sit back and listen.

"Frame" both your questions and responses in a way that makes them contextual and relevant to both sides and the issues being discussed. Again it is something we have been taught to do from childhood so, whilst it's not something to make a big thing of, it is worth mentioning. The more complex the issue the more important getting the context right becomes. After all it helps if you both know what it is you want to discuss!

"Envision" and you take people with you. Show them your thoughts and dreams, explain them in a way that is exciting and people will want to hear more. It's what all great storytellers do. They take us into another world by speaking of and showing us what's possible. Develop your storytelling skills and you will naturally develop your level of trust.

"Commit", really commit to anything and our enthusiasm becomes self evident. There is nothing more infectious and contagious than genuine enthusiasm. In its presence we can explore absolutely anything.

As with Deepak Chopra's Seven Spiritual Laws Of Success, these concepts work not in isolation but in constant combination. As with the laws, they are innate principles which we need to understand but, once learnt, we need to use intuitively and instinctively. Make such things second nature and we will create the trust that is the bedrock of Love at Work.

Know what's important

Begin difficult things when they are easy, do great things when they are small. The difficult things of the world must once have been easy; the great things must once have been small... A thousand mile journey begins with one step."
Lao Tse

When we are running a business one thing we can never afford to do is nothing. Another is to focus on the unimportant. Using Pareto's principle can help us to focus on what really matters. What he originally discovered was that at least 80% of Italy's wealth was in the hands of only 20% of its population. Further research uncovered that this was so in almost every other country in the world. Over time people have applied this principle to disparate types of information: the same 80/20 split can be applied to everything from the time we spend with our friends and the clothes we wear to fixing computer bugs and quality control. It's usefulness to us in this case lies in applying it to time and effort, in helping us sift what is important and what is not, then focusing our attention on what is. Take a look at the diagram below and think about how it might help us prioritise what we have to do:

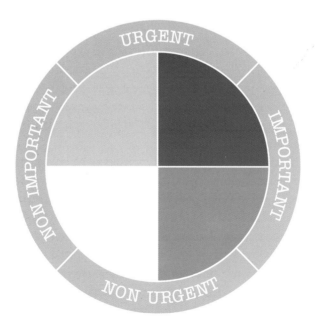

Using it to list and categorise the multitude of things anyone in a leadership role might think they have to deal with in a day can be extremely helpful. Admittedly it skews the 80/20 logic to 75/25 but it is near enough for our purposes. The degree of shading represents the degree of importance – the heavier the shading the more important the issue is. The most heavily shaded area is that of Urgent/Important. When you hear the other part of the business rule is that spending 80% of our time on the 20% that is truly Urgent/Important creates the best results, you will see that the only segment we need to worry about is that particular one. If you think about the other end of the scale, those things that are neither urgent nor important you may well be able to forget about them altogether. Ask yourself the question: are they worthy of my attention at all? It's a simple but useful trick. You may even find that it helps you create the time to think about your vision or how much more you can build a business based on Love at Work.

I guess what I am saying here is, if you want to grow your business rapidly, you will need to move away from its day-to-day running and into being with, and understanding those people on your team, as soon as possible. As I've said before, it really is all about the people. You need to get close to them, understand them and know what makes them tick.

Adding to the basics

Any good business person will tell you that one of the most important things they have is their ability to turn leads into opportunities, opportunities into business and then deliver them at a strong gross profit. All of which relies on effective marketing, effective sales, effective production and effective administration. To be able to do this we need a team that understands the whole process, applies it rigorously and feels accountable. What this model misses of course is the head/ heart connection – but not in our businesses. We understand that winning hearts is at least as important as any process because it's what creates strong teams and happy clients or customers. That's why we need to apply as much rigour to winning hearts as we do to any part of the process. It's also why our core values need to be constant and our strategies changeable and flexible. Know too that it applies equally in any other type of organisation and in our families and personal relationships.

There is no room for excuses when we are building a business. We simply can't afford the easy way out of being let off the hook. Anyway, when we are the leader we are on the hook and have no alternative but to stay there. By this time of course we have worked hard on ourselves and are way beyond playing victim and well established in witness consciousness. Success is not about luck. When the chips are down, it is about digging deeper, working harder and particularly thinking harder than anyone else. As leader you are your own champion, your own hero. Difficult times happen to everyone and it is our strength and resilience in these circumstances that sorts the winners from the losers.

Another never ending cycle

It is thinking harder, deeper, more creatively, more rigorously that makes the real difference. The fact is, the old chestnut of "Work smarter, not harder" is absolutely true and becomes more so the larger our business gets. We need to release ourselves from all the tasks that other people can do as well as we can and create the time and space to think about how we can maintain the values we set very early on, even when we were thinking about setting up a business. You have seen and understood how Maslow's hierarchy can help us understand not only how we and others operate but also, when we reach for its higher levels, how it can help us grow. What we need to think about now is how we can go on doing this as we grow as an organisation from one, to two, to four, to eight to 16, to 24, to 40 people and beyond. There are no magic answers so I have none to give you. In the same way all human beings are different and need to think through their own growth, every organisation is different and its leaders need to think through its growth too. All businesses are a combination of; job getting, job doing and job supporting; or product selling, product making and product supporting. Charities and NFPs are no different in principle. For example a charity has to raise the funds (selling), carry out its research or for example, save people from the sea, or work in the local community (doing) and the admin common to all work (supporting). They form yet another never ending and interlocking cycle without which there is no business. These are the underlying facts of any organisation but they are not what make it grow with love. It is the people involved in it that do that, which is why using the Maslow framework is such a useful tool when we are thinking about growth.

As an organisation grows, so its needs and aspirations change. Like a child, it grows stronger with age and becomes more capable of meeting its own physical needs, or knowing how to get them met. If you follow a path of Love at Work you will also be looking after everyone's emotional needs too – and of course their mental and spiritual ones. All of which will reach full expression eventually in the wider world. What really matters is that you recognise that your company and its people will need all these stages of growth if it and they are to be fulfilled and make a real contribution, not only to your business, but also to the world in which it sits and we live.

Profit or growth

There are so many important issues which you will face as your company develops, not least of which is that of profit or growth. Obviously you don't have to choose one or the other but they are interlinked. They are also influenced by your resources and your ability to access funds for growth if you really want to push forward. If you decide on this latter approach then do absolutely make sure your business model is not just sound but copper bottomed. This is the one place where you need to be absolutely rigorous in your thinking. For example, your sales forecasts need to be extremely conservative because you are going to have to rely on them to ensure you are in a strong financial position. On Maslow's physical level you need to know the money will come in when you say or you simply will not survive. Every other aspect of your business plan needs to be tested too. If possible check it out against other businesses in your field and place of business. I have seen companies, and big ones, fall badly when they have based their business model even on what has worked well for them elsewhere. Be prepared to be flexible, to readjust constantly, not through panic but through careful thought. Keep your thinking independent and keep it focused.

Firm foundations

Design and run your organisation to be agile and sitting on foundations of strong social and intellectual capital and you won't go far wrong. Do what you love and you won't go wrong at all. Sadly it is too easy to forget this and we need our antennae constantly up if we are not to follow false trails. You already have your dream, your vision, so keep your focus and take action every single day. Lots of people are in the wrong job or the wrong business or the wrong organisation. They may or may not recognise it in this lifetime but I hope they do for they will have so much more fulfilled lives and the world will be so much richer. If you have read this far, it's unlikely you are one of them. To those who know they don't want to do what they are doing but say they don't know what they do want to do I say this – "Yes you do!". It's simply that you haven't thought clearly enough or rigorously enough about it and then trusted your answer. Empowerment is something which fundamentally we need to give to ourselves, so why not do that now? I dare you! Then go out and grow your business.

Beware the myths of change

Now seems a good time to talk about change because, as has often been said, the only thing that is constant is change. It happens all day, every day and in our 21st century world the speed of it seems to increase and increase. Change is all around us. We know it and we feel it and we accept so much of it simply because either it doesn't appear to affect us directly or we can see its benefits. If we didn't accept change as a principle we simply wouldn't be able to go on learning. We'd be back with that idea of us all still living in caves wrapped in animal skins to keep warm.

There has been a myth going around for a long time that people don't like change. Personally I don't believe it – in fact I believe the complete opposite. I am sure people don't want to be told to change, but then who likes being told to do anything? Give people the choice to change something that isn't working and they will grab it with both hands. Use crisis, fear and unshakable facts to try and initiate change and they are more likely to make us freeze. On the other hand vision and emotional appeal drive us forward. I believe this is because there is a part of all of us that is a dreamer in search of a brighter future. It is this spark that drives us forward and if that's so then change is a part of that. Change does work, has always worked and we need to embrace it.

So much in life depends not on what we say but how we say it – on our communication. Getting across the need for change is no different. Here are some key myths we may need to dispel:

"Change has to be imposed" No it doesn't! We know that by now, don't we? It de-motivates and alienates people. Not only that, in involving others we create the opportunity for them to come up with ideas and methods we hadn't thought of. What a bonus that can be!

"It's only a small change" There's no such thing! Change affects people differently and we never quite know how, so don't play it down. Talk with everyone about the personal impact it may have – this way you will avoid any negativity.

"Not everyone needs to be involved" Of course they do. Neglect this and you neglect a fundamental principle of Love at Work. Not everyone feels the way you do but involving them in the change and how it is going to happen will certainly make it easier for them – and you.

"They'll come round in the end" No they won't. Don't involve people and they will go behind your back creating their own underground and do everything they can to destroy your changes, no matter how good they are.

"It's not personal" Of course it is. Anything that affects the way we are used to doing things is personal. We simply don't like not being consulted and why should we – we are adults, aren't we?

"We only need to do this once" You don't know that. What if it doesn't work? However, if you create a culture where change is the norm and where everyone knows they are welcome to suggest it you are close to instant buy-in.

"It's obvious why we are doing this" No, it isn't. Making assumptions is one of the most debilitating actions any of us can take – of others and ourselves. Take the time to explain the background and what you hope to achieve and people will walk with you. Don't take the time and you walk the knife edge alone.

"Let's make it radical" If it can be avoided, don't do it this way. So much of the best change is incremental – one small step after another with the previous one monitored and analysed. Evolution not revolution is so often the way forward.

In short, follow the principles and ideas that have been building chapter by chapter in this book and you won't go far wrong. Change isn't necessarily comfortable but it is so often necessary. Remember, presented properly it is exciting and people must love excitement or there would be no fairground rides.

**God grant me the serenity
to accept the things I cannot change;
courage to change the things I can;
and wisdom to know the difference."**
Reinhold Niebuhr

Planning for the future

One area where we will really need to take people with us is when we start to think about what HR departments are fond of calling succession planning. I find it an unfortunate term because on the one hand it explains everything and on the other nothing. Ideally we should succession plan for everyone in the organisation from the receptionist to the managing director. In reality most of us are so wrapped up in the day to day running of our businesses that we nearly always put it to the bottom of the pile, believing that it will wait. That's a huge assumption that will affect everyone. The reason we don't deal with it may well be because we think that it only affects the top leadership. We couldn't be more wrong. It affects every career minded person in every business across the country. Bright people want to know where their futures lie and good succession planning let's them see that. We're not talking old fashioned, "When I retire/die you get to take over the business" stuff here because modern, technology savvy, ambitious people don't stick around to find out. We are talking about straight forward, clearly laid out plans put where everyone who is interested can see them.

Should we choose not to think about succession planning, or think about it only in terms of our personal demise, we could be in for a rude awakening. One scenario could be that if we were to die the whole business might collapse. I have seen it happen and I know of other businesses where I am convinced it will happen if something is not done about it and soon. Perhaps people don't do it because, as their company grows, they begin to believe their own publicity, to believe they are invincible. Well, if they die they are clearly not and nor is their company. Without the right people in place to take over as smoothly as possible the company will die with them. It happens so often in the case of charismatic leaders where, for example, much of the business is there because of their personal relationships, or because they have a special relationship with their bank. Take them away and confidence disappears overnight.

No matter how big the business has grown, if it is still in the hands of the original owners, it is extremely susceptible to failure of this sort - if not this, then to conflict from within. In any substantial organisation there are power struggles going on all the time, both overt and covert. Our job as leaders is not just to have them where we can see them, but to teach those we work with that there is another way – a way with heart. That way, the likelihood of the business being ripped apart at some point is far more remote.

Things to do today:
Inhale
Exhale
Inhale
Exhale
Inhale
Exhale..."
Anon

Planning for change

As I said, succession is not just about those at the very top of the organisation, however flat the leadership style may be. Whenever anyone leaves an organisation, it has an effect on the business and an effect on the people. The more key that person is to the organisation, the more profound the effect. Sometimes it can be quite devastating. All the more reason therefore to do two things; work hard at ensuring everyone knows where they stand and that you know where they stand and: put that succession plan in place in order to alleviate problems as they occur.

When people do understand how an organisation is built and can equate that to what it means to them, its growth can happen organically, like that of a healthy plant. Planting the right seeds, whether those are actually the right people or the right thoughts, and watering and nurturing them to full bloom is one of the most rewarding jobs in the world.

One day while pondering both my own succession and the growth of the organisation I was responsible for, I came up with the idea of disciples. "Not a new one," I hear you say and you would be right but then, as I have said before, it pays to learn from the best. My thought was to gather round me a small group of people who felt the same as I did, held the same values and wanted the same long term goals. There would be no guarantee that it would work after I left the business but at least I was giving it my best shot. Not only that, such a strategy would support everything I held dear whilst I was there. It meant I would need at least one disciple in each of the areas of the company – marketing, professional and administration. In a relatively small business (an office of around 40 people in an international organisation of around 400) it wasn't too difficult, particularly as everyone at senior level had been picked not just for their professional skills but also for their people skills.

It's one thing knowing intuitively that you are on the same wavelength. It's totally another ensuring that those values are so well aligned that you really are singing from the same hymn sheet. The thing is, leaders like to do things their way and need to be allowed to do so. If I was to create Love at Work then it was essential that right across business getting, business doing and business administering, the people responsible clearly knew what the values were and what would make a real difference to achieving and perpetuating them. Fail in one area and you fail overall – it really tests your resolve. Each of those people needed to understand the principles and find meaning in them and in their work.

Making it work

The way I went about it was to find some common ground and that turned out to be the ability for people to think clearly for themselves. First of all I set about persuading Nancy Kline to personally teach them the principles of a thinking environment and the difference it could make in both their business and personal lives. Over a period of several months and several sessions we made this happen in a way that even the most sceptical person came on board. We started running our quarterly leadership meetings according to these principles and then our monthly management meetings. By this time, it was much easier to introduce the whole company to the transforming meetings methodology because the leadership team was so used to it.

Up to this time we had only had a loose principle of line management. It's a term I hate because it doesn't reflect the values I wanted to imbue. You can see what I mean about loose in the diagram below – there is very little "line" management in it but it does give people a clear understanding of whom to speak to about such things as holidays and sickness as well as their career development and professional skills.

Organic Reporting Structure

On its own this wasn't enough so, in collaboration with our HR Manager, she and I introduced something we at first called Coffee Catch Ups and later came to call Quarterly Catch Ups. Deliberately different from appraisals, these were informal one to ones, fully diarised where a coach/mentor (we never did find a satisfactory word for it even though it didn't stop it working) and their coachee/mentee (see what I mean?) could relax and talk over whatever issues they needed to. I'm not saying everyone took to it but there's no doubt in my mind that those few who didn't were the losers. Despite the informality it was always possible to follow the principles of non-interruption, the listener asking as few questions as possible and the thinker arriving at their own answers. Of course they could ask the other person for their thoughts but they would be couched in terms of experience rather than instruction.

There were people who naturally enough felt they didn't have the time, but we just kept on insisting and because the setting up of the meetings was always handled by HR, it worked. If a meeting didn't happen it was rearranged until it did. Eventually even the most intransigent got the message. The knock on effect was that there were never any surprises at annual appraisals. Both appraisers (there were always two at such meetings) and the person being appraised were up to speed so the whole session could focus first on success, then on what might need working on and then the future. Again, these sessions were held under the same agreements as the Quarterly Catch Ups mentioned earlier, which meant that both parties felt heard and that they had had the opportunity to say whatever they wanted or needed to say.

Knowing your business

Another reason I believe this worked – and a big one – is that the business was being run by a professional rather than a pure business person. Now this principle may be peculiar to the sorts of professional service firms I spent my career in but I can't see why it shouldn't equally apply to any other form of business. The reason I think it fundamentally important is this: when someone who understands only the financials or has never served a customer or sat in a client meeting they are at an immediate disadvantage. They simply do not know what it is like to be in that position, nor do they know from direct experience what it is that the customer or client might want. There comes a point when it is vital to have got your hands dirty. I am so hard pressed to think of a single successful business person across the board to whom this does not apply that I can't think of one at all! It's another principle of Love at Work – we need to know what it feels like to do whatever it is we are asking someone else to do on the front line of our business.

The dreaded curse

Lastly in this chapter let's briefly talk about email. For me it's the killer of communication and the easiest way to misunderstand and be misunderstood. The Internet has come upon us so fast that we cannot possibly have taken on board all its social and professional ramifications. People use it to write in a style as though they are talking directly to someone else when they are not. They use it to copy in as many other people as they can so they can never be accused of not informing people. They use it to abrogate responsibility and to directly or indirectly accuse others of not being up to the mark or to make a public example of them. There are even people who attempt to control their whole company via email. I have only three words of advice – don't do it!

Communication deteriorates exponentially as we move from face-to-face to telephone to written word. Add the speed of the Internet and the constant possibility of sending something before you have really considered it and disasters are simply waiting to happen. Have you never sent an email you regretted? If so, I'd love to meet you! I know I have. My first boss had a rule about letter writing and it was, "If it's a contractor whose upset you, reply today. If it's a client, leave it until tomorrow." He was half way right – I believe we should leave both until tomorrow and then think again. I also believe that the more important the message you want to impart, the more important it is to do it face-to-face. Can you imagine how those poor people felt who, a couple of years back, were fired by simultaneous text message? It must have been devastating. Of course the principle applies just as much to positive messages as negative ones. Even though the urban myth about over 90% of what we communicate face to face being unspoken has been exposed as just that – a myth, there is no substitute for looking someone in the eye.

When I was first in business, if you wanted to communicate with someone you either picked up the phone or wrote to them. In fact the standard form of business communication was by letter. The great thing about it was that it gave you time to think (those three words again). Someone wanted to ask you a question and they wrote you a letter. It took a day to arrive and it took you a day to reply, much of which gave you thinking time. You sent your reply and it took another day to arrive and so on. First came fax and then email, along with mobile phones rather than fixed lines and finally Blackberry and Iphone, so we became available any time anywhere. Can this ever be a good thing? I don't think so, simply because it has taken away our thinking time. People expect an immediate response and when they don't get it they become upset and even angry – "What do you mean, you haven't had time? I sent it to you fifteen minutes ago!".

None of this can be good for any of us. If we don't have time to think we certainly can't give of our best, whatever it is we do. I believe that someone, somewhere needs to sit down and establish a whole new protocol and etiquette around email, mobile phones and our accessibility. Without it, we will disappear in our own vortex. All we can really do is start from where we are, go as far as we can and then see how far we can go. Have faith in yourself, because there is always another step.

> **If we have the opportunity to be generous with our hearts, ourselves, we have no idea of the depth and breadth of love's reach."**
>
> **Margaret Cho**

What to take with you from this chapter

- Create a clear vision
- Be open-hearted – always
- Build trust
- Focus, focus, focus
- Plan ahead
- Communicate, communicate, communicate

Notes

Chapter 10

What's in this chapter:

- The connection between success, trust, intelligence and emotion
- The will to win
- Developing a great networking model

Winning and succeeding

" If there is something you want in life, then you've got one of two things. You've either got it or you've got a story about why you haven't got it. Drop the story."

Anthony Robbins

The basis of trust

The principles of Love at Work, properly imbued in your business, will do more to help you win business and continually succeed than any other single factor. If you have read this far you now have all the tools and ideas you will need to both win and succeed.

By now you know how important it is to understand and like your customers and clients. It doesn't matter what your product or service is or what its unit cost. All that matters is that they know that you want their long term business and will go out of your way to help them in order to achieve that. When they know you have their interests at heart as well as your own and that you are on their side they will feel comfortable, relaxed and safe in your company.

 Embed a desire for others to succeed in your DNA and you will succeed too."

Anon

Part of how we can do this is by helping them think for themselves, to reach their own conclusions. All decisions are a mixture of logic and emotion, so it may never be clear when we/they are justifying our emotions with logic or vice versa. It doesn't really matter as long as we are using our free will to make whatever decisions we need to make, whether it's buying a book, appointing our accountant or commissioning a huge building. Giving people the time and space to think things through and to choose for themselves, without pushing them in a particular direction, is a wonderful gift and it will be recognised. We should always seek out at least win/win in any negotiation. Once the deal has been struck the greatest thing we can do is to honour our promises. Everyone we deal with must be able to depend on us. They will feel this when we tell them the truth and act with integrity. After all, this is the whole basis of trust.

Success breeds success

 A winner never quits and a quitter never wins.”
Anon

Success breeds success and people like to feel that they are working with or buying from successful people and organisations. Confirm this to them and winning business becomes so much easier, so make it easy for them in the first place. Be clear about what you do or what it is you are selling and let your customer or client know just what is unique about your proposition. Talk to them about the benefits of working with you or buying from you rather than what it is you are selling. Love what you do and be passionate when taking every opportunity to talk about it. We all need to spread the word and people get a kick out of knowing people who are both buzzy and passionate. Once they not only like you but understand what you do they will spread the word for you, helping build the network you need to grow your business. There really isn't a substitute for getting out there and meeting people. My dear friend, George Metcalfe, who has spent a lifetime building businesses for himself and for others, goes as far as to say that in the early days of a business we need to spend as much as 85% of our time networking – a staggering thought but true.

We would be wasting our time though if we didn't know what was likely to push the decision making buttons of the majority of our prospective clients and customers. Those highest on the list are the quality and enthusiasm of our staff. Why on earth then do companies use low paid staff in their call centres? Particularly when next on the list is reputation. Reputations are incredibly difficult to build and notoriously easy to destroy. It simply cannot be worth the risk. Next, everyone wants to be listened to and everyone wants a response that demonstrates capability and initiative, so why not give it to them. Lowest on the list, believe it or not, comes price. By now you will know that I believe that this is because people want to talk with real people, feel comfortable with them and build a level of rapport. Our decisions around so many things are made from the heart rather than the head more often than many of us would like to admit.

IQ and EQ

In today's highly competitive world, those of us who understand the need to use not just our IQ but also our EQ can be up to twice as effective at winning business. It is this that can give us access to those vital decision making buttons. However, it will come as no surprise that this is not an intellectual exercise or understanding we are dealing with. We will only get the results we want when we work through our hearts, through Love at Work. It is this overall context that makes knowledge like this so powerful. Combining our client/customer knowledge with our product knowledge presents only one half of the equation. Our people skills and sales skills are the other half. Without them and our understanding of the difference that influence, awareness, confidence, empathy and all the other elements make, the first half becomes worthless. This is a fact now recognised by many multi-national companies and, of course, something that all of us involved in Love at Work have always known.

The use of our EQ doesn't answer all the questions though. Another aspect of winning and succeeding is that winners don't like losing; in fact they hate it. This doesn't make them bad sports; it makes them win more often. Bad sports sulk; winners take that energy and turn it around. It fires them up rather than depresses them. They learn from their losses and become even more determined to win. They achieve by repeating what worked and making adjustments to what didn't. They know that fortune favours the brave and that luck is no more than a combination of preparation and opportunity. What's more the greatest winners know that competitiveness need not eliminate kindness, humility or humanity.

The will to win

The will and desire to win comes in many different forms, not all of which are useful or helpful. Those that want to win simply for the sake of winning can easily become the bad apple aboard the ship I wrote of in Chapter 9. Take the case, for example, of someone we will call Jason. For weeks he took up my time badgering me to give him sales responsibilities along with his other roles. His main argument always was that nobody knew as well as he how to win business. Eventually I gave in on condition that we set targets to measure his skills. He totally surprised me with his response: "No thanks – all I really wanted was to see if I could get you to agree." Sadly this wasn't the only time he tried these sorts of tactics with me and with his colleagues. Covertly and sometimes not so covertly he found ways of getting his own way – of "winning" until eventually he tried it once too often and I decided, for the good of the team, to fire him. There's no doubt he did a lot of important work but his high opinion of himself and his ways of getting what he wanted certainly didn't fit with my concept of Love at Work. High maintenance people are not good for us as individuals and certainly not good for us as a team.

 Out of need springs desire and out of desire springs the energy and the will to win."
Denis Waitley

We cannot underestimate the importance of winning though. Everyone at every level of an organisation is happy when they are winning business. It can affect all of us in everything we do and say at work. Winning means we all have jobs. Understanding what we individually and collectively need to do to win business is the only way forward. My contention is that at the end of the day, provided we are highly competent, the majority of business is won on the strength of the relationships we build with others. We come back to the issue of EQ again and the fact that our professional expertise alone is never enough.

There will always be people out there who are at least as able if not better able than we are professionally. As Tom Peters says, we live in "A sea of high quality sameness". A good product or service is no more than an entry point. Therefore "normal" equals "nothing". How we stand out from the crowd is vital to our success. The way to do this is to continually act in a way that allows our potential clients and customers to move from liking us to respecting us to trusting us. Whenever we are with them we need to continually demonstrate our integrity through everything we say, do and show to them. On a practical level, the skills we need to be able to do this are: a strong understanding of the client's issues; responsiveness, adaptability and flexibility; and delivering what we say we will, when we say we will and at a realistic price. Do all of this and we will discover that winning in itself creates more wins.

Don't become a statistic

It's a salutary fact that 80% of businesses fail within the first five years. Of those that survive, less than 5% will reach a turnover of more than £500,000 and less than 1% will ever reach £5,000,000. These are the very real hurdles that separate us from our goals. Hard work alone is not enough. Holding the vision, focusing on what needs to be done and taking all the action you need to take will get you over the first few hurdles but it will never be enough Add to this all the people skills your team possesses, all its EQ, to win work and you will undoubtedly become one of the one percent. To remain there (which has to be our goal) means having an ever stronger product or service by discovering what we can do better and making sure we do – because today's excellence is tomorrow's norm.

Ability is what you are capable of doing.
Motivation determines what you do. Attitude determines
how well you do it."
Raymond Chandler

The power of networking

Some chapters back I wrote that the more important the message the more important the directness of the communication. In an ideal world all our communication would be direct and we would not need letters, faxes, emails and texts. Because, in our high-speed world, this isn't possible we need to optimise the time we have to communicate directly. The many forms of written communication are ideal for imparting things like facts, figures and abstract ideas. What we can't do through them is impart feelings and subtleties of our verbal and non-verbal messages. Never is this truer than in the area of networking. Whilst certain areas of it can be dealt with through email and text, there is no real substitute for individual face-to-face meetings, small group meetings or at organised networking events. But why is networking so important? Did you know that a (network) referral generates 80% more results than a cold call – and is so much better for our soul? Did you know that around 70% of all professional work is found through networking? Did you know that anyone you really want to meet is only five people away from you? No wonder Ivan Misner, the founder and chairman of BNI, places so much store by it.

Much of this book has been focused on the more esoteric aspects of building a business that truly create Love at Work. It would be remiss of me though, because of its importance, not to include some practical facts and ideas on networking. After all, it is an area so many of us find difficult yet is vital to building our businesses. Here, first of all, are the best of the tips I have picked up over the years:

- *Networking is about building long term relationships, not about going after a quick sale*
- *Be genuinely interested in the other person*
- *Talk to everyone, whatever you think they can or cannot do for you*
- *Busy people are never too busy to help others*
- *Keep on circulating and then circulate again*
- *Think of the other person in terms of what you can do for them, rather than what they can do for you*
- *Ask open ended questions (how?, what?, why?, where?, when?)*
- *Listen more than you speak on a ratio of at least 5:1*
- *Prepare yourself with relevant questions – the more you do, the easier networking becomes*
- *Think about who you can introduce to whom – then act*
- *Introduce people to each other even if you have only just met them*
- *Always ask for the other person's card before offering your own*
- *Always feed back when someone has made a useful introduction for you*
- *Nurture your network constantly*

Combine these with the many other understandings I have written of in this book and you should find networking will no longer hold the fear it holds for so many of us. The fact is, that like charity, communication (and therefore great networking) begins at home. We know now that leadership starts with self knowledge and self leadership. The more we learn about ourselves, the more able we are to lead, help and support others. Once we can communicate well and positively with ourselves we will be able to listen, empathise with and understand others so much more, all of which enhances our networking skills.

Just listen

 A winner listens. A loser just waits until it's their turn to talk."
Pat Williams

All the skills we talked through around enhancing our thinking apply here. You may be surprised how many of Time To Think's Ten Components of a Thinking Environment you can invoke in a social situation. Good eye contact and appropriate amounts of gentle nods and quiet murmuring will establish Attention. The very fact that you are at the same gathering suggests Equality and both of you having a glass of something hospitable in your hand goes a long way to creating Ease. There is always something to Appreciate about someone and in doing that, it will give them Encouragement to tell you more. All of which is designed to help them share their Feelings or elicit Information from them. Diversity and acknowledgement of it comes naturally in a room full of people. All that remains is for you to ask Incisive Questions in a Place which has been set up to be supportive and you simply cannot fail. There you are – all ten of them!

But what if you feel you can't think of suitable questions? Then here are a few easy to memorise starters that seem to work every time in both social and business situations – and after all, we now know there is very little difference between the two:

- *How did you two first meet?*
- *That's interesting – tell me more?*
- *How did you come to be a (lawyer, accountant, mechanic, IT specialist)?*

- *What's the biggest change you have seen in your field in the last five years?*
- *What help can I be to you in obtaining business?*
- *What do you enjoy most about your role?*
- *How do you see your field of business changing over the next five years?*
- *Where were you before you joined … and what did you do there?*
- *What drove you to set up your own business?*

Any time, any place, anywhere

Of course networking can happen any time, any place, anywhere. Most of the time, it's something we all do perfectly naturally and don't even think about. If this is the case then all we really need to do is to take those unconscious, informal skills into the formal situations and stop worrying about it. That's when we will stop feeling uncomfortable and covering it by being either pushy and aggressive on the one hand or weak and needy on the other. An easy way to overcome this is, simply to be genuinely more interested in the other person than in yourself or anyone else in the room. I rather like the way my friend George Metcalfe sums it all up:

- *Be there!*
- *Be more interested in the person you are talking to than in yourself*
- *Be genuinely enthusiastic about the other person's ideas and plans*
- *When you tell your story, make it really short and really interesting*
- *Record details of relevant meetings and follow up fast*
- *Do everything to give rather than to gain*
- *Confidently refer/introduce people to others*
- *Understand that asking questions actually makes you more interesting*
- *There's no such thing as selling – only research*
- *You are terrific! But forget it when talking to the other person*

Just do it

There really is no substitute for just doing it. The champion golfer Gary Player's maxim of "It's funny but the more I practice, the luckier I get" was never truer than in this situation. First of all therefore we need to join some appropriate organisations like Chambers of Commerce, Business Referral Exchange (BRX), Business Network International (BNI), local networking groups or professional or trade bodies. The great thing about all of these is that everyone is there for the same reason and the more experienced networkers are always willing to share their knowledge. That alone will help you adjust your attitude, overcome shyness and gain confidence through repetition. It will help you learn to work a crowd and, at the best groups, hone your 60 second presentation or "elevator pitch". If we really do find it excruciating then we can try hypnosis and NLP but, even after all that, ease really will come only through experience.

If you still aren't convinced then perhaps hearing it not from me but once more from George Metcalfe, known in the coaching fraternity as The Wild Elder Coach. A past Vice-President of the UK International Coach Federation amongst many other things, his depth of experience is boundless – he has been in the business world even longer than me! What's more he is an arch networker, always willing to pass on that knowledge for anyone to use. He explains the power of networking by citing the invention of the Ethernet by his distant kinsman, Bob Metcalfe, who proposed that the value of a network grows by the square of the size of the network (Metcalfe's Law). In brief and simple terms this principle means that a network which is twice as large as another will be four times more valuable because of the increasing number of interconnections. Even if a smaller network has some unique benefits the larger one will eventually win out because the square factor tips the balance in its favour. It's a law which explains the principle of virtually any network, not least of which is the largest of them all, the Internet.

Develop a powerful network

Winners get to the top and turn around to see who they have defeated. Leaders get to the top and turn around to help others achieve the same."
Dan Churches

For this reason alone it's worth developing the most powerful network we can. George would argue that with any start up business the most important thing we can do is spend as much as 85% of our time marketing through networking – and I believe he is absolutely right. Perhaps the real reason that this is true is because whilst you sit at the centre of your sphere of influence, everyone you know sits at the centre of theirs.

exercise

Just for a moment (in fact several moments) stop and either make a list of everyone you know, or go to your database, be it paper with something like Filofax or electronic with Outlook, Access, ACT or any other, and count up the number of entries. You will find, as Joe Girard (the "Worlds Greatest Salesman" according to the Guinness Book Of World Records) found, that you have upwards of 250 people on your list or in your database. If this is true (and it is) then everyone else you know has that number too – it's called Girard's Law of 250. What he went on to say was that this makes everyone on your database invaluable, people you can't afford to lose as contacts. Why? - Because you will lose the potential access to their 250 people too. In total that's 62,500 people. Add each of their 250 and the figure is incomprehensible. Now can you see why networking is one of the most important things you can ever do? ♥

You may well be wondering as you near the end of this book, "Why on earth is he banging on about networking when all the time he's been writing about the head-heart connection and Love at Work?" The answer is straightforward. It comes back to my assertion at the very beginning of the book that we are all here on this earth to learn about relationship, that the key relationship we need to learn about is the one with our self and that there is no better place to learn about it than at work. "Now you've really lost me!" I can hear you say, but I promise you I haven't. To learn to be Love at Work we need the workplace to eventually be it in. Networking is just another form of relationship. This is where the majority of our best colleagues, suppliers, consultants, customers and clients will come from. Without them we cannot make the friendships we need to feed and sustain our businesses or create the opportunities we need to learn about relationship. Without our businesses there is nowhere for us to learn about Love at Work because they form the sea in which we learn to swim. So, to paraphrase part of John F Kennedy's inaugural speech, don't think about networking in terms of what the world can do for you, but in terms of what you can do for the world.

What to take with you from this chapter

- Winning and trust are inseparable
- Winning is not a dirty word
- EQ is more valuable than IQ
- Prepare, prepare, prepare,
- Communicate, communicate, communicate
- Network, network, network
- Learn to be Love at Work

and to remind you to...

- *Complete the exercise in this chapter*

Notes

....

....

....

....

....

....

Chapter 11

What's in this chapter:

- Drawing everything together
- A reminder about meditation
- The vital role of coaches and mentors
- One last word

... and finally

" Let us reflect on what is truly of value in life, what gives meaning to our lives, and set our priorities on the basis of that."
The 14th Dalai Lama

It's an old story but one well worth repeating. Here it is, adapted from the original in the book by Ken Keyes, written in the late 1950s:

The Japanese monkey, Macaca Fuscata (or Macaque), has been observed in the wild for a period of about 30 years. In 1952 on the island of Koshima, scientists were providing monkeys with sweet potatoes dropped in the sand. The monkeys liked the taste of the raw sweet potatoes, but they found the dirt unpleasant.

An 18-month old female named Imo found she could solve the problem by washing the potatoes in a nearby stream. She taught this trick to her mother. Her playmates also learned this new way and they taught their mothers too. This cultural innovation was gradually picked up by various monkeys before the eyes of the scientists. Between 1952 and 1958 all the young monkeys learned to wash the sweet potatoes to make them more palatable. Only the adults who imitated their children learned this social improvement. Other adults kept eating dirty sweet potatoes.

Then something startling took place. By the autumn of 1958, a certain number of Koshima monkeys were washing sweet potatoes – the exact number is not known. Let us suppose that when the sun rose one morning there were 99 monkeys on Koshima Island who had learned to wash their sweet potatoes. Let's further suppose that later that morning, the hundredth monkey learned to wash potatoes. Then it happened! By that evening almost everyone in the tribe was washing sweet potatoes before eating them. The added energy somehow created an ideological breakthrough.

But notice: the most surprising thing observed by these scientists was that the habit of washing sweet potatoes then spontaneously jumped over the sea. Colonies of monkeys on other islands and the mainland troop of monkeys at Tagasakiyama began washing their sweet potatoes.

Thus, when a certain critical number achieves an awareness, this new awareness may be communicated from mind to mind. Although the exact number may vary, this Hundredth Monkey Phenomenon means that when only a limited number of people know of a new way, it may remain the conscious property of these people. But there is a point at which if only one more person tunes-in to a new awareness, a field is strengthened so that this awareness is picked up by almost everyone!

The Hundredth Monkey Phenomenon points out our responsibility and our power. Be informed, hopeful and energetic! Be vigilant with your thoughts of peace and love. Sense your power to lift the mood of despair. Let your enthusiasm seep in and penetrate the collective consciousness. Take a new look at your priorities. This does not necessarily mean leaving your work or your present lifestyle. It means giving an increased energy and priority to expanding your own awareness, to communicating with other people who are now "asleep" and to withdrawing all thoughts and actions which create human alienation, separateness, destruction and death. Do not wait until others around you are opening their hearts. Instead begin doing things now that are so desperately needed for the conscious unfolding of your life – and the survival of our species.

This story may happen to be apocryphal and mythic rather than pure scientific fact, but it matters not. Even if it is true in principle and not in detail, it doesn't lessen my reason for including it at this point. We need to constantly remind ourselves that whatever the difference is that we want to make in the world, we can. Our whole planet has been arranged for us so that we can. All we need to know is that. Malcolm Gladwell explains it brilliantly in his book, The Tipping Point, as the magic moment when ideas, trends and social behaviours cross a threshold, tip and spread like wildfire. Let's do it with Love at Work!

We've covered a lot of ground in the last ten chapters and, if you are at all like me, you will by now have forgotten much of what I have said. If you haven't then we are both blessed – you with your amazing memory and me because you have been able to remember much of it and use it in your life, gently spreading the word. I shall feel even more blessed if reading the book has kindled in you a spark to make you want to become part of the ground swell that is needed to make a difference in the world of work. In my mind there is no difference between that world and our personal world. We cannot act with integrity in either if we see them as separate places or having different values and ethics.

We must be the change we want to see in the world."
Mahatma Gandhi

A heart and mind set

Love at Work is not just a mind set, it's a heart set as well. It embraces every aspect of our being – physical, emotional, mental and spiritual – eventually taking us to a place of transcendence. This is the space from which we truly can make a difference. The scale of the difference we wish to make isn't important, any more than our place in our organisation is. All that matters is that we want to do it. Mind set and heart set is of course just another way of saying head-heart connection, the very presence of which supports our well-being. If we are to take these principles and use them we need above all to be able to trust ourselves. Knowing that we are fit on all four levels is part of that trust and it will flow outwards in all our dealings and meetings. When we know ourselves and trust ourselves, we are walking the talk and others will know they can trust us too.

Cornerstones

The cornerstone of Love at Work is those clear, strong moral values demonstrated by people who get their ego out of the way and live their lives with integrity. They achieve this through rigour in their thinking, rigour in their questioning of self and others and rigour in their outlook. Because of this they are supported by a realistic and well-developed world view. They know that everything in their world is the way that it is and not the way that it is not.

Such people have come to understand that the patterns they developed in their early lives may or may not serve them and are no longer willing to be ruled by the reactionary rebel and conform assumption we all grow up with. They work hard to uncover and witness those patterns and take every opportunity to change those that don't work for them. Amazing things happen to their perspective on the world as they move from agreement to alignment to attunement, not least of which is that as they change, those around them begin to change too. All the time they know that there is no one and no thing to change but themselves.

The power of meditation

Many of them have learned that meditation is a powerful and transformative tool that takes them to places and heights they might only previously have dreamed of. People who meditate regularly know how important it is to continue with their practice, particularly when they are going to have an exceptionally busy day. Getting up that extra 20 minutes early in order to meditate will repay them in additional energy many times over during that day. Meditation gives them a clarity of mind that they can use to discover what they want and to visualise it, focus on it and take action on it. They know that they can always have what they want by using the power of their mind in combination with the power of their heart.

I guess every single one of them aims for Love at Work because they know in their hearts that it is the only thing there is that is real. So, like them, hold your values, live your dreams and do whatever it takes to be the best you can. Listen to others, but learn to listen to and trust your instincts and intuition. I have always, always found that I ignore mine at my peril and sometimes even to the peril of my dearest friends. In this way you will build a life that is sustainable in every way, not just for now but for your children's future – and your children's children.

All great leaders know the importance of keeping a clear head and of leading by example. People will follow only those they trust and so for them to see people who are prepared to put themselves on the line is important to them. They spot the leader's focus, their lack of ego and their personal rigour and follow them because they want some of that too. They admire their commitment and, never settling for second best, they admire their love of people and their celebration of diversity which comes with this and in all they do and are. Not least though we admire great leaders because they recognise the need to do the things that they do best and willingly leave others to do the things they do best.

I am still learning."
Michelangelo

Coaches and mentors

Coaching and mentoring comes easily to those who lead through Love at Work and they recognise the difference between the two roles. They take the time and make the effort to support, enable and mentor others and they do it with care and love. We all need coaches in our lives and we all need mentors. We all need to learn how to coach and how to become great mentors. We can all do this for one another given time and experience. If you are early in your career, learn as much as you can from such people. The time will come when the situation is reversed, the time when you will be able to give rather than receive – although my experience is that the whole process ends up as natural as breathing – receiving on the in-breath and giving on the out, doing what the universe does in every moment.

The best coaches and mentors spend most of their time listening rather than speaking. It is the greatest gift we can give anyone. If we really must speak, let us phrase our words in the form of a question whenever we can. Then listen to what the other person has to say with 100% rapt attention. Silence really is golden. Their mind is thinking at its best when we ask questions but ask as few as possible. Help others to think for themselves, to think independently and you will be doing the world a great service. There is nothing we and our world can't achieve when this happens. Then help them (and yourself) to learn how to fully express those thoughts in a way that others can really hear. Clear expression reduces any likelihood of conflict, particularly when our thoughts are of a peaceful nature in the first place.

A last word

I would urge you to bear all of this in mind as you build your job, your business and, most important of all, your life. There really is no difference –all three are one and the same, as we are all one. Our vision, our open-heartedness and our willingness to trust and be trusted are the foundation stones upon which we can build a better world. Base your will to win, to be successful, in these attributes and there will be no boundaries to what you can achieve. Winning is a fabulous ideal. Success is a fabulous idea. Their essence is full of all the power, energy and vitality we need to mix with every drop of our creativity and intelligence (both intellectual and emotional). Do this well, wisely and with loving responsibility and we will have Love at Work. What fun that will be! I wish you a lifetime filled with excitement, love and learning.

Nigel

 The future may be made up of many factors but where it truly lies is in the hearts and minds of men."
Li Ka Shing

Notes

About the author

Born in Rotherham, Yorkshire towards the end of the Second World War, Nigel Cutts was educated at Scarborough High School for Boys, Leeds College of Art and Kingston College of Art.

His career in the design world spanned more than forty years. His first job was as an assistant to Don Ashton, the hotel and film designer of the Fifties and Sixties who designed the original Mandarin Hotel in Hong Kong and won an Oscar for "Bridge Over The River Kwai". At his second firm he was made their youngest ever Associate. During the late Seventies and through the whole of the Eighties he ran his own substantial design business and latterly set up the UK office of an international firm of architects, ending up as an International Director before retiring from main stream business in early 2009.

Nigel is someone who has always believed that to be the best you need to be with the best – even in his childhood days, when he learned to water ski with the Cambridge University Water Ski Club. From this he became a founder member of his local club where he was chief instructor and club champion for several years, teaching people like Dickie Henderson and Nicholas Parsons. Slightly later he took the same view of competing in ballroom dancing and was taught by, amongst others, Harry Smith-Hampshire and Doreen Casey, the then current World Champions.

In adulthood he became interested in, if not obsessed by, Obedience Dog Training for over 25 years, again seeking out the best instructors. Whilst in the sport he subsequently trained his own Obedience Champion, bred another and competed at Crufts no less than four times. He was also a Championship judge and coached and taught across the UK and Northern Europe.

It's not surprising then, that when it came to his personal growth and development he took a similarly powerful approach, immersing himself in the work of Walter and Gita Bellin at The Bellin Partnership as well as in the work of people like Denise Lynn, John Bradshaw, Bill Spear and Tony Robbins. He is also a qualified Conflict Resolution trainer as well as a coach and consultant with Nancy Kline's Time to Think organisation.

The natural progression of his life has been towards a combination of excellence and people. He now brings all this knowledge and experience together and runs, with his wife Gilly, Cutts & Cons, a consultancy specialising in coaching, counselling and mentoring business leaders specifically in the area of improving the quality and independence of their thinking and giving that full expression.

He lives in Surrey with his wife Gilly and between them they have seven children and nine grandchildren.

Appendix

Recommended reading

"The Moving Finger writes, and having writ,
Moves on: nor all your Piety nor Wit
Shall lure it back to cancel half a line,
Nor all your tears wash out a Word of it."
The Rubaiyat of Omar Khayyam

In anticipation of you wondering what it might be useful to read next, here is a brief list of those books I have from time to time recommended when a friend or colleague felt they wanted to know more about a particular issue around the principles of Love at Work. I guess therefore they are my personal favourites. There were some difficult choices and for this reason I have chosen just one title from each author. This list differs from the bibliography because that represents nearly, if not all of the books I have read over many years and which are relevant in someway to the development of the thought processes in the book. Happy reading!

Author	Book	Publisher
BACH Richard	*Jonathan Livingston Seagull*	Pan Books
BANDLER Richard, **GRINDER** John	*Frogs Into Princes*	Real People Press
BERNE Eric	*The Games People Play*	Penguin
BLY Robert	*Iron John*	Element Books
CARNEGIE Dale	*How To Win Friends And Influence People*	Vermilion
CHOPRA Deepak	*The Seven Spiritual Laws Of Success*	Bantam Press
COLLINS Jim	*Good To Great*	Random House
COLLINS Jim, **PORRAS** Jerry	*Built To Last*	Random House
CORNELIUS Helena, **FAIRE** Shoshana	*Everyone Can Win*	Simon and Schuster
COVEY Stephen R	*The 8th Habit*	Franklin Covey
DALAI LAMA His Holiness The	*Four Noble Truths*	Thorsons
DASS Ram	*Be Here Now*	Kingsport Press
DETHLEFSEN Thorwald, **DAHLKE** Rudiger	*The Healing Power Of Illness*	Element Books
EHRMANN Max	*Desiderata*	Random House
FOUNDATION FOR INNER PEACE	*A Course In Miracles*	Arkana
FRANKL Victor E	*Man's Search For Meaning*	Washington Square Press
GAWAIN Shakti	*Creative Visualisation*	Bantam
GIBRAN Kahlil	*The Prophet*	Pan Books
GLADWELL Malcolm	*Outliers*	Penguin

GOLEMAN Daniel	*Emotional Intelligence*	Bloomsbury Press
HAICH Elisabeth	*Initiation*	Mandala
HARRIS Amy & Thomas	*I'm OK, You're OK*	Pan Books
HAY Louise L	*You Can Heal Your Life*	Eden Grove
IMPLICATE TECHNOLOGY CENTRE	*Beyond The Personality*	Implicate Technology Centre
JAMPOLSKY Gerald	*Love Is Letting Go Of Fear*	Celestial Arts
JEFFERS Susan	*Feel The Fear And Do It Anyway*	Random Century
KITTO H D F	*The Greeks*	Pelican Originals
KLINE Nancy	*Time To Think*	Cassell
KORNFIELD Jack	*A Path With Heart*	Rider Books
KRYSTAL Phyllis	*Cutting The Ties That Bind*	Element Books
LEWIS Thomas, **AMINI** Fair, **LANNON** Richard	*A General Theory Of Love*	Vintage
PECK M Scott	*The Road Less Travelled*	Arrow
PETERS Thomas J, **WATERMAN** Robert H	*In Search Of Excellence*	Harper & Row
PIRSIG Robert M	*Zen And The Art Of Motorcycle Maintenance*	Corgi
REDFIELD James	*The Celestine Prophecy*	Bantam Books
RINPOCHE Soghal	*The Tibetan Book Of Living And Dying*	Rider Books
ROBBINS Anthony	*Awaken The Giant Within*	Simon and Schuster
ROSENBERG Marshall B	*Nonviolent Communication*	Puddle Dancer Press
SKINNER Robin, **CLEESE** John	*Families And How To Survive Them*	Mandarin
TAGORE Rabindranath	*The Religion Of Man*	Mandala
THE ARBINGER INSTITUTE	*An Anatomy Of Peace*	Berrett-Koehler
TICH NAHT THAN	*The Present Moment* (Audio)	Sounds True
TOLLE Eckhart	*The Power Of Now*	Hodder and Stoughton
TWYMAN James	*Emissary Of Light*	Hodder and Stoughton
VEAL Debra	*Rowing It Alone*	Robson Books
WALSCH Neale Donald	*Conversations With God*	Hodder & Stoughton
WEISS Bryan	*Many Lives, Many Masters*	Piatkus
WILBER Ken	*Kosmic Consciousness* (Audio)	Sounds True
WILSON-SCHAEF Anne	*Escape From Intimacy*	Yhorsona

Bibliography

> " If you want to be truly successful, invest in yourself to get the knowledge you need to find your unique factor. When you find it and focus on it and persevere, your success will blossom."

Sydney Madwed

Author	Book	Publisher
ALEXANDER Matthias	*The Alexander Technique*	Thames and Hudson
AL-JAJJAKA Sam	*Professional Level Psychometric Tests*	Kogan Page
APPLETON George	*Journey For A Soul*	Fontana
ARBINGER Institute	*The Anatomy Of Peace*	Berrett-Koehler
ARDEN Paul	*It's Not How Good You Are, It's How Good You Want To Be*	Phaidon
ARONSON Elliot	*The Social Animal*	W H Freeman
Ashton Anthony	*Harmonograph*	Wooden Books
ASSARAF John, **SMITH** Murray	*The Answer*	Simon & Schuster
AYER A J	*The Problem Of Knowledge*	Pelican
BACH Richard	*Jonathan Livingston Seagull*	Pan Books
BACH Richard	*A Gift Of Wings*	Pan Books
BACH Richard	*The Bridge Across Forever*	Dell Publishing
BACH Richard	*Illusions*	Pan Books
BACH Richard	*Out Of My Mind*	William Morrow
BACH Richard	*Running From Safety*	William Morrow
BACH Richard	*One*	Pan Books
BAN BREATHNACH Sarah	*Simple Abundance*	Bantam Books
BANDLER Richard, **GRINDER** John	*Frogs Into Princes*	Real People Press
BARRETT Richard	*Building A Values Driven Organisation*	Elsevier
BAYS Brandon	*The Journey*	Thorsons
BEEKEN Jenny	*Don't Hold Your Breath*	Polair Publishing
BEEKEN Jenny	*Your Yoga Body Map*	Polair Publishing
BEEKEN Jenny	*Yoga Of The Heart*	White Eagle Publishing
BERNE Eric	*The Games People Play*	Penguin
BERNERS-LEE Tim	*Weaving The Web*	Orion Business Books
BHAKTIVADANTA Swami Prabhupada	*The Nectar Of Devotion*	Bhaktivadanta Book Trust
BHAKTIVADANTA Swami Prabhupada	*Srimad Bhagavatam*	Bhaktivadanta Book Trust
BLOOMFIELD Caine, **JAFFE** Tim	*Discovering Inner Energy And Overcoming Stress*	Delacorte Press

BLY Robert	*Iron John*	Element Books
BRADSHAW John	*Healing The Shame That Binds You*	Health Communications
BRENNAN Barbara Ann	*Hands Of Light*	Bantam Books
BRENNAN Barbara Ann	*Light Emerging*	Bantam Books
BRYSON Bill	*A Short History Of Nearly Everything*	Doubleday
BUTLER W E	*How To Develop Clairvoyance*	Aquarian
BUTLER W E	*How To Read The Aura*	Aquarian
BYRNE Rhonda	*The Secret*	Simon & Schuster
BYRON Katie	*Loving What Is*	Rider Books
CAMERON Julia	*God Is No Laughing Matter*	Pan Books
CAMERON Julia	*The Right To Write*	Macmillan Press
CAMERON Julia	*Walking In This World*	Rider Books
CAMERON Julia	*The Artist's Way*	Pan Books
CAREY Ken	*The Starseed Transmissions*	Harper Collins
CARLSON Richard	*Don't Sweat The Small Stuff*	Hodder & Stoughton
CARNEGIE Dale	*How To Win Friends And Influence People*	Vermilion
CARNINGTON Patricia	*The Book Of Meditation*	Element Books
CARTER Philip, **RUSSELL** Ken	*Psychometric Testing*	Wiley
CASTLE Fina	*What A Wonderful World*	Hodder & Stoughton
CHANDU Jack F	*The Pendulum Book*	C W Daniel
CHOPRA Deepak	*Boundless Energy*	Random House
CHOPRA Deepak	*Ageless Body, Timeless Mind*	Random House
CHOPRA Deepak	*Synchro Destiny*	Random House
CHOPRA Deepak	*The Deeper Wound*	Random House
CHOPRA Deepak	*The Seven Spiritual Laws Of Success*	Bantam Press
CHOPRA Deepak	*Everyday Immortality*	Random House
CHOPRA Deepak	*The Way Of The Wizard*	Random House
CHOPRA Deepak	*Unconditional Life*	Bantam Books
CHOPRA Deepak	*Quantum Healing*	Bantam Books
CHOPRA Deepak	*The Path To Love*	Random House
CHOPRA Deepak	*The Return Of Merlin*	Harmony Books
CHOPRA Deepak	*Peace Is The Way*	Random House
CHOPRA Deepak, **SIMON** David	*The Seven Spiritual Laws Of Yoga*	John Wiley and Sons
CLUTTERBUCK David **MEGGINSON** David	*Making Coaching Work*	CIPD
CLUTTERBUCK David	*Everyone Needs A Mentor*	CIPD
COELHO Paulo	*The Alchemist*	Harper Collins
COHEN Pete	*Fear Busting*	Thorson Element
COHEN Judith, **VERITY** Pete	*Lighten Up*	Random House
COLLINS Jim	*Good To Great*	Random House
COLLINS Jim, **PORRAS** Jerry	*Built To Last*	Random House
COOK Roger	*The Tree Of Life*	Thames and Hudson
CORNELIUS Helena **FAIRE** Shoshana	*Everyone Can Win*	Simon and Schuster
COVEY Stephen R	*Daily Reflections For Highly Effective People*	Simon & Schuster
COVEY Stephen R	*The 8th Habit*	Franklin Covey
COVEY Stephen R	*The 7 Habits Of Highly Effective People*	Free Press
COVEY Stephen R	*Living The 7 Habits*	Franklin Covey

CROMPTON Paul	*The Elements Of Tai Chi*	Element Books
CUMMINGS Joe, **WASSMAN** Bill	*Buddhist Stupas In Asia*	Lonely Planet
DALAI LAMA His Holiness The	**The Power Of Buddhism**	Newleaf Boxtree
DALAI LAMA His Holiness The	*Path To Bliss*	Snow Lion Publications
DALAI LAMA His Holiness The	*How To See Yourself As You Really Are*	Random House
DALAI LAMA His Holiness The	*The Four Noble Truths*	Thorsons
DALAI LAMA His Holiness The	*The Dalai Lama's Book Of Wisdom*	Thorsons
DALAI LAMA His Holiness The	*The Dalai Lama's Book Of Transformation*	Thorsons
DASS Ram	*Journey Of Awakening*	Bantam Books
DASS Ram	*The Only Dance There Is*	Anchor Books
DASS Ram	*Grist For The Mill*	Celestial Arts
DASS Ram, **BUSH** Mirabai	*Compassion In Action*	Random House
DASS Ram	*Still Here*	Hodder and Stoughton
DASS Ram	*Be Here Now*	Kingsport Press
DASS Ram, **GORMAN** Paul	*How Can I Help?*	Rider Press
DAVIES Brenda	*The Rainbow Journey*	Hodder & Stoughton
DE BONO Edward	*Lateral Thinking*	Pelican
DE MELLO Anthony	*One Minute Wisdom*	Doubleday
DE MELLO Anthony	*The Heart Of The Enlightened*	Fount Paperbacks
DETHLEFSEN Thorwald **DAHLKE** Rudiger	*The Healing Power Of Illness*	Element Books
DOIDGE Norman	*The Brain That Changes Itself*	Viking
DROIT Roger-Pol	*101 Experiments In The Philosophy Of Everyday Life*	Faber & Faber
DUNNE Desmond	Yoga For Everyone	Four Square
EARLS Mark	Welcome To The Creative Age	John Wiley
EGAN Gerard	The Skilled Helper	Brooks/Cole
EHRMANN Max	Desiderata Random House	
ENGLISH Jane, **FENG** Gia-Fu	*Tao Te Ching*	Wildwood House
EVANS Richard, **JUNG** Paul I	*On Elementary Psychology*	Routledge & Keagan
FARNSWORTH Scott	Closing The Gap	SunBridge
FONTANA David	The Medititator's Book	Element
FORD Bill	*High Energy Habits*	Pocket Books
FOUNDATION FOR INNER PEACE	*A Course In Miracles*	Arkana
FRANKL Victor E	*Man's Search For Meaning*	Washington Square Press
GAWAIN Shakti	*Creative Visualisation*	Bantam
GENDLIN Eugene T	*Focusing*	Bantam
GERHARDT Sue	*Why Love Matters*	Routledge
GHAZI Polly, **JONES** Judy	*Downshifting*	Hodder Mobius
GIBRAN Kahlil	*The Thoughts And Meditations Of...*	Arrow Books
GIBRAN Kahlil	*The Prophet*	Pan Books
GLADWELL Malcolm	*The Tipping Point*	Abacus Books
GLADWELL Malcolm	*Outliers*	Penguin
GOLEMAN Daniel	*Emotional Intelligence*	Bloomsbury Press
GREY Margot	*Return From Death*	Arkana
GRIFFITHS Bede	*The Marriage Of East And West*	Fount Paperbacks
GRUWELL Erin	*The Freedom Writers Diary*	Broadway Books
HAANEL Charles	*Master Key System*	Ishtar Publishing

HAICH Elisabeth	*Initiation*	Mandala
HALL Judy	**The Art Of Psychic Protection**	Findhorn Press
HALLEY Ned	*The Complete Prophecies Of Nostradamus*	Wordsworth Editions
HAMEL Gary	*Leading The Revolution*	Harvard Business School Press
HANH Tich Naht	*Old Path, White Clouds*	Rider Books
HANH Tich Naht	*Creating True Peace*	Rider Books
HANH Tich Naht	*The Present Moment* (Audio)	Sounds True
HANH Tich Naht	*The Pine Gate*	White Pine Press
HANH Tich Naht	*The Sun My Heart*	Rider Press
HANH Tich Naht	*Touching Peace*	Parallax Press
HANH Tich Naht	*Transformations And Healing*	Parallax Press
HANH Tich Naht	*Our Appointment With Life*	Parallax Press
HANH Tich Naht	*Present Moment, Wonderful Moment*	Parallax Press
HANSARD Christopher	*The Tibetan Art Of Living*	Hodder and Stoughton
HARPER Jennifer	*Nine Ways To Body Wisdom*	Thorsons
HARRIS Amy & Thomas	*I'm OK, You're OK*	Pan Books
HARRIS Amy & Thomas	*Staying OK*	Pan Books
HARRIS Bill	*Thresholds Of The Mind*	Centerpointe Press
HAWKING Stephen	*A Brief History Of Time*	Bantam Books
HAY Louise L	*You Can Heal Your Life*	Eden Grove
HAY Louise L	*Inner Wisdom*	Hay House
HAY Louise L	*Heal Your Body*	Hay House
HEMENWAY Priya	*Eastern Wisdom*	Evergreen
HEWITT Peter	*The Coherent Universe*	Linden House
HODGKINSON Liz	*The Alexander Technique*	Piatkus
HODGKINSON Neville	*Will To Be Well*	Rider
HOFF Benjamin	*The Tao Of Pooh And The Te Of Piglet*	Methuen
HONORE Carl	*In Praise Of Slow*	Orion
IMPLICATE TECHNOLOGY CENTRE	*Beyond The Personality*	Implicate Technology Centre
IMPLICATE TECHNOLOGY CENTRE	*Towards Effortless Activity*	Implicate Technology Centre
ISHERWOOD Christopher **PRABHAVANANDA** Swami	*How To Know God – The Yoga Aphorsims Of Patanjali*	Mentor
ISRAEL Martin	*Summons To Life*	Hodder & Stoughton
ISRAEL Martin	*The Pain That Heals*	Arthur James
ISRAEL Martin	*The Spirit Of Counsel*	Mowbray
JAMES Oliver	*Affluenza*	Vintage Books
JAMPOLSKY Gerald	*Love Is Letting Go Of Fear*	Celestial Arts
JEFFERS Susan	*Feel The Fear And Do It Anyway*	Random Century
JOHNSON Steven	*Emergence*	Scribner
JUDGE William Q *(interpreted by)*	*Patanjali's Yoga Aphorisms*	The Theosophy Company
KARCHER Stephen	*The Elements Of The I Ching*	Element Books
KARPINSKI Gloria D	*Where Two Worlds Touch*	Ballantine Books
KEEN Sam	*Fire In The Belly*	Piatkus
KENNEDY Eugene, **CHARLES** Sara	*On Becoming A Counsellor*	Gill and MacMacMillan

KHANNA Madhu	*Yantra*	Thames and Hudson
KINGSLAND Kevin & Venika	*Hathapradipika*	Grael Communications
KITTO H D F	*The Greeks*	Pelican Originals
KLINE Nancy	*Time To Think*	Cassell
KLINE Nancy	*More Time To Think*	Fisher King
KOEHLER Wolfgang	*The Mentality Of Apes*	Pelican Books
KORNFIELD Jack	*A Path With Heart*	Rider Books
KORNFIELD Christina **FELDMAN** Jack	*Soul Food*	Harper Collins
KRISHNA Gopi	*Kundalini – The Evolutionary Energy In Man*	Shambala
KRYSTAL Phyllis	*Cutting The Ties That Bind*	Element Books
KRYSTAL Phyllis	*Cutting More Ties That Bind*	Element Books
KUMAR Satish	*The Buddha And The Terrorist*	Green Books
LABORDE Genie Z	*Fine Tune Your Brain*	Syntony
LANSDOWNE Zachary F	*The Rays And Esoteric Psychology*	Samuel Weiser
LEONARD Thomas J	*Becoming A Coach*	Coach U Press
LESHAN Lawrence	*How To Meditate*	Crucible Press
LEWIS Thomas, **AMINI** Fair **LANNON** Richard	*A General Theory Of Love*	Vintage
LINN Denise	*Sacred Space*	Rider Books
LINN Denise	*Pocketful Of Dreams*	Triple Five Publishing
LITVINOFF Sarah	*The Relate Guide To Better Relationships*	Vermilion
LUEN Lam Kam	*The Way Of Energy*	Gaia Books
MAHARISHI MAHESH YOGI	*Transcendental Meditation*	Kenyon Printing Co
MAISTER David H, **GREEN** Charles H **GALFORD** Robert M	*The Trusted Advisor*	Free Press
MARCUM David, SMITH Steven	*Egonomics*	Simon and Schuster
MAY Rollo	*Man's Search For Himself*	Delta Publishing
MCALL Kenneth	*Healing The Family Tree*	Sheldon Press
McGRAW Phillip	*Life Strategies*	Vermilion
McROBIE George	*Small Is Possible*	Abacus
MILLER Alice	*The Drama Of Being A Child*	Virago Press
MING-DAO Deng	*365 Tao Daily Meditations*	Harper Collins
MISNER Ivan R, **DAVIS** Robert	*Business By Referral*	Bard Press
MOOKERJEE Ajit	*Kundalini – The Arousal Of The Inner Energy*	Thames and Hudson
MOORE Thomas	*The Re-Enchantment Of Everday Life*	Harper Collins
NEILL Michael	*You Can Have What You Want*	Hay House
NELSON-JONES Richard	*Practical Counselling And Helping Skills*	Cassell
NOONAN Ellen	*Counselling Young People*	Tavistock Routledge
O'FLAHERTY Wendy *(translated by)*	*The Rig Veda, An Anthology*	Penguin
PAGELS Elaine	*The Gnostic Gospels*	Penguin Books
PASSONS William R	*Gestalt Approaches In Counselling*	Holt Rinehart & Winston
PECK M Scott	*A World Waiting To Be Born*	Arrow Books
PECK M Scott	*The Road Less Travelled*	Arrow
PECK M Scott	*Further Along The Road Less Travelled*	Pocket Books
PECK M Scott	*Golf And The Spirit*	Pocket Books
PECK M Scott	*People Of The Lie*	Touchstone
PETERS Tom, **AUSTIN** Nancy	*A Passion For Excellence*	Fontana

PETERS Thomas J, **WATERMAN** Robert H	*In Search Of Excellence*	Harper & Row
PIRSIG Robert M	*Zen And The Art Of Motorcycle Maintenance*	Corgi
POPENOE Cris	*Books For Inner Development*	Random House
RADHAKRISHNAN Sarvepalli **MOORE** Charles	*A Sourcebook Of Indian Philosophy*	Princeton University Press
REDFIELD James	*The Celestine Prophecy*	Bantam Books
REDFIELD James **ADRIENNE** Caroline	*The Celestine Prophecy – An Experiential Guide*	Bantam Books
REDFIELD James	*The Celestine Vision*	Bantam Books
REDFIELD James	*The Secret Of Shambala*	Bantam Press
REDFIELD James	*The Tenth Insight*	Bantam Press
RINPOCHE Soghal	*The Tibetan Book Of Living And Dying*	Rider Books
ROBBINS Anthony	*Awaken The Giant Within*	Simon and Schuster
ROGERS Carl R	*Client Centred Therapy*	Constable
ROMAN Sanaya, **PACKER** Duane	*Creating Money*	H J Kramer
ROSENBERG Marshall B	*Nonviolent Communication*	Puddle Dancer Press
ROSENBERG Marshall B	*Being Me, Loving You*	Puddle Dancer Press
SADLER William E	*The I Ching Of Management*	Humanics
SANKARA Paul	*Sankara On The Yoga Sutras (Vols 1 And 2)*	Routledge and Kegan
SCHLEMMER Phyllis **JENKINS** Palden	*The Only Planet Of Choice*	Gateway Books
SCHUMACHER E F	*A Guide For The Perplexed*	Sphere Books
SHAH Idries	*The Sufis*	Doubleday
SHARMA Chandra	*Homeopathy And Natural Medicine*	Dutton
SHEARER Alistair	*The Hindu Vision*	Thames and Hudson
SHEARER Alan *(translated by)*	*Effortless Being- The Yoga Sutras Of Patanjali*	Biddles
SHREEVE Caroline & David	*The Healing Power Of Hypnotism*	Thorsons
SIMON Edith	*The Saints* Pelican Books	
SIMONS T Raphael	*Feng Shui – Strategies For Business Success*	Rider Books
SKINNER Robin, **CLEESE** John	*Life And How To Survive It*	Arrow Books
SKINNER Robin, **CLEESE** John	*Families And How To Survive Them*	Mandarin
SOUTHON Mike, **WEST** Chris	*The Beermat Entrepreneur*	Pearson
SPEAR William	*Feng Shui Made Easy*	Thorsons
TAGORE Rabindranath	*The Religion Of Man*	Mandala
TEMPLAR Richard	*The Rules Of Life*	Pearson Education
THE ARBINGER INSTITUTE	*An Anatomy Of Peace*	Berrett-Koehler
THOMSON Peter	*The Secrets Of Communication*	Simon and Schuster
TOLLE Eckhart	*The Power Of Now*	Hodder and Stoughton
TOO Lilian	*Chinese Numerology In Feng Shui*	Konsep Books
TOTH Max, **NEILSEN** Greg	*Pyramid Power*	Aquarian
TRUNGPA Chogyam **FREMANTLE** Francesca	*The Tibetan Book Of The Dead*	Shambala Publicaitons
TWYMAN James	*Emissary Of Light*	Hodder and Stoughton
TWYMAN James	*The Secret Of The Beloved Disciple*	Findhorn Press
TWYMAN James	*Emissary Of Love*	Hampton Roads Publishing
URY William	*Getting Past No*	Random House

URY William, **FISHER** Roger	*Getting To Yes*	Random House
VAN DER POST Laurens	*Jung And The Story Of Our Time*	Penguin
VAN DUSSEN Wilson	*The Country Of Spirit*	J Appleseed & Co
VARIOUS	*Return Of The Buddha*	Royal Academy
VARIOUS	*Make It Stick*	Group Publishing
VEAL Debra	*Rowing It Alone*	Robson Books
VENKATESANANDA Swami	*Enlightened Living*	Chiltern Yoga Trust
VENKATESANANDA Swami	*Meditation And Its Methods*	Vedanta Press
VENKATESANANDA Swami	*The Universal Religion*	Ramakrishna Vedanta Centre
WALL Vicky	*The Miracle Of Colour Healing*	Aquarian Thorsons
WALSCH Neale Donald	*Applications For Living*	Hodder and Stoughton
WALSCH Neale Donald	*Conversations With God*	Hodder & Stoughton
WATTS Alan	*The Meaning Of Happiness*	Rider and Co
WEISS Bryan	*Many Lives, Many Masters*	Piatkus
WEISS Brian	*Same Soul, Many Bodies*	Piatkus Books
WILBER Ken & Freya	*Grace And Grit*	Shambala Publications
WILBER Ken & Freya	*The Atman Project*	Quest
WILBER Ken & Freya	*Kosmic Consciousness* (Audio)	Sounds True
WILBER Ken & Freya	*The Collected Works Of Ken Wilber*	Shambahla
WILBER Ken & Freya	*Grace And Grit*	Shambhala
WILBER Ken & Freya	*One Taste*	Shambala Publications
WILSON Colin	*The War Against Sleep*	The Aquarian Press
WILSON Paul	*The Quiet*	MacMillan Press
WILSON-SCHAEF Anne	*Escape From Intimacy*	Yhorsona
WOLF Fred Alan	*Parallel Universes*	Paladin
YOGONANDA Paramahansa	*Autobiography Of A Yogi*	Self Realisation Fellowship
YOUNG Meredith L	*Agartha*	Gateway Books
YUKTESWAR Swami Sri	*The Holy Science*	
ZELDIN Theodore	*An Intimate History Of Humanity*	Vintage Books

Index

Notes

Notes

Notes

Notes

Notes

Notes

Notes

Notes

Notes

Notes

Notes

Notes

Notes

Notes

Notes

Notes

Notes

Notes

Notes

Notes

Notes

Notes

Notes